KU-216-780

AN ORDINARY DAY WITH JESUS

Experiencing the Reality of God in Your Everyday Life

AN ORDINARY DAY WITH JESUS

Experiencing the Reality of God in Your Everyday Life

Leader's Guide

John Ortberg and Ruth Haley Barton

GRAND RAPIDS, MICHIGAN 49530

An Ordinary Day with Jesus Leader's Guide
Copyright © 2001 by Willow Creek Community Church

Requests for information should be addressed to:
Willow Creek Association
P.O. Box 3188
Barrington, IL 60011

ISBN: 0-310-24585-0

All Scripture quotations, unless otherwise indicated, are taken from the *Holy Bible: New International Version®*. NIV®. Copyright ©1973, 1978, 1984 by International Bible Society. Used by permission of Zondervan . All rights reserved.

Scripture quotations marked (NLT) are taken from the *Holy Bible,* New Living Translation, copyright © 1996. Used by permission of Tyndale House Publishers, Inc., Wheaton, IL 60189. All rights reserved.

All rights reserved. No part of this publication may be reproduced, stored in a retrieval system, or transmitted in any form or by any means—electronic, mechanical, photocopy, recording, or any other—except for brief quotations in printed reviews, without the prior permission of the publisher.

Interior design by Rick Devon

Produced with the assistance of the Livingstone Corporation. Project staff includes: Ashley Taylor, Christopher D. Hudson, Carol Barnstable, and Paige Drygas.

Printed in the United States of America

06 /VG/ 10 9 8 7 6 5 4

Dedication

Dallas Willard has been a teacher, mentor, and friend to many people—including the authors of this course—who seek to follow the way of Christ. The whole idea of building a course around spending the day with Jesus came from Dallas' teaching and we use it with his characteristic gracious permission.

With deep appreciation and much love, *An Ordinary Day with Jesus* is dedicated to Dallas Willard. "The . . . secret of the ordinary is that it is made to be a receptacle of the divine, a place where the life of God flows."*

* *The Divine Conspiracy*, Dallas Willard.

Contents

Preface

What does it take to make a day great? Often we think it takes some piece of extra-ordinary news—winning the lottery, getting a huge promotion, driving home during rush hour and not hitting any traffic jams.

But the truth is, any ordinary day can become extra-ordinarily great by doing one simple thing—spending it with God.

Too often people spend months or years or even decades feeling guilty about how they're approaching their spiritual lives. But this is not God's will for any of his children. He has another plan. His great desire is to walk together with each child of his through the ordinary days of their lives.

And this is his plan for you as well. You can do this. God would not have commanded it if it were not so.

You have a great privilege—to learn and teach about life with God:

- how to begin and end our days with God
- how to give our everyday relationships to him, and to be alone with him in a way that feeds our souls
- how to actually work with him right alongside us
- how to listen to the Holy Spirit
- how to identify the spiritual pathways that can aid us in experiencing ongoing connection with God
- how to reflect on the pace of our lives and hear God address us through Scripture
- how to plan for and commit to spending an entire day with Jesus

But the greatest learning will happen outside this course. It will emerge in the minutes and hours of daily living. Every moment is an opportunity to say, "Here's my chance to learn from Jesus. He's right here, right now, ready to live in magnificent partnership with me."

Here's your chance.

Acknowledgments

There is nothing more exciting than a church full of people who are experiencing the reality of God in the midst of the ordinary. And so it is with deepest gratitude that we acknowledge the community of faith in which we have learned and practiced the truths presented in this course.

To the elders and the congregation at Willow Creek Community Church for providing the context for the creation of this course. Hundreds of people made themselves available as "guinea pigs" to experience the course in various phases of its development and to provide us with thoughtful and valuable feedback.

To Bill Hybels for providing guidance during the initial phases of shaping the content.

To Jim Mellado, Joe Sherman, and Christine Anderson of the Willow Creek Association for believing in this project and coming alongside us with the resources and expertise needed to publish this course. Christine has shepherded, managed, and prodded this project with skill, persistence, and love. It would not have come to fruition without her.

To Wendy Seidman and Sue Drake for contributing the instructional design expertise that neither one of us has!

To Judson Poling for going beyond the call of duty in capturing this course in written form throughout *multiple* iterations and revisions. His mind and soul are part of each session.

To Steve Pederson, Mark Demel, Scott Dyer, and the staff of IMS Productions for their expertise and enthusiasm in working with us to create video segments that touch the heart.

To our volunteer team, including Keri Kent, Jim Pio, Dalene Strieff, Bill Hayes, Diana Searls, Art Holton, and Linda Bryant. We are grateful for their prayers and support as we developed the content and ministry of this course within the walls of Willow Creek.

To Jodi Walle, Karen Dickson, and Tiffany Staman for their patient administrative support throughout the various developmental phases of this project.

And to our families: John—Nancy, Laura, Mallory, and Johnny; Ruth—Chris, Charity, Bethany, and Haley. Thank you for bearing with the sacrifices of time necessary to carry out this project and, most of all, for providing us with ordinary moments made extraordinary by your love and presence in our lives.

How to Use the Leader's Guide

This Leader's Guide has been prepared to help you present this course in the most effective manner possible. These introductory pages provide ideas for presenting the sessions and list the materials and equipment required.

Group Size

An Ordinary Day with Jesus works with any size group:

- Large groups of 10 to 150 people or more
- Small groups of 4 to 9 people

Although the directions for the various group activities throughout this course have been written for medium- to large-sized groups, the instructions are easily transferred into small group situations. For example, when the Leader's Guide suggests breaking into groups of four, you can segment your small group into one, two, or three subgroups as needed. Also, when the Leader's Guide asks you to solicit feedback from each of the groups, you can simply ask for input from any of the individuals in your small group who would like to respond.

Small groups provide an excellent forum for presenting *An Ordinary Day with Jesus* because members of the group know each other, can encourage each other, and can hold each other accountable to apply the principles and skills they learn.

Format Options

An Ordinary Day with Jesus can be presented successfully in a number of delivery formats:

Weekend seminar—two sessions on Friday evening and six sessions on Saturday

The recommended presentation format for this course is a weekend seminar—6:30 p.m. to 9:00 p.m. on Friday evening, and 9:00 a.m. to 4:45 p.m. on Saturday. Although each session can be presented in 50 minutes, the weekend seminar format allows 60 minutes for each session, which is a slightly more relaxed pace. You may wish to use the following as a suggested schedule:

Friday Evening

6:30 p.m.	Arrival, welcome, and introductions
6:45 p.m.	Session 1: *Living in Jesus' Name*
7:45 p.m.	*Break*
8:00 p.m.	Session 2: *Everyday Relationships*
9:00 p.m.	Evening concludes

Saturday

9:00 a.m.	Arrival and welcome
9:15 a.m.	Session 3: *Work*
10:15 a.m.	*Break*
10:30 a.m.	Session 4: *Leadings*
11:30 a.m.	Session 5: *Solitude*
12:30 p.m.	*Lunch*
1:15 p.m.	Session 6: *Spiritual Pathways*
2:15 p.m.	*Break*
2:30 p.m.	Session 7: *Pace of Life*
3:30 p.m.	*Break*
3:45 p.m.	Session 8: *Making the Ordinary Extraordinary*
4:45 p.m.	Day concludes

Eight sessions of 50 minutes each

This Leader's Guide is written to accommodate an eight-session format smoothly. Teaching the sessions over eight weeks gives participants time to absorb the material and put into practice what they have learned each week.

Although the amount of time shown for each session is approximately 50 minutes, we encourage you to allow more time. If you are teaching a medium to large group, allow at least 1 hour per session.

As written, the material doesn't allow for extra time. The time allotted is intended to keep you and the participants moving quickly through the material. The 50 minutes does not include any time for questions and answers, storytelling (of what participants may have experienced that week as a result of the course), nor extra time needed by some people to complete the activities. To present a session in 50 minutes, it is necessary to maintain a brisk pace and strictly observe the times indicated in the Leader's Guide.

At the beginning of each session, you may want to allow additional time to take questions or, more importantly, to listen to stories of what participants experienced during the past week as a result of the course. You may also find you need additional time for the individual or small group activities.

Four sessions of 2 hours and 15 minutes each

By pairing up Sessions 1 and 2, Sessions 3 and 4, Sessions 5 and 6, and Sessions 7 and 8, you can effectively present the course in four sessions. If you present the course in this format, allow at least 1 hour for each session, with an additional 15 minutes for a break between the two sessions.

One-, two-, or three-day retreats

The material in this course is especially conducive to the relaxed pace and environment of a spiritual retreat. In this setting you have the flexibility to present the material in the format that best accommodates your retreat schedule.

How this Leader's Guide Is Organized

Each of the eight sessions is divided into the following parts:

Session Snapshot

Provides a brief summary of the content to be discussed in the session and the overall context into which the session fits.

Objectives

Describes what participants are to accomplish and learn in that session.

Outline

Provides an overview of the content and sequence to be covered in the session.

Session Introduction, Discovery, and Summary

Describes the actual "teaching" part of the session containing the content to be presented, which is keyed to the visual aids to be used in the session. This material is presented in two columns as shown in the following example:

TIME & MEDIA	CONTENTS
3 MINUTES	**WELCOME AND INTRODUCTION** • Call the group together. • Welcome participants to *An Ordinary Day with Jesus.* • Introduce yourself. Welcome to the first session of *An Ordinary Day with Jesus.* I want you to imagine something. I'd like you to think about what it would be like to spend an ordinary day of your life doing the things you normally do but actually doing them *with* Jesus. What if, for one day, you were to work and eat and sleep just like normal—except somehow Jesus was by your side each moment?

The Time and Media Column

The TIME notations indicate suggested times for each content block (which totals approximately 50 minutes). Caution: These times include just the CONTENTS portion of each session. They do not allow for any question-and-answer time, storytelling time, nor extra time participants may need to complete activities. If possible, we recommend expanding your schedule to allow for more of these elements.

The MEDIA graphics indicate when the PowerPoint slides (or overhead transparencies, if you're using that option) should be presented.

Included on the *An Ordinary Day with Jesus* CD-ROM are two folders. If your facility is equipped with the computer equipment required to use PowerPoint software, the folder named "Sessions for Viewing" contains files for a four-color, electronic presentation.

If you will be using a standard overhead projector and transparencies, the folder "Sessions for Printing" contains files for black-and-white transparencies. To make overhead transparencies, you may use one of two methods.

1. Print out the files on your computer printer, using the appropriate type of transparency for your particular printer.
2. First print the files on white paper. Place a sufficient number of overhead transparency sheets (the kind specifically made for copiers) in the paper tray of a photocopier, and then run the printout through the copier. Your local full-service copy center should be equipped to make transparencies if you do not have access to the necessary equipment.

The Contents Column

The CONTENTS column is a detailed guide to the course material. If you had to, you could read this column start to finish, word for word, and the material would be presented completely and in the correct order. However, the more effective way is for you to use this information as a resource as you prepare to present the eight sessions.

We recommend that you personalize this material by using your own words and illustrations. You might want to highlight key words and phrases so you'll be able to teach without having to read it word for word. If you prefer to write down your own material, there is space provided under the NOTES area (see "Notes" on page 25). Practice each session—including PowerPoint and video—at least once before presenting it to make sure you are comfortable with the material and are able to keep to the time you have allotted for the session. Also, be sure to have all visual aids organized and ready to use.

The CONTENTS column includes the following key elements:

1. The instructor narrative is shown in this standard typeface:

> Whatever the reason, many of us find it difficult to live an ordinary day in close connection with Jesus. If this has been true in your experience, you're in the right place. Wherever you are on your spiritual journey, Jesus really does want to be with you in your everyday life.

2. Statements the instructor should read *verbatim* are set off with the following symbol: . Example:

>  The heart of spiritual life is to do everything with Jesus, *in* his name—the way he would do it in our place, knowing he *is* actually present.

3. Words shown in ALL CAPITAL LETTERS are words participants need to fill in the blanks found on the corresponding pages in their Participant's Guides.

 FATIGUE is one of the greatest barriers to prayer and spiritual growth.

4. If you are using PowerPoint slides (rather than transparencies), the slides corresponding to content appear in the TIME & MEDIA column as shown in the example below. When a slide has multiple points and "builds," the following symbol ▶ appears as a prompt to advance to the next point:

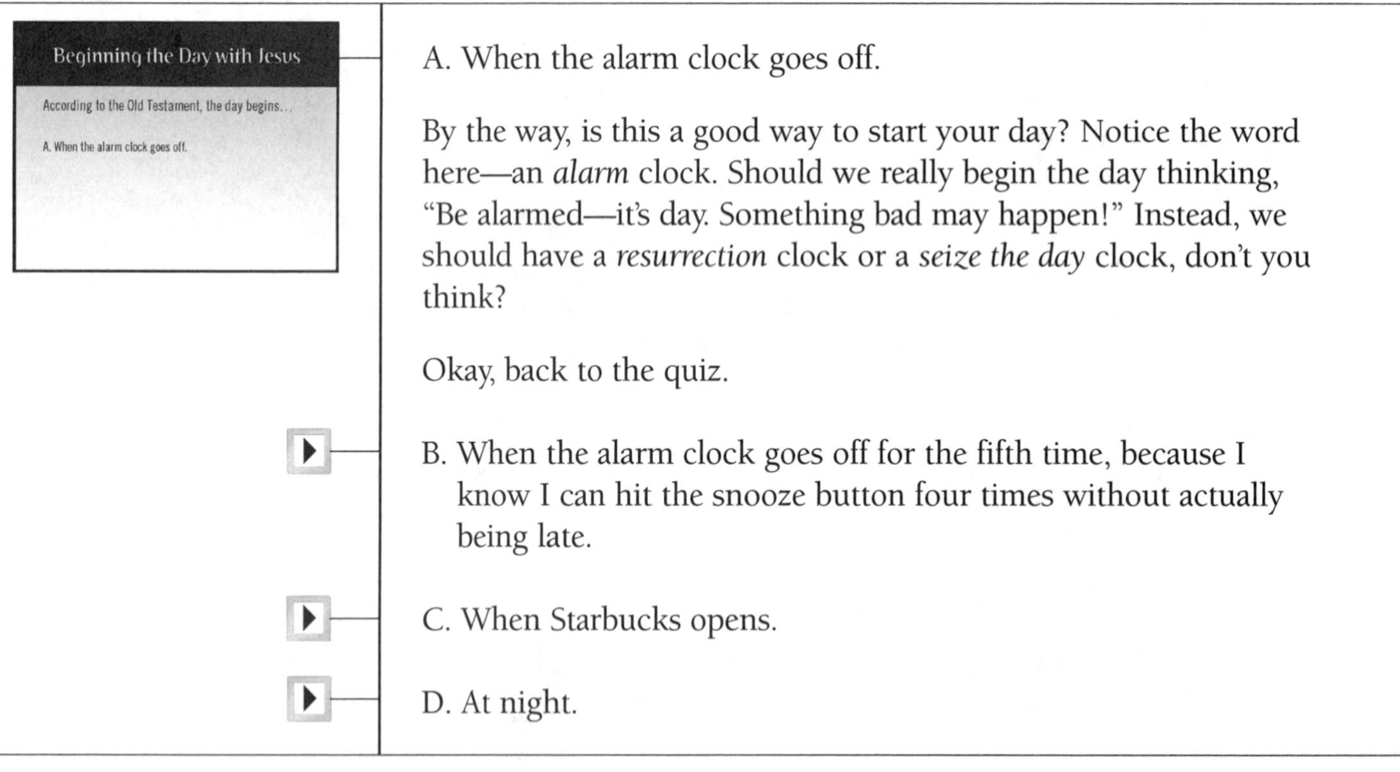

A. When the alarm clock goes off.

By the way, is this a good way to start your day? Notice the word here—an *alarm* clock. Should we really begin the day thinking, "Be alarmed—it's day. Something bad may happen!" Instead, we should have a *resurrection* clock or a *seize the day* clock, don't you think?

Okay, back to the quiz.

B. When the alarm clock goes off for the fifth time, because I know I can hit the snooze button four times without actually being late.

C. When Starbucks opens.

D. At night.

5. Scripture verses, other quotes, prayers, and words and phrases to be emphasized are italicized.

In Colossians 3:17, Paul writes:

Whatever you do, whether in word or deed, do it all in the name of the Lord Jesus, giving thanks to God the Father through him.

6. Directions to the instructor are shown in a contrasting typeface and enclosed in a shaded box. These directions are *not to be spoken* by the instructor.

> Because this portion of the teaching is set up as a multiple-choice quiz, be sure to actually say the letters—A, B, C, and D—that precede each answer.

7. A variety of activities are included throughout the course to help participants learn by talking to each other or reflecting on their own experiences. These include individual and small group activities.

Notes

Provides space to write your own words and illustrations to customize your presentation and replace portions of the instructor narrative.

Participant's Guide Pages

Allows you to view the page(s) participants are seeing as you talk without having to hold two books at the same time. It also helps you immediately know where the participants are in their books when someone asks.

Master Materials List

To present *An Ordinary Day with Jesus*, the following materials and supplies are needed:

- Leader's Guide
- Participant's Guides
- Name tags and markers
- Computer and projection equipment with CD-ROM disk if using PowerPoint slides; overhead projector, pens, and transparencies if using overheads. Make sure ahead of time that all equipment is in working order.
- *An Ordinary Day with Jesus* video cassette
- Video player and monitor, set up and ready to play

Optional: tape or CD player for music. Use this before and after sessions, as well as during breaks, to create a welcoming and relaxed atmosphere. Also, there are leader notes within some sessions suggesting that meditative instrumental music be played quietly in the background during certain individual activities.

Facility Setup

To create a comfortable and relaxed atmosphere, we recommend using round tables. Seat six people at each table, leaving an open space at the front so no one has their back to the instructor.

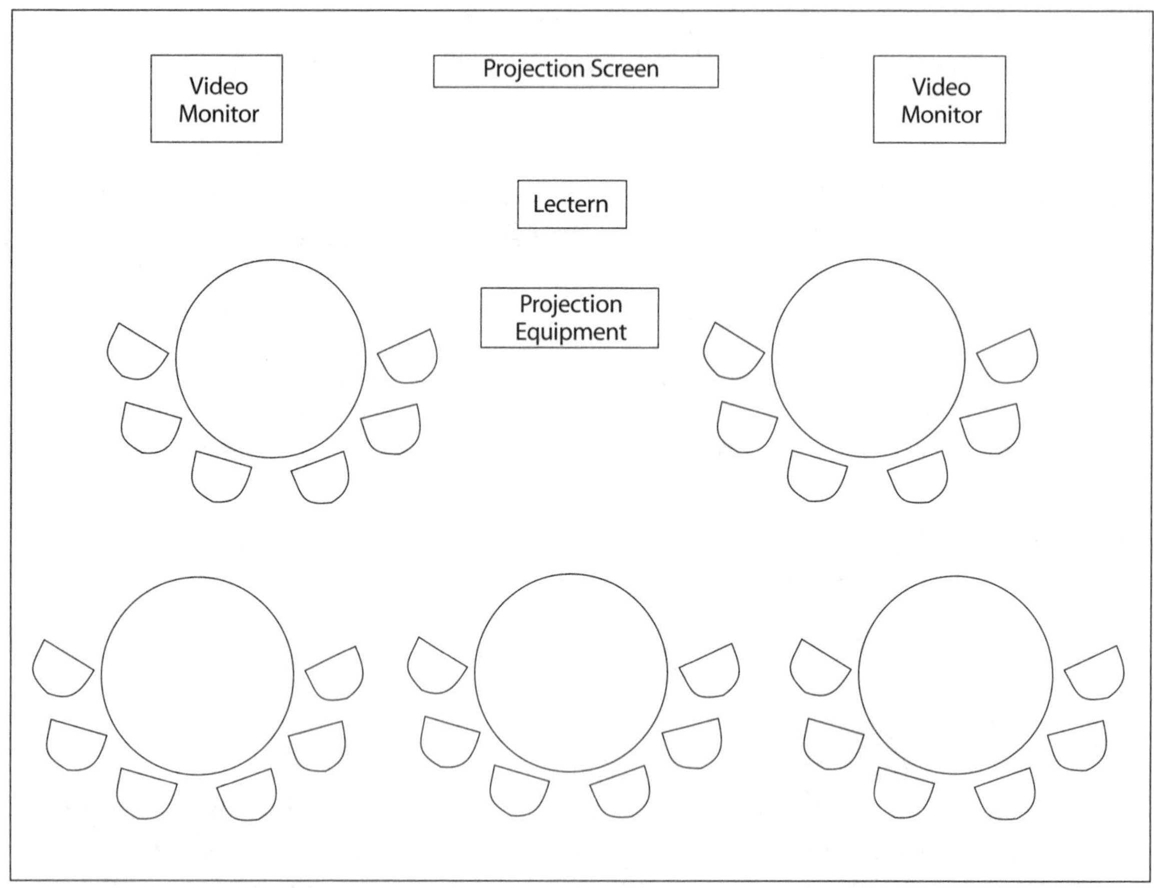

LIVING IN JESUS' NAME

SESSION SNAPSHOT

Overview

Jesus offers us the possibility of doing life with him, day by day. Participants may be surprised to discover that, although by necessity we spend much of life in routine activities, these are perfectly suited for God's work in us. Participants will also learn helpful practices they can use to make two everyday moments—falling asleep and waking up—times when they connect with the Lord.

Objectives

In this session, participants will:

1. Learn that the Christian life is an invitation to do everything in Jesus' name
2. Identify challenges to living in Jesus' name
3. Learn simple steps for beginning and ending each day with Jesus

SESSION OUTLINE

I. Welcome and Introduction

Video: *Something Missing*

II. Discovery

A. Every Ordinary Day in Jesus' Name

1. What Living in Jesus' Name Might Look Like in Your Life
2. One Day at a Time
3. Ground Rules for Discussions
4. Small Group Activity: *Challenges to Doing Life in Jesus' Name*

B. Beginning the Day with Jesus

1. Sleep
2. Waking Up

C. Learning to Find God in Each Moment of the Day

1. Review the Day with God
2. Individual Activity: *Review the Day with God*

III. Summary and Course Overview

LIVING IN JESUS' NAME

1

Monday

TIME & MEDIA

CONTENTS

2 MINUTES

WELCOME AND INTRODUCTION

- Call the group together.
- Welcome participants to *An Ordinary Day with Jesus.*
- Introduce yourself.

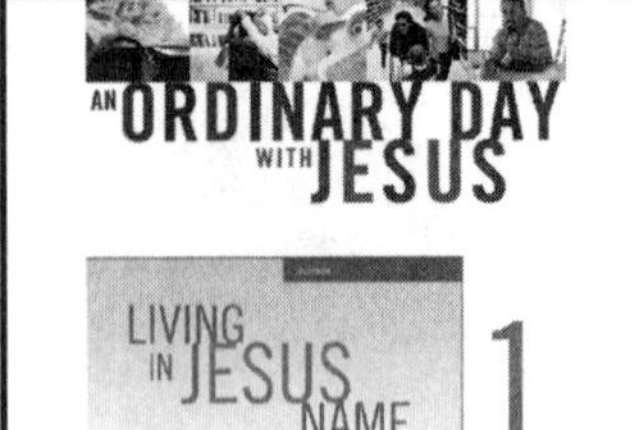

Welcome to the first session of *An Ordinary Day with Jesus.*

I want you to imagine something. I'd like you to think about what it would be like to spend an ordinary day of your life doing the things you normally do but actually doing them *with* Jesus. What if, for one day, you were to work and eat and sleep just like normal—except somehow Jesus was by your side each moment?

When it was all over and you put your head on the pillow that night, what would you look back on with excitement or joy? What would make you cringe? Here is one thing we can say for certain: most of us would acknowledge that such a day would feel *different.*

However we describe our lives right now, very few of us would say we live in unbroken, close connection with God. Many of us have compartmentalized our lives with "spiritual" activities in one place, and daily activities somewhere else. Doing *everything* in Jesus' name seems impossible.

NOTES

SESSION ONE

LIVING IN

JESUS' NAME

This course is going to help us bring together our fragmented experience. We're going to learn simple ways to experience the reality of God consistently throughout all the moments of our lives—one ordinary day at a time.

Let's watch a video that captures how many of us experience our relationship with God.

VIDEO: *SOMETHING MISSING*

Participant's Guide, page 14.

View video: *Something Missing.*

2 MINUTES

Wrap-up

What's your reaction to what you just saw?

Solicit three or four comments from the group. Be sure to repeat their answers so everyone hears the response.

Possible responses:

- *I really identify with it.*
- *I didn't realize these feelings are so common.*
- *I wonder why we all feel so disconnected from God.*

Whatever the reason, many of us find it difficult to live an ordinary day in close connection with Jesus. If this has been true in your experience, you're in the right place. Wherever you are on your spiritual journey, Jesus really does want to be with you in your everyday life.

Before we go any further in this session, I'd like to lead us in a prayer to ask for Jesus' help.

You may wish to substitute your own prayer for the prayer below.

Lord Jesus, we have come to this course because we want to know you more and experience your presence in our everyday lives. Some of us need hope, some of us need guidance, and all of us need to be transformed. We invite you to be present with us now. In your name we pray, amen.

NOTES

LIVING IN JESUS' NAME

AN ORDINARY DAY

VIDEO

Something Missing

Notes:

Every Ordinary Day in Jesus' Name

The Apostle Paul believed the place to grow close to God is precisely in our__________________ lives.

> *Whatever you do, whether in word or deed, do it all in the name of the Lord Jesus, giving thanks to God the Father through him.*
> (Colossians 3:17)

> *I am with you always ...*
> (Matthew 28:20)

The heart of spiritual life is to do everything *with* Jesus, *in* his name—the way he would do it in our place, knowing he *is* actually present.

14

DISCOVERY

5 MINUTES

Every Ordinary Day in Jesus' Name

Many people think that to get close to God they have to resign from life and become a monk or a hermit somewhere. If only the pressures of everyday life were lifted—such as going to a job or taking care of small children—*then* they could be the kind of people God wants them to be. Yet for the Apostle Paul, the reverse was true.

Every Ordinary Day in Jesus' Name

The Apostle Paul believed the place to grow close to God is precisely in our EVERYDAY lives.

He believed the place to grow close to God is precisely in our EVERYDAY lives!

In Colossians 3:17, Paul writes:

Whatever you do, whether in word or deed, do it all in the name of the Lord Jesus, giving thanks to God the Father through him.

Paul's concept of doing ordinary, daily activities in Jesus' name is at the very core of what this course is about.

Let's think for a moment about what it means to do everything in Jesus' name. In Paul's day, a name wasn't just something to call a person. A name signified the whole person—it was a label for the person's character or essence. So when Paul says to do everything in Jesus' name, he's saying to do these things according to Jesus' character—to do something the same way Jesus would do it if he were in our place.

What's striking is how *comprehensive* Paul's statement is. "*Whatever* you do," he says. Then, in case we miss how broad that is, he adds, "in word or deed." And if anyone is still looking for loopholes, he says, "do it *all*" in the name of Jesus.

Of course, this isn't something we attempt in our own power. We don't just do things *for* Jesus in his name—as if he were far away, like a spectator watching while we act on stage. When we become Christians, Jesus takes up residence within us. We do life *with* him, in a partnership, not as a performance.

NOTES

VIDEO

Something Missing

Notes:

Every Ordinary Day in Jesus' Name

The Apostle Paul believed the place to grow close to God is precisely in our__________________ lives.

> *Whatever you do, whether in word or deed, do it all in the name of the Lord Jesus, giving thanks to God the Father through him.*
> (Colossians 3:17)

> *I am with you always . . .*
> (Matthew 28:20)

The heart of spiritual life is to do everything *with* Jesus, *in* his name—the way he would do it in our place, knowing he *is* actually present.

In Matthew 28:20 Jesus said to his friends:

I am with you always.

He is here, in us, right now.

Every Ordinary Day in Jesus' Name

The heart of spiritual life is to do everything *with* Jesus, *in* his name—the way he would do it in our place, knowing he *is* actually present.

The heart of spiritual life is to do everything with Jesus, *in* his name—the way he would do it in our place, knowing he *is* actually present.

Several phrases come up repeatedly throughout this course, such as, "living in Jesus' name," or "partnering with God," or "being led by the Holy Spirit." They all mean the same thing, because Jesus, God, and the Holy Spirit are all part of the triune God.

What Living in Jesus' Name Might Look Like in Your Life

Participant's Guide, page 15.

Think about what living in Jesus' name might look like in your life. What would happen if you were to spend a whole, ordinary day doing everything in Jesus' name?

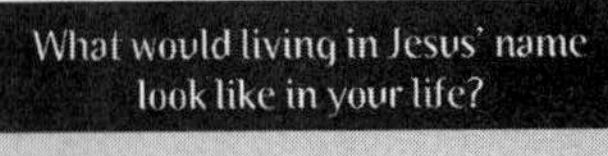

• Waking up

Read this list with a lighthearted feel; many of these points will conjure up amusing mental images.

- Let's start with the morning. If someone were to observe you waking up, would they say it was pretty much like seeing Jesus wake up?

- Eating breakfast. What would it mean to eat breakfast in Jesus' name? Maybe it means you'd actually eat breakfast! Would that affect the amount of gratitude you feel or the pace at which you eat?

- Driving. What would it look like to drive in Jesus' name? If you could actually see Jesus in the passenger seat next to you, would he look nervous? Would you drive any slower than normal?

NOTES

LIVING IN JESUS' NAME

AN ORDINARY DAY

VIDEO

Something Missing

Notes:

Every Ordinary Day in Jesus' Name

The Apostle Paul believed the place to grow close to God is precisely in our__________________ lives.

> *Whatever you do, whether in word or deed, do it all in the name of the Lord Jesus, giving thanks to God the Father through him.*
> (Colossians 3:17)

> *I am with you always ...*
> (Matthew 28:20)

The heart of spiritual life is to do everything *with* Jesus, *in* his name—the way he would do it in our place, knowing he *is* actually present.

14

WITH JESUS

SESSION ONE

What Living in Jesus' Name Might Look Like in Your Life

- *Waking up*
- *Eating breakfast*
- *Driving*
- *Working*
- *Watching TV*
- *Worrying*
- *Doing ordinary household tasks*
- *Shopping*
- *Doing everyday relationships*

15

- Working. How about your work? Whether you work in an office, work at home, go to school, or are retired, how might your daily work be different if you were to do it in Jesus' name?

- Watching TV. How would you watch TV in Jesus' name? Do you think he would only watch nature programs?

- Worrying. A huge part of an ordinary day consists of concerns and worries. Scientists have actually identified a gene—labeled SLCA64—that can predispose people to worry.[1] Now that you know that, how many of you are worried that you might have it!?

- Doing ordinary household tasks. What would it mean to vacuum the carpet or pay bills in Jesus' name?

- Shopping. How would you shop in Jesus' name? Would you buy different things—or fewer things—if he were present?

- Doing everyday relationships. Think about your relationships with your family, friends, and neighbors. Paul said whatever we do "in word or deed" should be done in Jesus' name. Think of the words you've spoken so far today. If you only uttered words in Jesus' name, how many words would you have to take back? Are there any you know of right now that you wish you could take back? What would it mean to relate in Jesus' name to people you dislike?

We've just looked at several components of an ordinary day. Now we're going to consider why starting with just one day at a time is so important.

Turn to page 16.

One Day at a Time

Participant's Guide, page 16.

Living in Jesus' name is like the manna God gave to the Israelites in the desert—it comes in one-day doses.

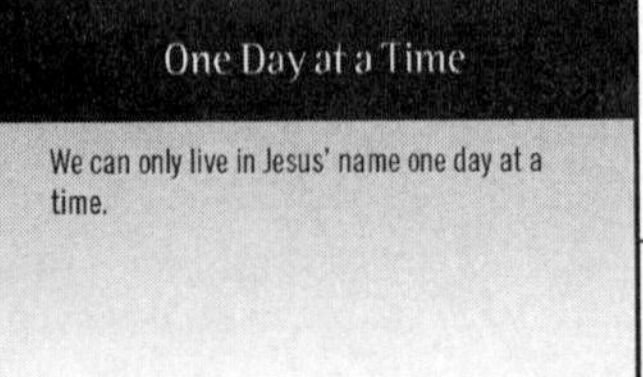

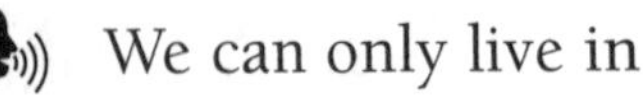

We can only live in Jesus' name one day at a time.

[1] Edward M. Hallowell, M.D., *Worry: Hope and Help for a Common Condition* (New York: Ballantine, 1998), xiv.

NOTES

What Living in Jesus' Name Might Look Like in Your Life

- *Waking up*
- *Eating breakfast*
- *Driving*
- *Working*
- *Watching TV*
- *Worrying*
- *Doing ordinary household tasks*
- *Shopping*
- *Doing everyday relationships*

One Day at a Time

We can only live in Jesus' name one day at a time.

> *Do not worry about tomorrow,*
> *for tomorrow will worry about itself.*
> *Each day has enough trouble of its own.*
> (Matthew 6:34)

> *This is the day the* LORD *has made;*
> *let us rejoice and be glad in it.*
> (Psalm 118:24)

If I am going to learn to spend an ordinary day with Jesus, it will have to be *this* day.

It doesn't mean doing new things.

It means doing things you're ______________ doing, but in new ways—*in Jesus' name.*

 In Matthew 6:34 Jesus said:

Do not worry about tomorrow, for tomorrow will worry about itself. Each day has enough trouble of its own.

Psalm 118:24 says:

This is the day the LORD *has made; let us rejoice and be glad in it.*

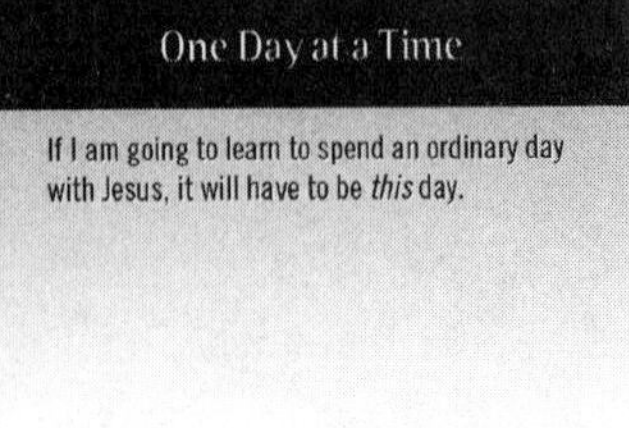

It doesn't say "yesterday." It doesn't say "tomorrow."

 If I'm going to learn to spend an ordinary day with Jesus, it will have to be *this* day. For this day is all I have.

One Day at a Time

It doesn't mean doing new things.

It means doing things you're ALREADY doing, but in new ways—in Jesus' name.

It does not require heroic measures—that's one of the encouraging things about this course.

 For the most part, it doesn't even mean doing new things. It means doing things you're ALREADY doing, but in new ways—*in Jesus' name.*

Hopefully that's freeing for you.

SMALL GROUP ACTIVITY: *CHALLENGES TO DOING LIFE IN JESUS' NAME*

Participant's Guide, page 17.

Objective
For participants to identify an activity that is difficult for them to do in Jesus' name.

Ground Rules for Discussions

- No pressure

In a moment we're going to break up into small groups. During discussion times, there are three very important ground rules.

 First, no *pressure.*

If you don't want to talk, take a pass.

 Second, no *advice.*

If someone shares a problem, the rest of the group members should listen, but don't try to fix the person or offer solutions to the problem.

NOTES

LIVING IN JESUS' NAME — AN ORDINARY DAY

One Day at a Time

We can only live in Jesus' name one day at a time.

> *Do not worry about tomorrow, for tomorrow will worry about itself. Each day has enough trouble of its own.*
> (Matthew 6:34)

> *This is the day the LORD has made; let us rejoice and be glad in it.*
> (Psalm 118:24)

If I am going to learn to spend an ordinary day with Jesus, it will have to be *this* day.

It doesn't mean doing new things.

It means doing things you're ______________ doing, but in new ways—*in Jesus' name.*

16

WITH JESUS — SESSION ONE

SMALL GROUP ACTIVITY

Challenges to Doing Life in Jesus' Name

Ground rules for discussions:

No pressure

No advice

No faking

Directions:

1. Introduce yourself to the people at your table.
2. Share one or two of the activities listed below that are the hardest for you to do in Jesus' name, and explain why.

- ☐ *Sleeping*
- ☐ *Waking up*
- ☐ *Eating*
- ☐ *Doing everyday relationships* (*kids, spouse, neighbor, etc.*)
- ☐ *Working*
- ☐ *Handling conflict*
- ☐ *Spending money*
- ☐ *Driving*
- ☐ *Doing household chores*
- ☐ *Watching TV*
- ☐ *Recreational activities*

17

 Finally, no *faking*.

This is a safe place to talk about your life as it *really* is, not how you wish it were or want others to think it is.

So . . . no pressure, no advice, no faking.

Now we're ready to have our small group discussion.

Directions

1. Introduce yourself to the people at your table.
2. Share one or two of the activities listed below that are the hardest for you to do in Jesus' name, and explain why.

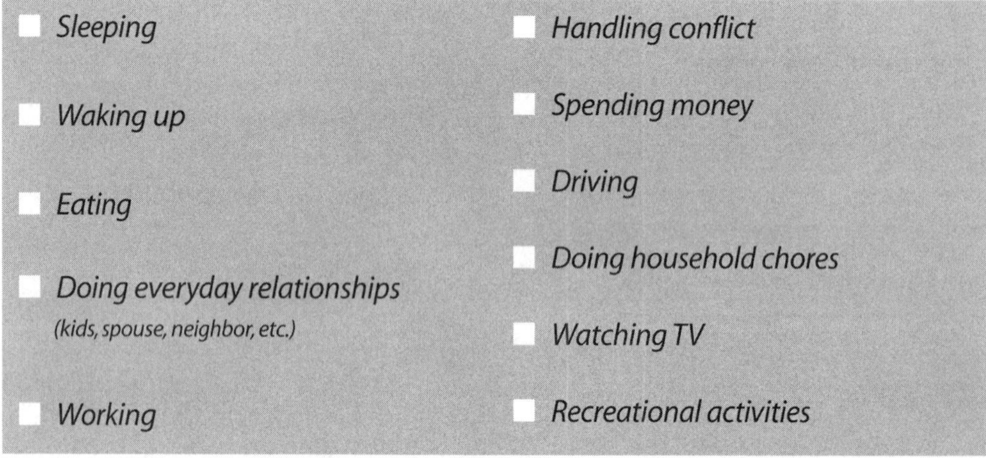

- *Sleeping*
- *Waking up*
- *Eating*
- *Doing everyday relationships* *(kids, spouse, neighbor, etc.)*
- *Working*
- *Handling conflict*
- *Spending money*
- *Driving*
- *Doing household chores*
- *Watching TV*
- *Recreational activities*

One of the best things you can do to help participants feel comfortable answering this question in their groups is to model vulnerability by first answering this question yourself. Briefly share with the class the activity that is the hardest for you to do in Jesus' name and how it impacts your life. Be specific. For example:

"The activity that's hardest for me to do in Jesus' name is handling conflict, especially at work. I find myself resenting the people who disagree with me. I sometimes end up avoiding them rather than meeting with them to work through things, which often makes the problem worse and strains our relationship."

Any questions on the directions?

NOTES

WITH JESUS

SESSION ONE

SMALL GROUP ACTIVITY

Challenges to Doing Life in Jesus' Name

Ground rules for discussions:

No pressure

No advice

No faking

Directions:

1. Introduce yourself to the people at your table.
2. Share one or two of the activities listed below that are the hardest for you to do in Jesus' name, and explain why.

- ☐ *Sleeping*
- ☐ *Waking up*
- ☐ *Eating*
- ☐ *Doing everyday relationships* *(kids, spouse, neighbor, etc.)*
- ☐ *Working*
- ☐ *Handling conflict*
- ☐ *Spending money*
- ☐ *Driving*
- ☐ *Doing household chores*
- ☐ *Watching TV*
- ☐ *Recreational activities*

17

You will have 10 minutes for your discussion.

After 5 minutes, notify the group, "We're at the halfway point." At 9 minutes, say, "One minute left." Then call the group back together after 10 minutes.

2 MINUTES

Wrap-up

What activities are hardest to do in Jesus' name?

Solicit two or three comments from the group. Be sure to repeat their answers so everyone hears the response.

Possible responses:

- *Driving—I'm a maniac at the wheel.*
- *Working—pressure at work keeps me from thinking about God.*
- *Eating—I'm always in a hurry.*
- *Sleeping—I have no idea what that would look like!*
- *Parenting—I lose patience so easily, I'm sure Jesus wouldn't parent like I do.*
- *Spending money—I'm terrible at controlling impulse spending.*
- *Handling conflict—All the models I have aren't very Christ-like.*

Now that we've identified areas where we struggle to live in Jesus' name, we're going to take a closer look at how we can begin to invite Jesus into an ordinary day from the moment the day begins.

Turn to page 18.

9 MINUTES

Beginning the Day with Jesus

Participant's Guide, page 18.

In order to live every moment of an ordinary day with Jesus, we have to begin the day with him. So let's consider how a day begins. Here's a multiple-choice quiz to get us started.

According to the Old Testament, when does the day begin?

NOTES

WITH JESUS SESSION ONE

SMALL GROUP ACTIVITY

Challenges to Doing Life in Jesus' Name

Ground rules for discussions:

No pressure

No advice

No faking

Directions:

1. Introduce yourself to the people at your table.
2. Share one or two of the activities listed below that are the hardest for you to do in Jesus' name, and explain why.

- *Sleeping*
- *Waking up*
- *Eating*
- *Doing everyday relationships* (kids, spouse, neighbor, etc.)
- *Working*
- *Handling conflict*
- *Spending money*
- *Driving*
- *Doing household chores*
- *Watching TV*
- *Recreational activities*

17

LIVING IN JESUS' NAME — AN ORDINARY DAY

Beginning the Day with Jesus

According to the Old Testament, the day begins ________________.

> *There was evening, and there was morning—the first day.*
> (Genesis 1:5)

> Thinking about night as the beginning of the day reminds us that everything doesn't depend on us. We go to sleep, but God is working all through the night. So we don't have to be anxious or rushed. When we wake up, we will simply join him in his work.
> Eugene H. Peterson

18

Because this portion of the teaching is set up as a multiple-choice quiz, be sure to actually say the letters—A, B, C, and D—that precede each answer.

Beginning the Day with Jesus

According to the Old Testament, the day begins...

A. When the alarm clock goes off.

A. When the alarm clock goes off.

By the way, is this a good way to start your day? Notice the word here—an *alarm* clock. Should we really begin the day thinking, "Be alarmed—it's day. Something bad may happen!" Instead, we should have a *resurrection* clock or a *seize–the–day* clock, don't you think?

Okay, back to the quiz.

B. When the alarm clock goes off for the fifth time, because I know I can hit the snooze button four times without actually being late.

C. When Starbucks opens.

D. At night.

What's the correct answer?

Pause.

Beginning the Day with Jesus

According to the Old Testament, the day begins AT NIGHT.

That's right—the answer is "D."

According to the Old Testament, the day actually begins AT NIGHT.

Genesis 1:5 says:

There was evening, and there was morning—the first day.

Throughout the Bible's description of creation, each day begins with night.

This same principle also applies to observing the Sabbath. According to Jewish law, what signals the beginning of the Sabbath?

Pause.

NOTES

LIVING IN JESUS' NAME

AN ORDINARY DAY

Beginning the Day with Jesus

According to the Old Testament, the day begins ________________.

> *There was evening, and there was morning—the first day.*
> (Genesis 1:5)

> Thinking about night as the beginning of the day reminds us that everything doesn't depend on us. We go to sleep, but God is working all through the night. So we don't have to be anxious or rushed. When we wake up, we will simply join him in his work.
> Eugene H. Peterson

18

Sundown. So in the Hebrew way of thinking, the day always begins with night.

Author Eugene Peterson explains why this is important to understand. He says that thinking about night as the beginning of the day reminds us that everything doesn't depend on us. We go to sleep, but God is working all through the night. So we don't have to be anxious or rushed. When we wake up, we will simply join him in his work.[2]

When we acknowledge that the day begins at night, the first thing we need to do in order to spend an ordinary day with Jesus is make some changes in how we sleep.

SLEEP

Participant's Guide, page 19.

Believe it or not, the Bible does have things to teach us about sleep.

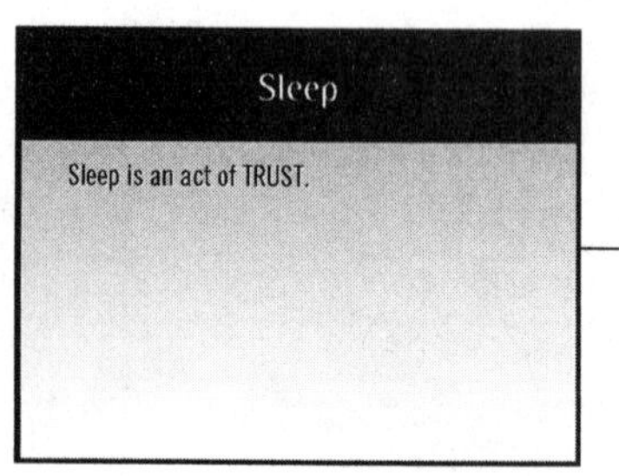

It tells us that sleep is an act of TRUST.

In Psalm 3:5 David writes:

I lie down and sleep; I wake again, because the LORD sustains me.

When we sleep, we acknowledge that God can run the world quite well without us. And that can be hard for some of us.

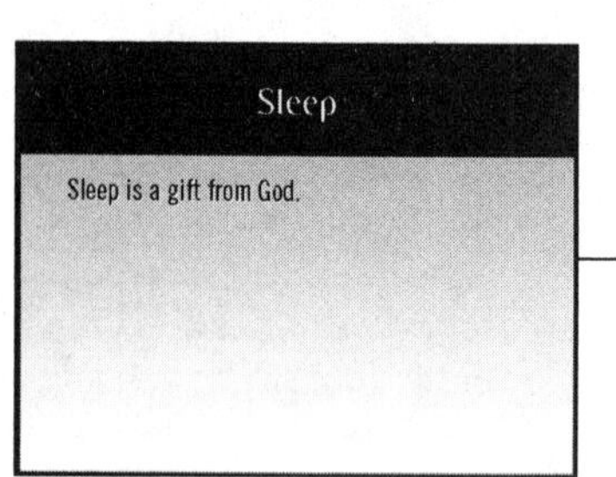

The Bible also teaches that sleep is a gift from God.

Psalm 127:2 says:

In vain you rise early and stay up late, toiling for food to eat—for he grants sleep to those he loves.

This should be a theme verse for many of us. In our day, sleep seems to be the gift nobody wants.

So how do we practice what we might call "sleep discipleship"?

Turn to page 20.

[2] Eugene H. Peterson, *Working the Angles: The Shape of Pastoral Integrity* (Grand Rapids: Eerdmans 1990), 42–49.

NOTES

LIVING IN JESUS' NAME

AN ORDINARY DAY

Beginning the Day with Jesus

According to the Old Testament, the day begins ________________.

> *There was evening, and there was morning—the first day.*
> (Genesis 1:5)

> Thinking about night as the beginning of the day reminds us that everything doesn't depend on us. We go to sleep, but God is working all through the night. So we don't have to be anxious or rushed. When we wake up, we will simply join him in his work.
> Eugene H. Peterson

18

WITH JESUS

SESSION ONE

Sleep

Sleep is an act of ________________.

> *I lie down and sleep; I wake again, because the* LORD *sustains me.*
> (Psalm 3:5)

Sleep is a gift from God.

> *In vain you rise early and stay up late, toiling for food to eat—for he grants sleep to those he loves.*
> (Psalm 127:2)

19

Get Enough Sleep

Sleep

Get enough sleep.

Participant's Guide, page 20.

 First, get enough sleep.

Despite the Bible's affirmation of sleep, many of us go to bed exhausted. In fact, some of us wake up that way too, and go through our whole day tired. *U.S. News and World Report* recently reported that Americans have a national sleep deficit that's bigger than the national financial deficit. One study found that approximately 24,000 people in the United States die every year in car accidents caused by sleep deprivation.[3]

And this isn't just a consequence of living in a fast-paced, modern society. Sleep deprivation was a problem in Jesus' day as well. Remember the disciples in the Garden of Gethsemene? What was it that kept them from praying with Jesus the night before his crucifixion?

Pause.

That's right, they kept falling asleep.

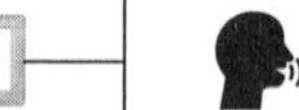 FATIGUE is one of the greatest barriers to prayer and spiritual growth.

It is hard to be like Jesus when you're sleep deprived. If you doubt this, try hanging out with a sleep-deprived person and see how well they do at living in Jesus' name.

Odd as it may sound, for some of you the single most spiritual thing you could do is get enough sleep. And you can say you heard it here first!

Resolve Conflicts before Going to Bed

 The second thing you can do to sleep in Jesus' name is resolve conflicts before going to bed.

What we think about as we drift off to sleep often shapes how we feel the next morning. That's one of the reasons it's beneficial to try to resolve any conflicts before we go to bed.

[3] Susan Brink, "Sleepless in America," *U.S. News and World Report* (October 16, 2000), 63–72.

NOTES

LIVING IN JESUS' NAME

AN ORDINARY DAY

Get enough sleep.

_______________________ is one of the greatest barriers to prayer and spiritual growth.

Resolve conflicts before going to bed.

It is a decisive rule of every Christian fellowship that every dissension that the day has brought must be healed in the evening. It is perilous for the Christian to lie down to sleep with an unreconciled heart.

Dietrich Bonhoeffer

Do not let the sun go down while you are still angry, and do not give the devil a foothold.

(Ephesians 4:26–27)

Invite Jesus to be with you when you wake.

Pray a simple prayer: "God, when I wake up, I want my first thoughts to be about you."

Great is his faithfulness; his mercies begin afresh each day.

(Lamentations 3:23, NLT)

20

 Dietrich Bonhoeffer, a German pastor martyred by the Nazis, wrote:

It is a decisive rule of every Christian fellowship that every dissension that the day has brought must be healed in the evening. It is perilous for the Christian to lie down to sleep with an unreconciled heart.[4]

The Apostle Paul puts it just as bluntly in Ephesians 4:26-27:

Do not let the sun go down while you are still angry, and do not give the devil a foothold.

This may be hard, but as much as it is humanly possible, be at peace with members of your family and others by the time you put your head on the pillow at night. You may only be able to say, "God, I can't fix this right now, so I need you to hold this problem for me until I awake." But whatever *is* in your power to do to bring reconciliation, do it.

Invite Jesus to Be with You When You Wake

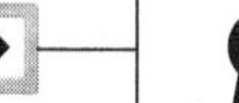

Once you're getting enough sleep and are resolving conflicts before going to bed, the final thing to do as you drift off to sleep is to invite Jesus to be with you when you wake.

You might pray a simple prayer like this: "God, when I wake up, I want my first thoughts to be about you."

 Lamentations 3:23 says:

Great is his faithfulness; his mercies begin afresh each day (NLT).

Ask God to remind you of the "fresh mercies" from him you can count on from the moment you open your eyes and tomorrow begins.

So, that's learning to sleep in Jesus' name.

Waking Up

Participant's Guide, page 21.

Now we come to what we typically think of as the start of the day—waking up.

[4] Dietrich Bonhoeffer, *Life Together* (San Francisco: HarperCollins, 1978), 74.

NOTES

LIVING IN JESUS' NAME

Get enough sleep.

________________ is one of the greatest barriers to prayer and spiritual growth.

Resolve conflicts before going to bed.

> *It is a decisive rule of every Christian fellowship that every dissension that the day has brought must be healed in the evening. It is perilous for the Christian to lie down to sleep with an unreconciled heart.*
>
> Dietrich Bonhoeffer

> *Do not let the sun go down while you are still angry, and do not give the devil a foothold.*
>
> (Ephesians 4:26–27)

Invite Jesus to be with you when you wake.

Pray a simple prayer: "God, when I wake up, I want my first thoughts to be about you."

> *Great is his faithfulness; his mercies begin afresh each day.*
>
> (Lamentations 3:23, NLT)

What are you normally like in the morning? Someone once said there are two kinds of people in the world: those who love to wake up in the morning, and those who hate people who love to wake up in the morning. Marriages usually have one of each.

Optional humor:
A newlywed wife was asked, "Now that you're married, do you sometimes wake up grumpy in the morning?" "No," she replied, "I let him sleep."

When you wake up, check in with yourself. What fears or anxieties are you carrying even before your feet hit the floor? Even while your head is still on the pillow, at the beginning of every day invite Jesus to spend the day with you.

Here's a suggested outline of a simple routine you can use to invite Jesus to be with you. Do this as soon as possible when you wake up.

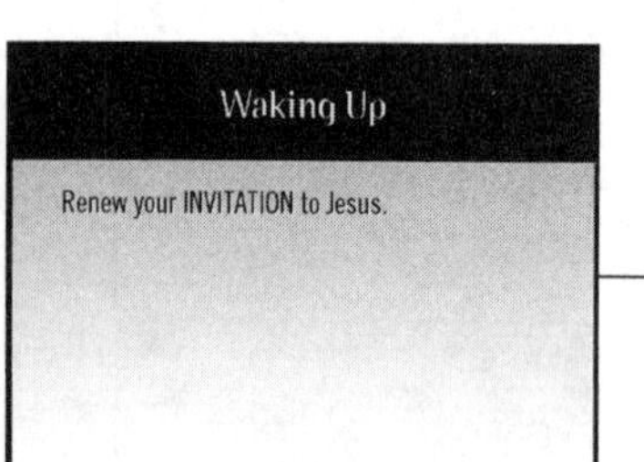

Renew Your Invitation to Jesus

 First, renew your INVITATION to Jesus.

Jesus honors our freedom, so he usually doesn't impose himself on people who aren't open to him. He goes where he's invited, so invite him into your day.

Your invitation could be as simple as, "Lord, before I get up I want to invite you to join me in everything I do today. Thank you for your willingness to live in and through me."

Speak to Jesus about Any Anxieties or Concerns You Feel

 Next, speak to Jesus about any anxieties or concerns you feel.

What are the first thoughts on your mind when you wake up? For many, they are thoughts that make us feel anxious, or fearful, or hurried. It does not need to be so!

NOTES

Waking Up

Renew your ______________________ to Jesus.

Speak to Jesus about any anxieties or concerns you feel.

For Christians, the beginning of the day should not be burdened and haunted by the various kinds of concerns that they face during the day. The Lord stands above the new day, for God has made it. All restlessness, all impurity, all worry and anxiety flee before him. Therefore, in the early morning hours of the day, may our many thoughts and our many idle words be silent and may the first word and the first thought belong to the one to whom our whole life belongs.

Dietrich Bonhoeffer

Cast all your anxiety on him because he cares for you.

(1 Peter 5:7)

Acknowledge your ________________ on Jesus.

Come to me, all you who are weary and burdened, and I will give you rest.

(Matthew 11:28)

 Dietrich Bonhoeffer wrote:

For Christians, the beginning of the day should not be burdened and haunted by the various kinds of concerns that they face during the day. The Lord stands above the new day, for God has made it. All restlessness, all impurity, all worry and anxiety flee before him. Therefore, in the early morning hours of the day, may our many thoughts and our many idle words be silent and may the first word and the first thought belong to the one to whom our whole life belongs.[5]

These words are all the more striking because Bonhoeffer wrote them while living under an oppressive Nazi regime.

This does not have to be a long, drawn-out prayer. Something like, "Lord, I have a meeting today, and I'm nervous about it." Or "Lord, I feel kind of distant from the kids; help me really pay attention when they come home from school." Or "God, I need wisdom for a tough decision."

 Do as 1 Peter 5:7 invites us to do:

Cast all your anxieties on him because he cares for you.

Acknowledge Your Dependence on Jesus

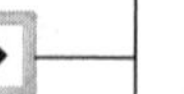

Finally, acknowledge your DEPENDENCE on Jesus.

You were not meant to carry the weight of the world on your shoulders. You weren't meant to carry even the weight of your own life by yourself.

 In Matthew 11:28 Jesus says:

Come to me, all you who are weary and burdened, and I will give you rest.

Take him up on his offer through a simple prayer each morning, and acknowledge your reliance on him.

Just as you've gotten in the habit of brushing your teeth in the morning, get in the habit of beginning your day with Jesus. Invite him into your day and surrender it to him. Let your pillow be a symbol to remind you that you need to go to sleep in Jesus' name and that you need to wake each morning deliberately choosing to begin your day with him.

[4] Dietrich Bonhoeffer, *Life Together* (San Francisco: HarperCollins, 1978), 43.

NOTES

WITH JESUS

SESSION ONE

Waking Up

Renew your ______________________ to Jesus.

Speak to Jesus about any anxieties or concerns you feel.

For Christians, the beginning of the day should not be burdened and haunted by the various kinds of concerns that they face during the day. The Lord stands above the new day, for God has made it. All restlessness, all impurity, all worry and anxiety flee before him. Therefore, in the early morning hours of the day, may our many thoughts and our many idle words be silent and may the first word and the first thought belong to the one to whom our whole life belongs.

Dietrich Bonhoeffer

Cast all your anxiety on him because he cares for you.

(1 Peter 5:7)

Acknowledge your ________________ on Jesus.

Come to me, all you who are weary and burdened, and I will give you rest.

(Matthew 11:28)

21

Turn to page 22.

2 MINUTES

Learning to Find God in Each Moment of the Day

Participant's Guide, page 22.

Another way to describe living in Jesus' name is that it involves learning to find God in each moment of the day—in every activity we're involved in.

Here's an example that may shed light on how this works. Does anyone remember a popular series of children's books that came out a few years ago called *Where's Waldo*? Raise your hand.

Pause.

These books were filled with page after page of very detailed cartoon drawings. Hidden in the details of every drawing was a little character named Waldo, in a red-and-white-striped ski cap and glasses.

The challenge was to become a master in the art of finding Waldo. You might have to search for quite some time to pick him out of the crowd, but Waldo was always there.

In many ways, our experience of God in an ordinary day is like reading the *Where's Waldo?* books.

Learning to Find God in Each Moment of the Day

We need to develop the skill of identifying God's presence in our lives.

We need to develop the skill of identifying God's presence in our lives.

So how do we do that?

REVIEW THE DAY WITH GOD

One of the best tools available to help you find God in each moment is through a review of your day with God.

Think of it as an exercise in looking for where God was at work in you that day.

NOTES

Learning to Find God in Each Moment of the Day

We need to develop the skill of identifying God's presence in our lives.

Review the day with God.

22

This practice of reviewing the day is actually a very ancient form of prayer.[6] Christians for many centuries have found it very helpful—as have many in our day.

Reviewing the day with God is a lot like what sports teams do. When athletes want to improve their performance, they often spend time watching game films. By reviewing what they did on the field, they can learn from mistakes and be encouraged by their progress. In the same way, you can review the game film of your day with God.

We're going to take some time to do this right now.

INDIVIDUAL ACTIVITY: *REVIEW THE DAY WITH GOD*

Participant's Guide, page 23.

Objective
For participants to experience reviewing their day with God.

On page 23 is an outline for reviewing the day with God. We're going to walk through it together step-by-step, and then you'll have some time to do this on your own.

Directions

1. Be still for a moment, and quiet your mind.
2. Acknowledge that Jesus is present. Invite him to guide you.
3. Recall the beginning of the day when you first woke up. Watch that scene, as if on video. What is your reaction to what you see? Talk to God about that.
4. Continue through the video of your day, going from scene to scene. As you reflect on each one, some scenes may fill you with gratitude, others with regret. Speak directly to God about this. You may also want to pray for some of the people you interacted with during the day.
5. End your review with a prayer of thanksgiving for God's mercy and love. Ask him to refresh you as you sleep.

[6] For a more detailed presentation, see Chapter 3 of Richard J. Foster's *Prayer: Finding the Heart's True Home* (San Francisco: HarperCollins, 1992).

NOTES

INDIVIDUAL ACTIVITY

Review the Day with God

1. Be still for a moment, and quiet your mind.

2. Acknowledge that Jesus is present. Invite him to guide you.

3. Recall the beginning of the day when you first woke up. Watch that scene, as if on video. What is your reaction to what you see? Talk to God about that.

4. Continue through the video of your day, going from scene to scene. As you reflect on each one, some scenes may fill you with gratitude, others with regret. Speak directly to God about this. You may also want to pray for some of the people you interacted with during the day.

5. End your review with a prayer of thanksgiving for God's mercy and love. Ask him to refresh you as you sleep.

Take 5 minutes to do this right now.

If you have audio equipment, you can create a more reflective atmosphere during this activity by playing soft instrumental music—no words—quietly in the background.

Call the group back together after 5 minutes.

3 MINUTES

Wrap-up

Let's come back together. Who found something to be thankful for? Raise your hand.

Pause.

That was a gift, wasn't it?

If anyone had some regrets, that's okay too.

What else did you learn about your day?

Solicit two or three comments from the group. Be sure to repeat their answers so everyone hears the response.

Possible responses:

- *I don't usually reflect on my life like that—it was enjoyable.*
- *I winced when I thought of something I'd said earlier.*
- *I found some blessings today I would have overlooked if I hadn't done this.*
- *I had a hard time staying focused.*

Turn to page 24.

Participant's Guide, page 24.

Reviewing Your Day with God Regularly

You will become aware of recurring negative patterns. This will:
—cause you to grow tired of your regrets
—increase your desire to grow and change

If you review your day with God regularly, two things will begin to happen.

First, you will become aware of recurring negative patterns in your life, which will cause you to grow tired of your regrets. This will increase your desire to grow and change.

NOTES

WITH JESUS SESSION ONE

INDIVIDUAL ACTIVITY

Review the Day with God

1. Be still for a moment, and quiet your mind.
2. Acknowledge that Jesus is present. Invite him to guide you.
3. Recall the beginning of the day when you first woke up. Watch that scene, as if on video. What is your reaction to what you see? Talk to God about that.
4. Continue through the video of your day, going from scene to scene. As you reflect on each one, some scenes may fill you with gratitude, others with regret. Speak directly to God about this. You may also want to pray for some of the people you interacted with during the day.
5. End your review with a prayer of thanksgiving for God's mercy and love. Ask him to refresh you as you sleep.

23

LIVING IN JESUS' NAME — AN ORDINARY DAY

Reviewing Your Day with God Regularly

Two things will begin to happen.

- You will become aware of recurring negative patterns. This will:
  —cause you to grow tired of your regrets
  —increase your desire to grow and change
- You will begin to be awed by God's presence in the ordinary moments of your life.

24

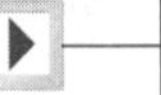

Second, you will begin to be awed by God's presence in the ordinary moments of your life.

You will realize that you really can live your day in Jesus' name. When that starts to happen consistently, life gets exciting—because when you start experiencing the reality of God's presence with you every day, it's not ordinary any more!

1 MINUTE

SUMMARY AND COURSE OVERVIEW

Participant's Guide, page 25.

Course Overview

Session 2: Everyday Relationships
Session 3: Work
Session 4: Leadings
Session 5: Solitude
Session 6: Spiritual Pathways
Session 7: Pace of Life
Session 8: Making the Ordinary Extraordinary

Let me end this session with an overview of the course. We're going to spend the next seven sessions looking at various aspects of an ordinary day—things like relationships and our work. We'll also learn about ways to connect with Jesus throughout an ordinary day by listening to and following leadings, by spending time alone with him in solitude, and by using our unique spiritual pathway to enjoy being with him. We'll look at how pace of life affects our ability to live in Jesus' name, and then in session eight we'll actually plan out an ordinary day with Jesus.

Course Overview

Course goal—to help you spend an ordinary day with Jesus.

And that's the goal of this course—to help you spend an ordinary day with Jesus.

As we've already seen, you can wake up in Jesus' name, you can go to sleep in Jesus' name, and you can do everything in between in Jesus' name.

The big idea is that it *is possible* for each of us to live *every day* with Jesus—one day at a time.

Before we move to the next session on everyday relationships, we're going to take a break.

Break.

NOTES

Reviewing Your Day with God Regularly

Two things will begin to happen.

- You will become aware of recurring negative patterns. This will:
  —cause you to grow tired of your regrets
  —increase your desire to grow and change

- You will begin to be awed by God's presence in the ordinary moments of your life.

Course Overview

Session 2: Everyday Relationships

Session 3: Work

Session 4: Leadings

Session 5: Solitude

Session 6: Spiritual Pathways

Session 7: Pace of Life

Session 8: Making the Ordinary Extraordinary

Course goal—to help you spend an ordinary day with Jesus.

It *is possible* to live *every day* with Jesus—one day at a time.

If you are teaching this course in an eight-week format rather than a weekend seminar format, you can close the session with the following prayer or substitute your own prayer.

Lord, thank you for the gift of each new day. May we learn to find you in every one. Help us lie down each night resting in you, putting our heads on our pillows in complete confidence you are still in control. And may we wake up ready to go into each morning surrendered to you, relying on your everyday grace to help us through each challenge. In Jesus' name, amen.

EVERY DAY RELATIONSHIPS

SESSION SNAPSHOT

Overview

We all have ideas about what constitutes spiritual maturity, but Jesus was absolutely clear: growth in the spiritual life is measured by an increasing capacity to love God and love others. Therefore, relationships are central to the life God wants us to live, and we have ample opportunity in an ordinary day to relate to people lovingly in Jesus' name. Our relationships *show* us the condition of our hearts, and they also help us to *grow* in Christlikeness.

Objectives

In this session, participants will:

1. Discover the ultimate gauge for spiritual maturity
2. Identify barriers to becoming a more loving person
3. Learn three ways to train to be more loving

SESSION OUTLINE

I. Introduction

II. Discovery

A. Spiritual Gauges

1. The Wrong Gauge
2. Small Group Activity: *Spiritual Gauges*
3. The Right Gauge
4. Video: *Flying Lesson*
5. Individual Activity: *Reflection on Flying Lesson*

B. Using the Right Gauge: Training vs. Trying

C. Three Ways to Train to Be More Loving

1. Listen
2. Use Touch
3. Speak Words of Love

III. Summary

EVERYDAY RELATIONSHIPS

TIME & MEDIA

CONTENTS

INTRODUCTION

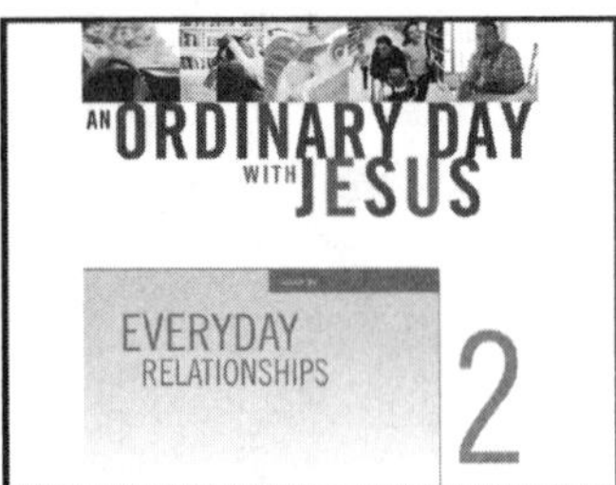

If you are teaching this course in an eight-week format rather than a weekend seminar format, you may want to begin by briefly discussing participants' experiences since the last session. Start the session as follows:

"In session one we learned about going to sleep and waking up in Jesus' name. Did anyone try that? What was it like for you?"

Solicit two or three comments from the group. Be sure to repeat their answers so everyone hears the response.

Possible responses:

- *I found it very enjoyable.*
- *I was surprised what a difference it made to focus on Jesus first thing.*
- *The review of the day made me recognize how my day was spent, and I was surprised by how much I worried.*

NOTES

SESSION TWO

EVERYDAY RELATIONSHIPS

In session one, we learned about going to sleep and waking up in Jesus' name. For most of us, the very next part of our day brings us into contact with other people. It might be a spouse, a roommate, a child, a neighbor, or a coworker. If we're going to continue to live an ordinary day with Jesus, we're going to have to learn how to experience his presence in these everyday relationships. That's what this session is about.

DISCOVERY

5 MINUTES

Spiritual Gauges

Participant's Guide, page 28.

We have many kinds of tools and gauges that tell us how well things are functioning. For example, if you want to know whether or not you have a fever, what instrument do you need?

Pause briefly for participants' responses.

Right, a thermometer.

If you want to know whether or not your car has adequate fuel, what do you need to look at?

Pause briefly for participants' responses.

Yes, the fuel gauge.

If you want to know if there is any relationship between your clothes feeling tighter and all those holiday cookies you ate, what do you use?

Pause briefly for participants' responses.

Right, a scale. Or a tape measure.

How about your soul?

If someone were to ask you how your soul is doing, what gauge would you look at?

EVERYDAY RELATIONSHIPS

Spiritual Gauges

The Wrong Gauge

____________________________ are external, superficial signs or practices that set one group apart from another.

For scribes and Pharisees: observing strict dietary laws, rigidly keeping the Sabbath, and circumcision.

> *Spirituality wrongly understood or pursued is a major source of human misery and rebellion against God.*
>
> Dallas Willard

28

Think about that for a moment. In a few minutes, we're going to have a chance to talk about it. Before we do that, let's take a look at the spiritual gauges people used back in Jesus' day.

The Wrong Gauge

The religious people in that time—scribes and Pharisees—were confident they knew the right gauges to assess not only their own spiritual health but also the spiritual health of everyone else. Using these gauges, they could be very sure who was in and who was out, spiritually speaking.

The scribes and Pharisees used what might be called "boundary markers" as their spiritual gauges.

BOUNDARY MARKERS are external, superficial signs or practices that set one group apart from another.

The scribes and Pharisees watched one another carefully, and they judged each other harshly based on how well they kept or failed to keep these boundary marker practices.

For them, the main issues were observing strict dietary laws, rigidly keeping the Sabbath, and circumcision.

Get these practices right, and your soul—as well as your standing before God—was gauged to be healthy. Get them wrong, and you could be sure you were in trouble.

Here's the problem. These highly trained, biblically literate, passionate believers-in-God were *passionately wrong!* In fact, Jesus aimed some of his harshest criticisms right at them and their legalistic approach to spiritual life.

Why? Why would Jesus—the Son of God who wanted people to care deeply about spiritual matters—come down so hard on those who were making every effort to be spiritual? The answer is that they were using the wrong gauge, and it had serious consequences for their relationship with God.

NOTES

EVERYDAY RELATIONSHIPS

Spiritual Gauges

The Wrong Gauge

______________________________ are external, superficial signs or practices that set one group apart from another.

For scribes and Pharisees: observing strict dietary laws, rigidly keeping the Sabbath, and circumcision.

> *Spirituality wrongly understood or pursued is a major source of human misery and rebellion against God.*
>
> Dallas Willard

28

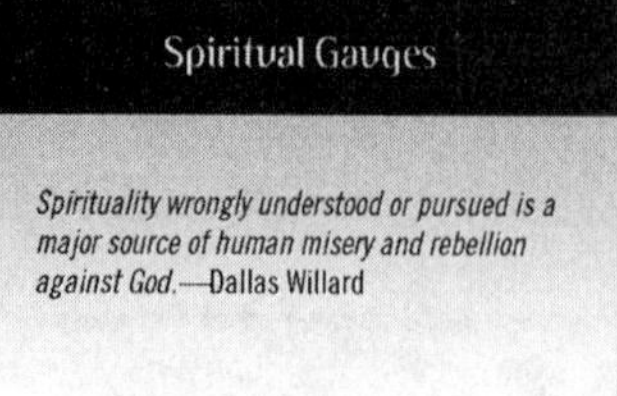

 Author Dallas Willard summed it up well when he wrote:

> *Spirituality wrongly understood or pursued is a major source of human misery and rebellion against God.*[1]

The focus of this session is to help us avoid that misery and rebellion by making sure we don't fall into the trap of using the wrong spiritual gauges.

We've talked about wrong spiritual gauges in Jesus' day, but what about today? Do Christians now have external boundary markers they use to gauge spiritual health and maturity?

Let's take a couple minutes to talk about this in groups.

SMALL GROUP ACTIVITY: *SPIRITUAL GAUGES*

Participant's Guide, page 29.

Objective
For participants to identify wrong spiritual gauges people use today.

Directions

1. Form a group with two other people.
2. Answer the following questions: What are some wrong ways people in our day gauge spiritual health and maturity? Do you sometimes use wrong spiritual gauges? What are they?

Any questions on the directions?

You will have about 10 minutes for your discussion.

Call the group back together after 10 minutes.

[1] Dallas Willard, *The Spirit of the Disciplines* (San Francisco: HarperCollins, 1991), 81.

NOTES

Spiritual Gauges

The Wrong Gauge

______________________ are external, superficial signs or practices that set one group apart from another.

For scribes and Pharisees: observing strict dietary laws, rigidly keeping the Sabbath, and circumcision.

> *Spirituality wrongly understood or pursued is a major source of human misery and rebellion against God.*
> Dallas Willard

SMALL GROUP ACTIVITY

Spiritual Gauges

1. Get in a group with two other people.
2. Answer the following questions:
   - What are some wrong ways people in our day gauge spiritual health and maturity?
   - Do you sometimes use wrong spiritual gauges? What are they?

2 MINUTES

Wrap-up

What are the wrong gauges we sometimes use?

Solicit three or four comments from the group. Be sure to repeat their answers so everyone hears the response.

Possible responses:

- *Busyness in church activities*
- *What you wear*
- *Knowledge of the Bible and doctrine*
- *Attending church services*
- *How early they get up in the morning to have their quiet time*
- *Comparing themselves to people who are not as spiritual*
- *Using the right spiritual buzz words*

Notice that in many of the wrong gauges people focus on external behaviors to assess how they are doing spiritually. For example, how their devotional life is going, or how often they're having quiet times, or if they're following a set of legalistic rules.

Turn to page 30.

1 MINUTE

THE RIGHT GAUGE

Participant's Guide, page 30.

If those are all the wrong gauges, what is the right gauge of spiritual health and maturity?

Fortunately, we don't need to be confused. Jesus made it crystal clear in Matthew 22:36-40.

When someone asked him:

"Teacher, which is the greatest commandment in the Law?" Jesus replied: "'Love the Lord your God with all your heart and with all your soul and with all your mind.' This is the first and greatest commandment. And the second is like it: 'Love your neighbor as yourself.' All the Law and the Prophets hang on these two commandments."

SMALL GROUP ACTIVITY

Spiritual Gauges

1. Get in a group with two other people.
2. Answer the following questions:
   - What are some wrong ways people in our day gauge spiritual health and maturity?
   - Do you sometimes use wrong spiritual gauges? What are they?

EVERYDAY RELATIONSHIPS

The Right Gauge

> *Teacher, which is the greatest commandment of the Law?*
> *Jesus replied, "Love the Lord your God with all your heart*
> *and with all your soul and with all your mind."*
> *This is the first and greatest commandment.*
> *And the second is like it: "Love your neighbor as yourself."*
> *All the Law and the Prophets*
> *hang on these two commandments.*
> (Matthew 22:36–40)

The right gauge is _____________________.

> *If I have not love—even if I am knowledgeable,*
> *even if I do miracles, or give myself up as a martyr—*
> *I am nothing.*
> (1 Corinthians 13:1-3, paraphrased)

God is not interested in some abstract thing called your *spiritual* life.

God is interested in your _____________________.

He wants you to be filled with love—love for him, and love for people.

According to Jesus, the right gauge is LOVE—love for God, and love for neighbors.

Paul echoed this theme in his famous love chapter, 1 Corinthians 13. He wrote, "If I don't have love—even if I am knowledgeable, even if I do miracles, or give myself up as a martyr—I am nothing" (paraphrased).

The Right Gauge

- God is not interested in some abstract thing called your *spiritual* life.
- God is just interested in your LIFE.
- He wants you to be filled with love—love for him, and love for people.

We must understand this important truth: God is not interested in some abstract thing called your *spiritual* life. God is interested in your LIFE—*all* of it. And he wants you to be filled with love—love for him, and love for people.

Love is the right gauge.

So how do we use the gauge of love in an ordinary day?

VIDEO: *FLYING LESSON*

Participant's Guide, page 31.

To get a picture of what this might look like, we're going to watch a video. It's a scene on an airplane that could take place in your life or mine. It's a great example of what the gauge of love might look like in our lives.

View video: *Flying Lesson.*

That puts things into perspective, doesn't it? We're going to take a few minutes individually to reflect on what we just saw.

6 MINUTES

INDIVIDUAL ACTIVITY: *REFLECTION ON FLYING LESSON*

Objective
For participants to reflect on the spiritual gauge of love and identify barriers that keep them from being a more loving person.

NOTES

EVERYDAY RELATIONSHIPS

The Right Gauge

Teacher, which is the greatest commandment of the Law?
Jesus replied, "Love the Lord your God with all your heart
and with all your soul and with all your mind."
This is the first and greatest commandment.
And the second is like it: "Love your neighbor as yourself."
All the Law and the Prophets
hang on these two commandments.
(Matthew 22:36–40)

The right gauge is ________________________.

If I have not love—even if I am knowledgeable,
even if I do miracles, or give myself up as a martyr—
I am nothing.
(1 Corinthians 13:1-3, paraphrased)

God is not interested in some abstract thing called your *spiritual* life.

God is interested in your ________________________.

He wants you to be filled with love—love for him, and love for people.

VIDEO

Flying Lesson

Notes:

INDIVIDUAL ACTIVITY

Reflection on *Flying Lesson*

Use the space below to write your answers to the following questions:

1. Think about the two men on the plane and their contrasting reactions to the young woman. How are you like the irritated passenger? How are you like the compassionate passenger? What does this reveal about the gauge of love in your life?

2. What barriers keep you from being a more loving person?

Directions

Use the space below to write your answers to the following questions:

1. Think about the two men on the plane and their contrasting reactions to the young woman. How are you like the irritated passenger? How are you like the compassionate passenger? What does this reveal about the gauge of love in your life?

2. What barriers keep you from being a more loving person?

You will have about 5 minutes.

Call the group back together after 5 minutes.

2 MINUTES

Wrap-up

What were some barriers you identified that keep you from being more loving?

Solicit three or four comments from the group. Be sure to repeat their answers so everyone hears the response.

Possible responses:

- *Busyness, hurried pace of life*
- *Fear*
- *Competing priorities*
- *Energy drain, fatigue*
- *Thinking my life is harder than others'*
- *Judgmental spirit*
- *Unsure how to act*
- *Want to get my own way*

Even when we've decided we want to become more loving, we still face a challenge. How do we actually go about pursuing this change, or using the right gauge?

Turn to page 32.

NOTES

VIDEO

Flying Lesson

Notes:

INDIVIDUAL ACTIVITY

Reflection on *Flying Lesson*

Use the space below to write your answers to the following questions:

1. Think about the two men on the plane and their contrasting reactions to the young woman. How are you like the irritated passenger? How are you like the compassionate passenger? What does this reveal about the gauge of love in your life?

2. What barriers keep you from being a more loving person?

4 MINUTES

Using the Right Gauge: Training vs. Trying

Using the Right Gauge: Training vs. Trying

Participant's Guide, page 32.

When it comes to using the gauge of love, one of the most important things we need to understand is the distinction of *training* versus *trying*.

Listen to what the Apostle Paul wrote in 1 Corinthians 9:24–25:

Do you not know that in a race all the runners run, but only one gets the prize? Run in such a way as to get the prize. Everyone who competes in the games goes into strict training. They do it to get a crown that will not last; but we do it to get a crown that will last forever.

Notice what he says: runners go into strict training so they can win a perishable crown. But we should *go into training* to get a crown that will last forever. There it is: God wants us to go into spiritual training.

Now, there is an enormous difference between *trying* to do something and *training* to do something. And there is a limit to what we can do on our own power. To get a clearer picture of the difference between training and trying, let's continue with Paul's running analogy. How many of you could leave this room right now and run—not walk, but run—an entire marathon? Raise your hand.

Pause.

How many of you who believe you couldn't run a marathon believe you *would* be able to run a marathon if you just tried really, really, really hard?

Pause.

Trying harder won't make it happen, will it? However, many of us here *could* run a marathon eventually if we really wanted to. What would we have to do first? We would have to train. We would have to eat differently and exercise and, if we had the right coaching, we could probably be ready to run a marathon eventually.

NOTES

EVERYDAY RELATIONSHIPS

Using the Right Gauge: Training vs. Trying

Do you not know that in a race all the runners run,
but only one gets the prize? Run in such a way as to get the prize.
Everyone who competes in the games goes into strict training.
They do it to get a crown that will not last;
but we do it to get a crown that will last forever.
(1 Corinthians 9:24-25)

Definition of Training:

To train means to ________________________ my life around activities I can do that will enable me, over time, to do what I cannot do by direct effort alone.—Dallas Willard

Train yourself to be godly.
(1 Timothy 4:7)

Everyone who is fully trained will be like [their] teacher.
(Luke 6:40)

32

Dallas Willard has a simple definition:

To train means to ARRANGE my life around activities I can do that will enable me, over time, to do what I cannot do by direct effort alone.

As a general rule, we human beings *overestimate* what we can do by trying and *underestimate* what we can do by training. Significant change in any area—physical, intellectual, and so on—usually involves training, not just trying. And this is no less true when it comes to spiritual life.

Paul wrote to a young pastor in 1Timothy 4:7:

Train yourself to be godly.

Jesus echoed the same thought in Luke 6:40 when he said:

Everyone who is fully trained will be like [their] teacher.

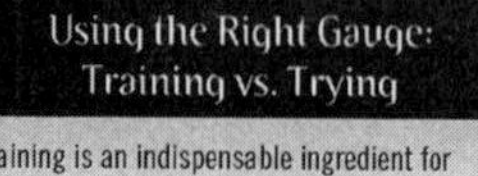

Participant's Guide, page 33.

Both Paul and Jesus make it clear: Training is an indispensable ingredient for pursuing spiritual transformation.

When they hear messages about Jesus' kind of life, many people think to themselves: "I must try harder to be like Jesus." They hear a message about love and say, "Tomorrow I will try really, really hard to be more loving." Then what happens? Have you ever tried really, really hard to be more loving with an overactive three-year-old or a cranky boss? It doesn't work very well, does it?

But it is possible for each one of us to become more loving. God would not have commanded it if it weren't possible. But what will we probably have to do first?

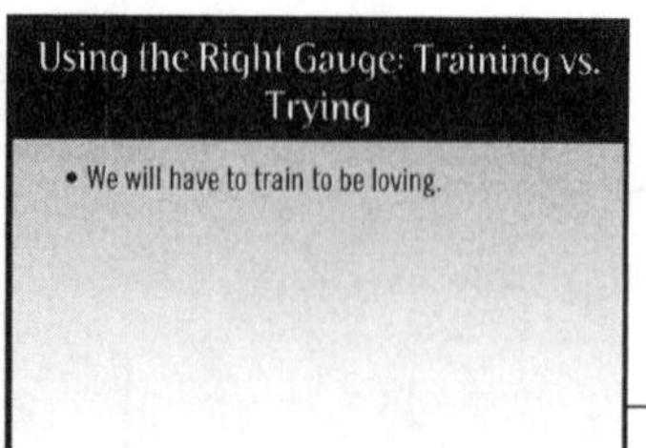

Train. We will have to *train* to be loving.

We will have to engage in some activities we *can* do at our current level of loving so that over time we will become even more loving.

The purpose of such activities is not to demonstrate how spiritual we are. Training activities exist to help us grow in love for God and other people and to become more like Christ.

NOTES

EVERYDAY RELATIONSHIPS

AN ORDINARY DAY

Using the Right Gauge: Training vs. Trying

Do you not know that in a race all the runners run,
but only one gets the prize? Run in such a way as to get the prize.
Everyone who competes in the games goes into strict training.
They do it to get a crown that will not last;
but we do it to get a crown that will last forever.
(1 Corinthians 9:24-25)

Definition of Training:

To train means to ______________________ my life around activities I can do that will enable me, over time, to do what I cannot do by direct effort alone.—Dallas Willard

Train yourself to be godly.
(1 Timothy 4:7)

Everyone who is fully trained will be like [their] teacher.
(Luke 6:40)

32

WITH JESUS

SESSION TWO

Training is an indispensable ingredient for pursuing spiritual transformation.

We will have to train to be loving.

The purpose of such activities is not to demonstrate how spiritual we are.

Training activities exist to help us grow in love for God and other people and to become more like Christ.

33

Turn to page 34.

6 MINUTES

Three Ways to Train to Be More Loving

Participant's Guide, page 34.

Believers over the centuries have used many practices to help them train to be like Christ. Several of them Jesus himself used. Using Jesus as our supreme example of how to show love, we're going to look at three ways we can train to be more loving in our everyday relationships.

Three Ways to Train to Be More Loving

1. Listen.

LISTEN

 First, we need to listen.

Jesus did a lot of that. He was certainly the greatest teacher who ever lived, yet he didn't just speak—he listened. He asked questions and then waited for people to answer. He paused in silence to give people time to think, and feel, and process.

Optional illustration:
One mother describes how her teenage daughter taught her the power of listening. One evening after dinner her daughter was especially disappointed and depressed about a situation at school. Although she was tired herself, the mother sat and listened as her daughter poured out her concerns. As the daughter continued, the mother wondered to herself, "What can I possibly say to help her? I feel so powerless right now." While she listened attentively, unable to come up with any words of comfort or wisdom, the daughter paused and said, "Thanks for sitting with me, Mom. I feel better now." And that was the end of it—the daughter's whole outlook on her situation had changed. The mother had done the very thing the daughter needed: she'd listened.

 James 1:19 says:

Everyone should be quick to listen, slow to speak and slow to become angry.

According to James, you can be more loving by listening more.

NOTES

EVERYDAY RELATIONSHIPS

Three Ways to Train to Be More Loving

1. ❑ Listen.

> *Everyone should be quick to listen, slow to speak and slow to become angry.*
> (James 1:19)

Use the phrase "Tell me __________________."

2. ❑ Use touch.

UCLA study: We need at least eight to ten meaningful touches a day for our emotional health.

3. ❑ Speak words of love.

> Jesus, the Word who became flesh, was *"full of grace and . . . truth."*
> (John 1:14)

Words of grace
- Comfort
- Encouragement
- Care and concern

Words of truth
- Forgiveness
- Reconciliation
- Addressing conflict

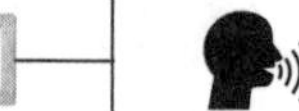

One of the simplest ways to train in listening is to use the phrase "Tell me MORE."

When someone is talking, resist the urge to comment on their words. Instead, when they've finished a thought, look at them and say sincerely, "Tell me more."

This phrase is so important, let's say it together.

Slowly say the phrase out loud together. This may seem a little awkward, but try it anyway. It works!

"Tell me more."

Of course, once you say that, you will need to actually listen! You can't love in a hurry, and you can't listen in a hurry—patience and love are bound together. If you use this simple phrase, over time you will become a more loving and patient person. And you can do this now, without special training—you really can!

Three Ways to Train to Be More Loving

1. Listen.
2. Use touch.

USE TOUCH

In addition to listening to people, a second way to train in love is to use touch.

It is important to be aware of any sensitivities your group may have about what constitutes appropriate touch. In some cultures, hugging and touching are common and acceptable forms of expressing love and care; in others, touch is appropriately expressed in some settings (e.g., during a Sunday morning greeting time at church) but not in others (e.g., in informal social situations or between men and women). You may need to address any unique social or cultural issues about touch in this section in order to make the teaching appropriate for your setting.

Jesus reached out and touched the untouchables in his world, including sick people. He held little children, which was completely out of character for respected rabbis in his day. He was comfortable being around both men and women, and they felt safe around him.

NOTES

AN ORDINARY DAY

EVERYDAY RELATIONSHIPS

Three Ways to Train to Be More Loving

1. ❑ Listen.

> *Everyone should be quick to listen, slow to speak and slow to become angry.*
> (James 1:19)

Use the phrase "Tell me ________________."

2. ❑ Use touch.

UCLA study: We need at least eight to ten meaningful touches a day for our emotional health.

3. ❑ Speak words of love.

> Jesus, the Word who became flesh, was *"full of grace and . . . truth."*
> (John 1:14)

Words of grace
- Comfort
- Encouragement
- Care and concern

Words of truth
- Forgiveness
- Reconciliation
- Addressing conflict

34

 A study at UCLA discovered that we need at least eight to ten meaningful touches a day for our emotional health.[2]

A warm handshake, a touch on the arm or shoulder, or a hug can be a huge blessing. I hope you've all had your quota of hugs today!

We need to use appropriate touch to connect with people as Jesus did—for our own sakes, as well as theirs. You will find it will help you become more loving, and people will experience you as a more loving person.

Speak Words of Love

We can train in love when we listen, when we use touch, and, finally, we can train when we speak words of love.

Jesus often spoke words of love to the people he came in contact with. Sometimes they were words of grace, other times they were words of truth. Both came from a heart of love.

 The Apostle John says that Jesus, the Word who became flesh, was "full of grace and truth."[3]

Notice that John describes him as both grace-giving and truth-telling. The same ought to be true of us.

 In the course of our everyday relationships, we need to speak words of grace. It might mean offering comfort, giving encouragement, or expressing care or concern. And we need to speak words of truth, even when truth is hard to hear. This might mean asking for forgiveness, seeking reconciliation, or addressing conflict.

Because it's often easier for most of us to speak grace than it is to speak truth, on page 114 in the Appendix is a step-by-step guide for navigating conflict based on Jesus' teaching in Matthew 18. If you need help in this area, you can take some time to look this over later.

[2] Gary Smalley and John Trent, *The Blessing* (New York: Pocket Books, 1990), 42.
[3] John 1:14

NOTES

EVERYDAY RELATIONSHIPS

Three Ways to Train to Be More Loving

1. ❑ Listen.

> *Everyone should be quick to listen, slow to speak and slow to become angry.*
> (James 1:19)

Use the phrase "Tell me ________________."

2. ❑ Use touch.

UCLA study: We need at least eight to ten meaningful touches a day for our emotional health.

3. ❑ Speak words of love.

> Jesus, the Word who became flesh, was *"full of grace and . . . truth."*
> (John 1:14)

Words of grace
- Comfort
- Encouragement
- Care and concern

Words of truth
- Forgiveness
- Reconciliation
- Addressing conflict

34

I want to encourage you. You do not have to start anything new in your life to do this. All you need to do is work at the relationships you have, using some simple steps that Jesus modeled. If you want to be more loving, don't just go out and say, "I'm going to be loving." Instead, try some of these simple exercises. Say to people, "Tell me more." Reach out and touch someone on the arm, or give them a hug. And say an extra kind thing daily, or speak a tough truth when needed. Over time, you will become a more loving person.

Take a moment now to look over the list of three ways to train to be more loving. Place a check mark next to the training activity you would like to use in an ordinary day.

Pause to allow participants to do this.

Now that you've identified a way to become more loving, imagine what it would be like to look back on your life and observe that you had consistently become a more loving person. This is something you can do. You can engage in simple training activities that really will help you to become more loving.

1 MINUTE

SUMMARY

Participant's Guide, page 35 .

To summarize this session, we can measure our life's successes in a lot of areas, but the one gauge we need to focus on above all others is the gauge of love.

Next session, we'll look at how we spend most of our hours each day: in work. We're going to learn how to do our work—paid or unpaid, at home, in the office, at a factory, or in a classroom—in Jesus' name. If you do something other than sleep all day, this session is for you!

Let's close this session with prayer.

NOTES

Three Ways to Train to Be More Loving

1. ❑ Listen.

> *Everyone should be quick to listen, slow to speak and slow to become angry.*
> (James 1:19)

Use the phrase "Tell me ______________."

2. ❑ Use touch.

UCLA study: We need at least eight to ten meaningful touches a day for our emotional health.

3. ❑ Speak words of love.

> Jesus, the Word who became flesh, was *"full of grace and . . . truth."*
> (John 1:14)

Words of grace
- Comfort
- Encouragement
- Care and concern

Words of truth
- Forgiveness
- Reconciliation
- Addressing conflict

Summary

You may wish to substitute your own prayer for the prayer below.

Lord, thank you for filling our lives with relationships. May we be open to the work you want to do in us through them. Make us brave, to see ourselves as we really are, looking intently at the gauge of love—which is the most important one of all. We ask this in Jesus' name, amen.

If you are teaching this course in the weekend seminar format, this concludes the Friday evening portion of the course. You may wish to say the following to close the evening:

"That's all for tonight. Thanks for being here. We'll see you tomorrow morning at ________ A.M. Sleep well, in Jesus' name!"

WORK

SESSION SNAPSHOT

OVERVIEW

Most people aren't very aware of Jesus' presence in their work. But because this is the largest part of our day, we need to include him at work if we are to live an ordinary day with him. This session will take participants through a typical workday. They will learn how to experience God's character-building activity in the relationships and experiences they encounter.

OBJECTIVES

In this session, participants will:

1. Consider ways to begin and end their workday in Jesus' name
2. Learn ways they can experience God's presence with them at work
3. Give themselves a performance review from God's perspective

SESSION OUTLINE

I. Introduction

II. Discovery

Video: *Work*

A. Why Work?

B. Beginning Your Workday

Small Group Activity: *Beginning My Workday*

C. During Your Workday

1. Setting
2. People
3. Take Mini-Breaks

D. Ending Your Workday

E. Two Additional Observations about Work

1. Unpaid Work
2. Wrong Fit
3. Individual and Small Group Activity: *The Ultimate Performance Review*

III. Summary

WORK

TIME & MEDIA

CONTENTS

2 MINUTES

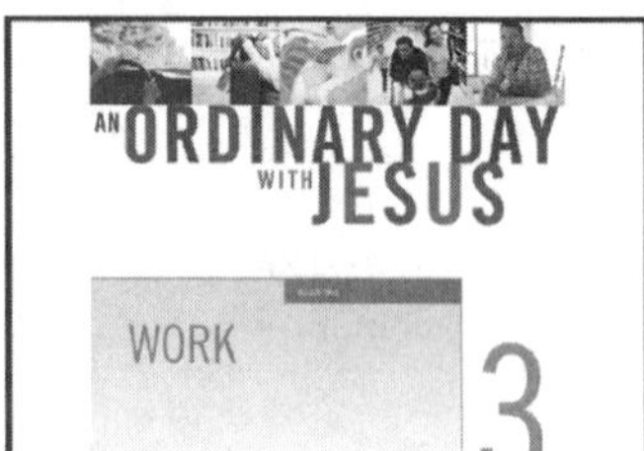

INTRODUCTION

Welcome to session three of *An Ordinary Day with Jesus.*

If you are teaching this course in the weekend seminar format, this is the first session of the Saturday portion of the course. You may want to ask participants about their experiences since the last session with the following question:

"Did anyone try going to sleep and waking up in Jesus' name? What was it like for you?"

Solicit two or three comments from the group. Be sure to repeat their answers so everyone hears the response.

Possible responses:

- *I found it very enjoyable.*
- *I was surprised what a difference it made to focus on Jesus first thing.*
- *The review of the day made me recognize how my day was spent, and I was surprised by how much I worried.*

NOTES

SESSION THREE

WORK

If you are teaching this course in an eight-week format rather than a weekend seminar format, you may want to begin by briefly discussing participants' experiences since the last session. Start the session as follows:

"In the last session we talked about everyday relationships and three ways we could train—by listening, using touch, and speaking words of love. Did anyone have a chance to use any of these training tools? What was it like for you?"

Solicit two or three comments from the group. Be sure to repeat their answers so everyone hears the response.

Possible responses:

- *I was amazed at how I really did feel like I was being more loving when I tried some of these.*
- *I was surprised what a difference simply saying "Tell me more" made—people really did tell me more!*
- *I have always been a little uncomfortable reaching out to people, but I was glad I tried.*

In the first session we talked about going to sleep and waking up in Jesus' name. In session two we looked at everyday relationships and how love is the right gauge of spiritual maturity. In this session we're going to explore what it means to be with Jesus in your daily work—not just how you feel about your job, or how to be more successful at it, but how to make your work an act of partnering between you and God through all aspects of your workday.

It's important to note that everyone here works. It may be at a job . . . it may be at home . . . it may be in school. You may get paid for your work or not. You may be a volunteer, or be retired, or be full-time at home. Your work is whatever you do daily. From a biblical perspective, everybody works. Paycheck or not—everybody works.

1 MINUTE

DISCOVERY

Let's begin with a trivia question.

Other than genetics, what do you think is the number one factor that determines how long you'll live? What most contributes to—or takes away from—your life span?

NOTES

SESSION THREE

WORK

Pause briefly for participants' responses.

Here's what the experts say: it's job satisfaction.

Studies have shown those who say they enjoy their work, live longer; those who don't, die sooner.[1]

Now that you know that—how many of you are convinced you could die at any moment?

Optional Activity:
If you have time, this one-minute activity is a fun way to get participants talking about work.

"Just for fun, turn to the person next to you and each of you take 30 seconds to convince the other person that your job—whether paid or unpaid—is harder than their job."

Call group back together after 1 minute.

"Which of you won?"

Pause.

5 MINUTES

VIDEO: *WORK*

Participant's Guide, page 38.

We're going to watch a video now that will help us see how work affects us.

View video: *Work.*

1 MINUTE

Wrap-Up

If you were to identify the one or two obstacles to doing your work in Jesus' name, what would they be?

[1] John Maxwell, "It's the Grind that Gets 'Em," a message given May 16, 1989, Injoy Life Club Lesson (June 1989).

NOTES

WORK

VIDEO

Work

Notes:

Why Work?

We work because we are made in the image of God.

> *My Father is always at his work to this very day, and I, too, am working.*
> (John 5:17)

Work is:

—not a curse but a blessing.

—partnering with God to care for his creation and serve others.

The most important thing you bring home from your work is __________.

Solicit three or four comments from the group. Be sure to repeat their answers so everyone hears the response.

Possible responses:

- *The fast pace*
- *Dealing with people*
- *Kids' needs*
- *Deadlines*
- *Huge responsibilities that weigh heavily*
- *Difficult coworkers*
- *Interruptions*
- *Lack of patience*
- *Job tasks feel "worldly"*

3 MINUTES

Why Work?

The truth is, work is *hard.* In fact, many people think of work as a necessary evil they have to do just to pay the bills. If you were to ask the average person, "Why do you work?" what do you think would be the number one response?

Pause briefly for participants' responses.

Most people say "money." You may have seen the bumper sticker: "I owe, I owe, so off to work I go." But money by itself is not a good enough reason to work. Stay-at-home parents already know this because they work very hard for no money at all!

Optional humor:
Consider this ironic fact: The guy who sang the song "Take This Job and Shove It" is named Johnny *Paycheck!*

According to Scripture, we work because we are made in the image of God.

NOTES

WORK

VIDEO

Work

Notes:

Why Work?

We work because we are made in the image of God.

> *My Father is always at his work to this very day, and I, too, am working.*
> (John 5:17)

Work is:

—not a curse but a blessing.

—partnering with God to care for his creation and serve others.

The most important thing you bring home from your work is __________.

If you think about it, what does God do all day? Ever ask yourself that question?

He works! We see this from the beginning of the Bible, where God is doing the work of creation. This continues throughout Scripture. The Bible is essentially a book about all that God has done in human history—all his *work*.

Jesus worked too. He spent most of his life as a carpenter.

Jesus said of his Heavenly Father in John 5:17:

> *My Father is always at his work to this very day, and I, too, am working.*

I don't know if you've ever thought about it, but the correct answer to that question of what God does all day is, he works. And he made us in his image, and that's why we're to work as well.

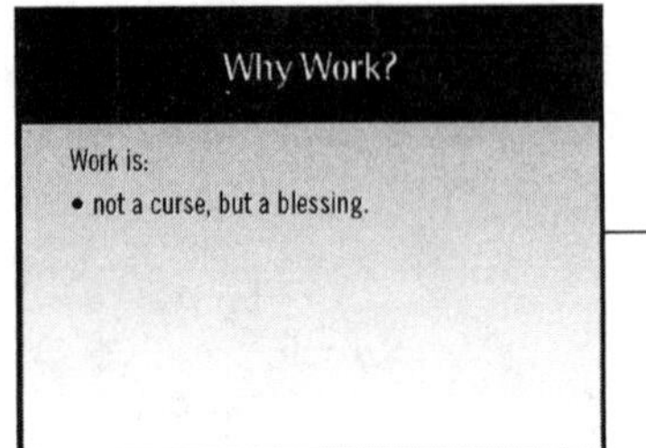

Work is not a curse but a blessing.

You were made to contribute value to others in your own unique way. That's one of the reasons why a sense of being useless or unnecessary is so painful to us. People sometimes think work entered the world because of the curse. It did not. *Frustration* over work came because of the curse—"thorns and thistles."[2] But work itself is a very good thing.

According to the Bible, work is partnering with God to care for his creation and serve others.

Doing the right work, with the right attitude and spirit, is immensely important. Because the most important thing you bring home from your work is not a paycheck—especially if you aren't paid in the first place!

The most important thing you bring home from your work is YOU.

Let's start with the big picture. From beginning to end, what would it look like for you to do what you do daily—a job, running a household, going to school, volunteering, caring for children—in Jesus' name?

[2] Genesis 3:18

NOTES

WORK

VIDEO

Work

Notes:

Why Work?

We work because we are made in the image of God.

> *My Father is always at his work to this very day, and I, too, am working.*
> (John 5:17)

Work is:

—not a curse but a blessing.

—partnering with God to care for his creation and serve others.

The most important thing you bring home from your work is __________.

38

Beginning Your Workday

Participant's Guide, page 39.

Beginning Your Workday

- Showing up on time
- Greeting your coworkers or family members differently

Beginning Your Workday

- Pray
  —Tell God about your attitudes or feelings.

Picture the beginning of your workday. How could you begin your work in Jesus' name?

For one thing, it would probably include showing up on time. It might well involve greeting your coworkers or your children differently—in a way that makes them glad you are part of their lives.

Begin your day by taking a moment to pray. First, you may want to tell God about your attitudes or feelings.

Are you hurried? Excited? Fearful? Bored? Joyful? Stressed? Talk to God about that.

Ask God to make you effective and successful in the work you are doing.

That is a good prayer to pray.

Also, ask God to partner with you throughout the day.

Ask him to help you with the challenges you face.

Let's take a few minutes to discuss this in small groups.

Small Group Activity: *Beginning My Workday*

Objective
For participants to consider how beginning their workday in Jesus' name might make a difference in their lives.

NOTES

Beginning Your Workday

Showing up on time

Greeting your coworkers or your children differently

Pray

—Tell God about your attitudes or feelings.

—Ask God to make you effective and successful.

—Ask God to partner with you throughout the day.

SMALL GROUP ACTIVITY

Beginning My Workday

1. Form a group with two other people.
2. Describe the beginning of your workday.
3. Share how you think it might be different if you were to begin your workday in Jesus' name.

Directions

1. Form a group with two other people.
2. Describe the beginning of your workday.
3. Share how you think it might be different if you were to begin your workday in Jesus' name.

Any questions on the directions?

You will have 9 minutes for your discussion.

Call the group back together after 9 minutes.

2 MINUTES

Wrap-up

What are some ways your workday might be different if you began it in Jesus' name?

Solicit three or four comments from the group. Be sure to repeat their answers so everyone hears the response.

Possible responses:

- *I'd be less crabby, more friendly.*
- *I'd pray and give my concerns to God.*
- *I'd do a heart check to start the day with a better attitude.*
- *I'd probably be more productive.*
- *I'd take a moment to be more grateful for my job and the people I work with.*

I think you'll find that if you begin the day well and pay attention to some of these ways to do it in Jesus' name, the rest of the day will be significantly improved. And you can do this—you really can.

Turn to page 40.

NOTES

WITH JESUS SESSION THREE

Beginning Your Workday

Showing up on time

Greeting your coworkers or your children differently

Pray

—Tell God about your attitudes or feelings.

—Ask God to make you effective and successful.

—Ask God to partner with you throughout the day.

SMALL GROUP ACTIVITY

Beginning My Workday

1. Form a group with two other people.
2. Describe the beginning of your workday.
3. Share how you think it might be different if you were to begin your workday in Jesus' name.

9 MINUTES

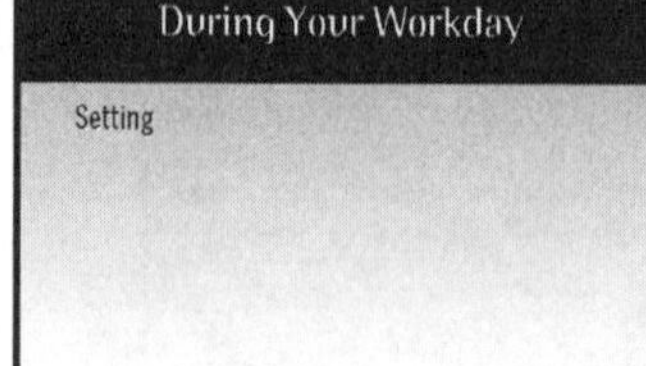

During Your Workday

SETTING

Participant's Guide, page 40.

Once you've started the day in Jesus' name, the next thing to do is consider the setting in which you work.

Does the setting at your desk or workspace help remind you that you are working in partnership with God?

If you don't have such a workspace, is there anything you carry that helps you be mindful of him?

One way to help you be more aware of God's presence with you is to place SYMBOLS or reminders in your work setting to help you remember you do not work alone.

You might write a single word on a piece of paper that represents what you're asking God to help you with, such as *Peace, Wisdom,* or *Serve.*

Or you could write the notation for a favorite Scripture. A good one for work would be "3:23," to remind you of Colossians 3:23, which says, "Whatever you do, work at it with all your heart, as working for the Lord."

If you don't have a designated workspace, you could carry a small stone in your purse or pocket as a reminder that your life is built on Jesus the Rock and your work can be secure in his care.

If you have a personal example of something you use in your setting to remind yourself that God is present with you at work, you may want to share it here.

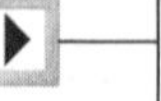

Another way to help you be aware of God's presence is to make sure your work setting is well ordered.

NOTES

WORK

During Your Workday

Setting

Place ______________________ or reminders in your work setting.

A single word on a piece of paper (*peace, wisdom, serve*)

A favorite Scripture verse

> *Whatever you do, work at it with all your heart, as working for the Lord.*
> (Colossians 3:23)

Make sure your work setting is well ordered.

People

Look for opportunities to do simple acts of ______________________.

"How may I serve you today?"

Learn from difficult people.

They help us grow in our ability to love.

They represent a learning opportunity.

Say to yourself, "School is in session; here's my chance to learn about love."

Maybe your workspace is too cluttered for you to find God—or anything else, for that matter. One study found that the average desk worker has thirty-six hours of work on his or her desk and spends three hours a week sorting through piles trying to find the next project to work on.[3] The Bible says that in the beginning of God's work he brought order out of chaos; maybe he's calling you to the same task.

So as best you can, create a setting that helps you be productive spiritually as well as occupationally.

People

PEOPLE

It is virtually impossible to do our work in the world and not come across people. For some of us, this may only be a few people—and the same people every day. Others of us are constantly meeting new people.

Whatever your situation, one of the most important aspects of working in Jesus' name is how you relate to the people your work brings you in contact with.

These could be coworkers, a boss, clients, children, teachers, or students. In order to experience God's presence in these relationships, we need to pay attention to how we treat people.

Look for Opportunities to Do Simple Acts of Service

One way to treat coworkers and others we encounter as Jesus would treat them is to look for opportunities to do simple acts of SERVICE.

These include things like holding an elevator open for a late passenger, offering to carry a heavy package, or opening a door. Or it might involve offering to help a coworker on a project.

When looking for this kind of opportunity, a great phrase to use is "How may I serve you today?"

Let's practice that phrase together:

Have participants repeat the phrase with you.

"How may I serve you today?"

[3] Richard A. Swenson, M.D., *The Overload Syndrome* (Colorado Springs: NavPress, 1999), 142.

NOTES

WORK

During Your Workday

Setting

Place ______________________ or reminders in your work setting.

A single word on a piece of paper (*peace, wisdom, serve*)

A favorite Scripture verse

> *Whatever you do, work at it with all your heart, as working for the Lord.*
> (Colossians 3:23)

Make sure your work setting is well ordered.

People

Look for opportunities to do simple acts of ______________________.

"How may I serve you today?"

Learn from difficult people.

They help us grow in our ability to love.

They represent a learning opportunity.

Say to yourself, "School is in session; here's my chance to learn about love."

That didn't hurt too badly, now, did it?

Just being willing to help can make a huge impact on people—and on you. It reminds us of how the New Testament often describes Christ-followers as servants of Jesus Christ.[4] And you and I can do this.

Learn from Difficult People

In addition to serving people, we also need to learn from them.

We especially need to learn from the difficult people we work with.

Has anyone ever had a difficult person in your life? Raise your hand.

Pause.

Believe it or not, you need people like this!

Difficult people help us grow in our ability to love.

Jesus said a very important aspect of following him is to love our enemies. So if you don't have any difficult people in your life right now, you're missing a chance to grow in love.

Optional humor:
In fact, if you don't have such a person, see me after class. Our church keeps a list of difficult people on file, and I'll assign you one!

Every difficult person represents a learning opportunity. A great phrase to keep in mind as you try to love these people is, "School is in session." As you wince when someone upsets you, you can say to yourself, "School is in session; here's my chance to learn about love."

You could be home with a difficult teenager; at work with a demanding boss or gossipy coworker; struggling with a customer's complaints. Whatever the interaction, remind yourself, "School is in session. I'm in God's school, and this person is the curriculum. What can I learn about love? What can I learn about myself?"

[4] Philippians 1:1

NOTES

WORK

During Your Workday

Setting

Place ______________ or reminders in your work setting.

A single word on a piece of paper (*peace, wisdom, serve*)

A favorite Scripture verse

> *Whatever you do, work at it with all your heart, as working for the Lord.*
> (Colossians 3:23)

Make sure your work setting is well ordered.

People

Look for opportunities to do simple acts of ______________.

"How may I serve you today?"

Learn from difficult people.

They help us grow in our ability to love.

They represent a learning opportunity.

Say to yourself, "School is in session; here's my chance to learn about love."

Receive Feedback Well

• Think of yourself with "sober judgment..."

Receive Feedback Well

Participant's Guide, page 41.

Finally, in addition to serving people, performing simple acts of service, and learning from difficult people, we can also experience God's presence in our work with people when we receive feedback well.

Paul says in Romans 12:3 that we are to think of ourselves with "sober judgment."

One of the best chances we'll have to gain sober judgment about ourselves is by paying attention to the feedback we receive from others—and how well we receive it.

Feedback may come in expected ways, such as a performance review from your boss or diagnostic tools that help you assess your skills and interests. You may also get unsolicited feedback from a coworker, a client, a teacher, or your kids telling you what they think of your parenting skills.

Most of us tend to find feedback difficult. We each have our own set of barriers that keeps us from receiving feedback well. Probably the most common obstacle is defensiveness. Anyone ever feel defensive when getting feedback?

Pause. Say the next line tongue-in-cheek.

How many of you are never defensive, and you resent the question?

Pause for laughter.

What would it look like for you to receive feedback in Jesus' name?

Maybe it would mean setting aside your fears long enough to really hear what's being said. Perhaps it would mean a greater level of humility and openness.

You could pray this prayer: "What is the truth I need to learn from this, Lord?"

NOTES

Receive Feedback Well

> Think of yourself with *"sober judgment."*
> (Romans 12:3)

Set aside your fears long enough to really hear what's being said.

Have a greater level of humility and openness.

Pray this prayer: "What is the truth I need to learn from this, Lord?"

Your work can become the center of your spiritual life.

Take Mini-Breaks

The Bible describes creation occurring with a daily rhythm:

Breaks in between

A day off at the end of every six

It is not more spiritual to work nonstop to exhaustion.

Take a short walk.

Make a brief phone call to a friend.

Take at least one day off out of every seven.

Then, even if you're fearful or defensive, you're giving God a chance both to shape you as he chooses and to improve your job performance.

So, people in our workplace give us lots of opportunities for growth—as we serve them, as we learn from difficult people, and as we get feedback. Doing these things in Jesus' name will make our jobs a virtual university of character development.

 Instead of feeling like your job has nothing to do with your spiritual life, it can become the center of your spiritual life.

TAKE MINI-BREAKS

 Another way to experience God's presence during the workday is to take mini-breaks.

In creation, God set a wonderful precedent for us. Creation is described as taking place in stages. It happened over six days, and then on the seventh, God rested.

 God could have created the universe in its final form in an instant, but instead the Bible describes creation occurring with a daily rhythm—and with breaks in between and a day off at the end of every six. That pattern is a good model for us.

It is not more spiritual to work nonstop to exhaustion.

God did not say, "Whew, I'm beat. Thank *me* it's Friday!" To follow God's pattern, we have to engage in diligent activity followed by regular breaks. We have to pause and see our work and declare it is good.

 It might be as simple as getting up and taking a short walk, or making a brief phone call to a friend, and if at all possible, taking at least one day off out of every seven.

We need a theology of rest or our work cannot be God-honoring.

Turn to page 42.

Participant's Guide, page 42.

NOTES

Receive Feedback Well

> Think of yourself with *"sober judgment."*
> (Romans 12:3)

Set aside your fears long enough to really hear what's being said.

Have a greater level of humility and openness.

Pray this prayer: "What is the truth I need to learn from this, Lord?"

Your work can become the center of your spiritual life.

Take Mini-Breaks

The Bible describes creation occurring with a daily rhythm:

Breaks in between

A day off at the end of every six

It is not more spiritual to work nonstop to exhaustion.

Take a short walk.

Make a brief phone call to a friend.

Take at least one day off out of every seven.

Take Mini-Breaks

Two or three times a day, take five to ten minutes to stop your work, be quiet, and FOCUS on God.

Two or three times a day, take five to ten minutes to stop your work, be quiet, and FOCUS on God.

You can do this. If you have an office, close the door; if you're at home, pick a comfortable chair or other location; if you're on the road, your car will do; if you have kids, take time while they're napping or engaged in some activity. At least once in the morning and once in the afternoon shut out the world and enjoy the presence of God.

Thank him for his care for you. Ask him for help with a challenge you're facing.

Have you ever gotten to the end of a day and realized that you worried about something for hours on end but never actually asked God for help?

Take Mini-Breaks

We don't want to just work *for* God; we want to work *with* him.

We don't want to just work *for* God; we want to work *with* him.

Taking mini-breaks is a way to make sure you *do* commit the matter to him and invite him to partner with you in your work so that you're working in Jesus' name.

We're going to practice doing this right now. I'm going to stop talking for about two minutes. Close your eyes and shut out everyone around you. Take these minutes to reconnect with God. Is there anything you'd like to say to him? Anything you'd like to ask from him? Open yourself up to him during these quiet moments, and then we'll continue.

If you have audio equipment, you can create a more reflective atmosphere during this activity by playing soft instrumental music—no words—quietly in the background.

Call the group back together after 2 minutes.

Anyone notice what happened to you in the last two minutes?

Pause.

NOTES

WORK

Two or three times a day, take five to ten minutes to stop your work, be quiet, and __________________ on God.

Thank him for his care for you.

Ask him for help.

We don't want to just work *for* God; we want to work *with* him.

Ending Your Workday

End each workday by taking a few moments to reflect on what you have done, and declare it ____________________.

End your day honestly.

Ask God for his help to work diligently the next day.

Pray and ask God for his strength to:

—be able to leave work behind

—enter fully into home life

End your workday in Jesus' name.

You started to relax. Most of us carry tension with us physically, in our bodies. Think of how much more you'd have if you were at work. God did not make us for that. We need to incorporate these breaks into our days as God did in his so we can rest in God.

This is something you can do—you really can take little breaks like the one we just experienced.

Another kind of break we need is for meals. Meals are a natural opportunity to stop and be grateful, and to acknowledge God's care. On page 118 in the Appendix there are additional guidelines on how to enjoy your mealtimes more and use them as breaks done in Jesus' name. You might want to take some time to read over those later.

Ending Your Workday

Once we know how to begin the workday, create the right setting, serve others, learn from difficult people, receive feedback well, and take mini-breaks, there's only one thing left to do: go home!

Ending your workday in Jesus' name is just as important as beginning your workday in Jesus' name.

Perhaps you find that you often end the day feeling frustrated for not having done more. You feel rushed and frenzied, and end up bringing work home with you.

God himself, at the end of each workday in creation, would pause, review what he had done, and declare it good.

Rather than focusing on what you haven't done and beating yourself up about it, end each workday by taking a few moments to reflect on what you *have* done, and declare it GOOD.

You also need to end your day honestly.

Maybe when you reach the end of the workday, you realize that you've wasted some of it. If that's true, talk to God about that.

NOTES

WORK

Two or three times a day, take five to ten minutes to stop your work, be quiet, and ____________ on God.

Thank him for his care for you.

Ask him for help.

We don't want to just work *for* God; we want to work *with* him.

Ending Your Workday

End each workday by taking a few moments to reflect on what you have done, and declare it ____________.

End your day honestly.

Ask God for his help to work diligently the next day.

Pray and ask God for his strength to:

—be able to leave work behind

—enter fully into home life

End your workday in Jesus' name.

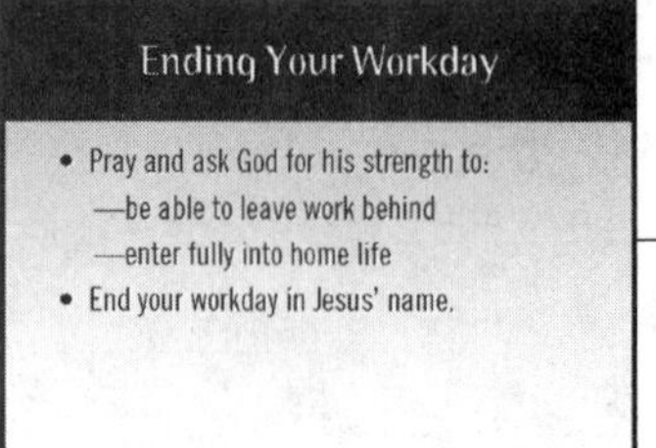

Ask him for his help to work diligently the next day.

However your day went, pray and ask God for his strength to be able to leave work behind and enter fully into the home life that you are leaving for. Then, end your workday in Jesus' name.

2 MINUTES

Two Additional Observations about Work

Participant's Guide, page 43.

We've discussed several ways we can be with Jesus in an ordinary workday, but before we end this session, we need to make two additional observations about work. One is about unpaid work; the other is about wrong fit with a job.

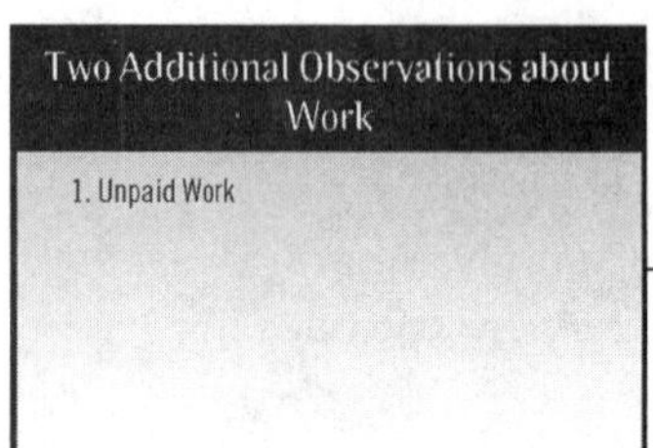

Unpaid Work

For some of us—and this is true for *all* of us at some point—our work is unpaid.

If this describes your situation, you may be tempted to devalue your work. In a society that measures almost everything in terms of money, doing unpaid work may seem less important. But this is not true and it's not biblical.

Tony Campolo has said that when his wife, Peggy, was at home full time with their children and someone would ask, somewhat condescendingly, "And what is it that *you* do, my dear?" she would respond: "I am socializing two Homo sapiens (hō-mō-sāp-ē-enz) into the dominant values of the Judeo-Christian tradition in order that they might be instruments for the transformation of the social order into the kind of eschatological (es-kat-el-äj-i-kel) utopia that God willed from the beginning of creation."

Pause.

Then Peggy would ask the other person, "And what do *you* do?"[5]

[5] Tony Campolo, *You Can Make a Difference* (Nashville: Word Publishing, 1994), 50–51.

NOTES

WORK

Two or three times a day, take five to ten minutes to stop your work, be quiet, and ________________ on God.

Thank him for his care for you.

Ask him for help.

We don't want to just work *for* God; we want to work *with* him.

Ending Your Workday

End each workday by taking a few moments to reflect on what you have done, and declare it ________________.

End your day honestly.

Ask God for his help to work diligently the next day.

Pray and ask God for his strength to:

—be able to leave work behind

—enter fully into home life

End your workday in Jesus' name.

Two Additional Observations about Work

1. Unpaid Work

Your work, too, matters to God.

Money is *not* the measure of the value of your work in God's eyes.

2. Wrong Fit

God wants you to use your skills and giftedness in your work.

> *It is wrong, it is sin, to accept or remain in a position that you know is a mismatch for you. Perhaps that's a form of sin you've never even considered—the sin of staying in the wrong job. But God did not place you on this earth to waste away your years in labor that does not employ his design or purpose for your life, no matter how much you may be getting paid for it.*
>
> Arthur Miller

Give yourself to your current work as diligently as you can.

At the same time, explore other job opportunities.

Think what would have happened if Jesus had decided that only work with a paycheck mattered. He never would have stopped being a carpenter to become an itinerant, unpaid rabbi and teacher.

If your work is unpaid, working in Jesus' name may include reminding yourself that your work, too, matters to God.

Everybody works, and money is *not* the measure of the value of your work in God's eyes.

Wrong Fit

The second additional observation about work concerns wrong fit.

Some of us experience real sadness about our jobs because we're involved in work that is a wrong fit for our skills and giftedness. If this describes your situation, you need to know that God cares about that!

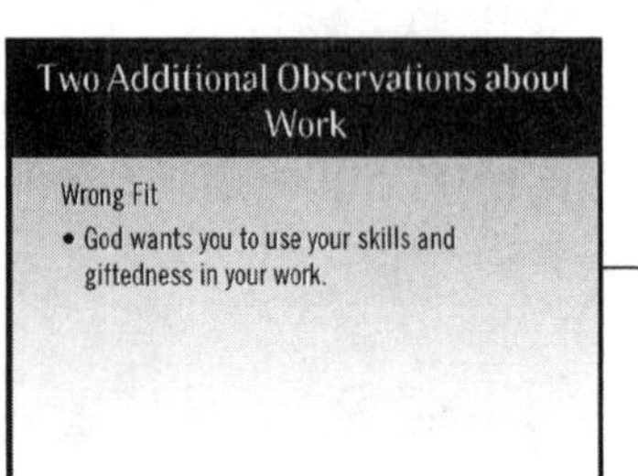

God wants you to use your skills and giftedness in your work.

One author puts it like this:

It is wrong, it is sin, to accept or remain in a position that you know is a mismatch for you. Perhaps that's a form of sin you've never even considered—the sin of staying in the wrong job. But God did not place you on this earth to waste away your years in labor that does not employ his design or purpose for your life, no matter how much you may be getting paid for it.[6]

If you are in a wrong fit situation, working in Jesus' name may mean you give yourself to your current work as diligently as you can each day, while at the same time you explore other job opportunities.

Turn to page 44.

[6] Arthur Miller, *Why You Can't Be Anything You Want to Be* (Grand Rapids: Zondervan, 1999), 115.

NOTES

Two Additional Observations about Work

1. Unpaid Work

Your work, too, matters to God.

Money is *not* the measure of the value of your work in God's eyes.

2. Wrong Fit

God wants you to use your skills and giftedness in your work.

> *It is wrong, it is sin, to accept or remain in a position that you know is a mismatch for you. Perhaps that's a form of sin you've never even considered—the sin of staying in the wrong job. But God did not place you on this earth to waste away your years in labor that does not employ his design or purpose for your life, no matter how much you may be getting paid for it.*
>
> Arthur Miller

Give yourself to your current work as diligently as you can.

At the same time, explore other job opportunities.

15 MINUTES

INDIVIDUAL AND SMALL GROUP ACTIVITY: *THE ULTIMATE PERFORMANCE REVIEW*

Participant's Guide, pages 44–45.

We're going to take a few minutes to reflect on and discuss our workdays with an activity called *The Ultimate Performance Review*.

Objective
For participants to assess their work performance from God's perspective and then discuss with their group how it might be different if they were to work in Jesus' name.

This activity has two parts—an individual activity on page 44 and a group activity on page 45.

Directions

For the individual activity:

Give yourself a performance review from God's perspective. Write your responses to the following questions:

- What would God say about my approach to my daily work?
- How is work affecting my heart?
- What would God affirm about my attitudes and habits?
- Where in my workday am I having the hardest time connecting with God?
- How might one ordinary day at work be different if I did it in partnership with God?

Any questions about the directions?

You will have 5 minutes for the individual activity, and then we'll come together for small group discussions.

If you have audio equipment, you can create a more reflective atmosphere during this activity by playing soft instrumental music—no words—quietly in the background.

Call the group back together after 5 minutes.

NOTES

WORK

INDIVIDUAL ACTIVITY

The Ultimate Performance Review

Give yourself a performance review from God's perspective. Write your responses to the following questions.

What would God say about my approach to my daily work?

How is work affecting my heart?

What would God affirm about my attitudes and habits?

Where in my workday am I having the hardest time connecting with God?

How might one ordinary day at work be different if I did it in partnership with God?

SMALL GROUP ACTIVITY

The Ultimate Performance Review

(continued)

1. Form a group with two other people.
2. Discuss answers to the last question on the performance review: How might one ordinary day at work be different if I did it in partnership with God?

SMALL GROUP ACTIVITY

Directions

For the group activity:

1. Form a group with two other people.
2. Discuss your answers to the last question on the performance review: How might one ordinary day at work be different if I did it in partnership with God?

Any questions?

You will have 10 minutes.

Call the group back together after 10 minutes.

1 MINUTE

Wrap-up

Let's hear what you came up with. How would your workday be different if you did it in partnership with God?

Solicit three or four comments from the group. Be sure to repeat their answers so everyone hears the response.

Possible responses:

- *I'd be less defensive.*
- *I would set good boundaries between work and home.*
- *I would be clear about what success would look like.*
- *I would take more risks because I know God is there to help me.*
- *I need to prayerfully make a daily plan.*
- *I am going to be open to what God might have for me in interruptions.*
- *I need to ask for God's help.*

You really can do this. Working in Jesus' name may mean making some changes. But you will see that if you actually partner with God at work, it will never be the same workplace again.

Turn to page 46.

NOTES

WORK

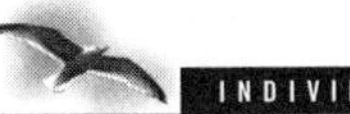

INDIVIDUAL ACTIVITY

The Ultimate Performance Review

Give yourself a performance review from God's perspective. Write your responses to the following questions.

What would God say about my approach to my daily work?

How is work affecting my heart?

What would God affirm about my attitudes and habits?

Where in my workday am I having the hardest time connecting with God?

How might one ordinary day at work be different if I did it in partnership with God?

SMALL GROUP ACTIVITY

The Ultimate Performance Review

(continued)

1. Form a group with two other people.
2. Discuss answers to the last question on the performance review: How might one ordinary day at work be different if I did it in partnership with God?

1 MINUTE

SUMMARY

Participant's Guide, page 46.

Summary

We work because we are made in the image of God.

We can experience God's presence with us at work.

Let's review:

 We work because we are made in the image of God.

We can experience God's presence with us at work by beginning and ending the workday in Jesus' name, by paying attention to our work setting and the people we work with, by taking mini-breaks, and by taking at least one day off.

This doesn't involve doing any new things; these are things you already do. It just means doing them in new ways.

 God invites us to join him in his work as we do our work.

You can do this. You can work in Jesus' name.

If you are teaching this course in an eight-week format rather than a weekend seminar format, you can close the session with the following prayer or substitute your own prayer.

Lord, thank you for making us in your image and for giving us meaningful tasks to do that express that image. May we learn to use our work to do your work, and may we be more open to the ways you want to shape us through our partnership with you at work. In Jesus' name, amen.

Break.

NOTES

WORK

Summary

We work because we are made in the image of God.

We can experience God's presence with us at work by:

- Beginning and ending the workday in Jesus' name
- Paying attention to our work setting
- Paying attention to the people we work with
- Taking mini-breaks
- Taking at least one day off

God invites us to join him in his work as we do our work.

46

LEADINGS

SESSION SNAPSHOT

Overview

This session introduces participants to the truth that leadings from God are an important part of doing life in Jesus' name. Some people claim foolish and harmful things as God's leadings. Others avoid the subject because they don't think God would communicate directly with them, or they are fearful of becoming like those who don't seem to know the difference between God's voice and their own. This session gives practical guidelines for discerning how the Holy Spirit gives us leadings.

Objectives

In this session, participants will:

1. Discover that leadings from the Holy Spirit can be a normal part of everyday life
2. Learn how to filter leadings so God's truth alone comes through

SESSION OUTLINE

I. Introduction

II. Discovery

A. Learning to Listen to God's Voice

1. How God Speaks

2. Video: *Leadings*

3. Small Group Activity: *Experiences with Leadings*

B. Three Key Learnings about Leadings

1. Hearing God's Voice Is Learned Behavior

2. God Can Speak to Anyone

3. God's Voice Has Distinguishing Characteristics

4. Video: *Competing Voices*

5. "The Whisper Test"

III. Summary

LEADINGS

TIME & MEDIA

CONTENTS

INTRODUCTION

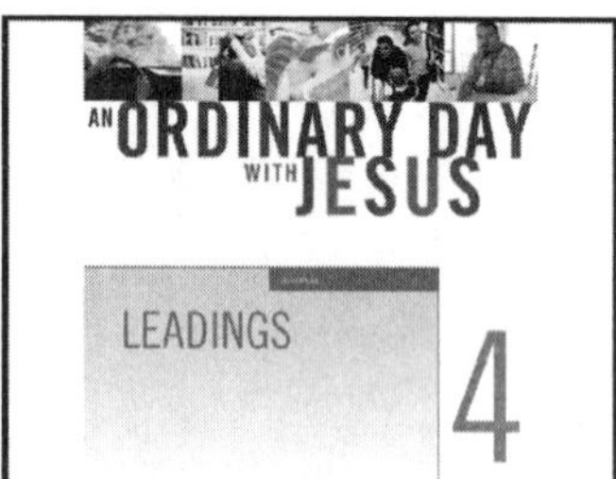

If you are teaching this course in an eight-week format rather than a weekend seminar format, you may want to begin by briefly discussing participants' experiences since the last session. Start the session as follows:

"In the last session we talked about being with Jesus at work. Did anyone have a chance to try any of the things we talked about? What was it like for you?"

Solicit two or three comments from the group. Be sure to repeat their answers so everyone hears the response.

Possible responses:

- *I tried to stay aware of Jesus, but by the end of the day things were pretty much as they always have been.*
- *I found I was able to really listen to a coworker when he talked to me about his financial problems.*
- *After I finished work, I stopped and reviewed what I had done that day and said, "It is good!" That was really encouraging for me.*

NOTES

SESSION FOUR

LEADINGS

So far in this course we've covered going to sleep and waking up in Jesus' name, everyday relationships, and work. In this session we're going to consider a very important truth—the fact that Jesus really does want to communicate with us. We're going to answer the question, How can I listen to Jesus and follow the leadings of the Holy Spirit in the course of an ordinary day?

3 MINUTES

DISCOVERY

Learning to Listen to God's Voice

Participant's Guide, page 48.

Learning to Listen to God's Voice

In a typical day, we are bombarded with sights and sounds that compete with what the Bible calls the still, small voice of God.[1]

If we decide we want to spend our ordinary days experiencing the reality of God, we need to learn to listen to God's voice. God *does* speak today. God *does* guide.

He wants a relationship with his children, and part of that relationship involves promptings and leadings from the Holy Spirit.

But we need to learn to hear his voice and to filter out the noise of the world so we can distinguish what is really from God.

Think of a cell phone to represent the main message of this session. Through the Holy Spirit, God has access to us twenty-four hours a day. He dials our number and wants us to answer.

But the ring on God's phone is not deafening. It is possible not to hear the ring. Or, if we do hear the ring, it is possible to look at the caller ID and decide we really don't want to hear from God. Or maybe we *do* want to hear from him, but we have trouble understanding what he might be saying. This session is about how to hear the ring, pick up the phone, and discern what God is saying.

How God Speaks

In his excellent book *Hearing God,* Dallas Willard describes how we receive God's thoughts.

[1] 1 Kings 19:11–13 (KJV)

NOTES

LEADINGS

Learning to Listen to God's Voice

We need to learn to:

Hear his voice

Filter out the noise of the world

How God Speaks

How human communication works:

When one person speaks, the listener is prompted to have new thoughts.

You allow the speaker to influence your thoughts.

Communication is simply _________________ someone's thoughts with their cooperation.

People can guide your thoughts only indirectly, through physical means like sounds or sights.

God can guide your thoughts by speaking directly to your heart and mind.

How God Speaks

How human communication works:
- When one person speaks, the listener is prompted to have new thoughts.

First, he points out how human communication works. When one person speaks, the listener is prompted to have new thoughts in his or her mind.

These new thoughts came about because the first person says something that triggered those thoughts.

When I speak to you—like right now, for example—you are having thoughts you wouldn't be having otherwise.

You are allowing me, the speaker, to influence your thoughts.

How God Speaks

Communication is simply GUIDING someone's thoughts with their cooperation.

If I weren't talking, your mind would be going in a different direction.

In its most basic form, communication is simply GUIDING someone's thoughts with their cooperation.

Because we're finite, we are limited to finite means to communicate. I make sounds, and when you hear them, you have certain thoughts—hopefully the ones I want you to have. Or I write down words, and when you see those visual images, you have certain thoughts and reactions.

- People can only guide your thoughts indirectly.
- God can guide your thoughts by speaking directly to your heart and mind.

We use these physical means with each other because we're physical creatures. But God is infinite. That means he can guide your thoughts without having to use things like sound waves on your eardrums or inkblots on a page.

People can guide your thoughts only indirectly, through physical means like sounds or sights.

God can guide your thoughts by speaking directly to your heart and mind.

What that means is that it really is possible for you to have a thought that God himself speaks to you. The Bible is full of stories where this really happens to people.

Participant's Guide, page 49.

NOTES

LEADINGS

Learning to Listen to God's Voice

We need to learn to:

Hear his voice

Filter out the noise of the world

How God Speaks

How human communication works:

When one person speaks, the listener is prompted to have new thoughts.

You allow the speaker to influence your thoughts.

Communication is simply __________________ someone's thoughts with their cooperation.

People can guide your thoughts only indirectly, through physical means like sounds or sights.

God can guide your thoughts by speaking directly to your heart and mind.

 Jesus reinforces this point in John 10:2–4, where he says:

A shepherd enters through the gate. The gatekeeper opens the gate for him, and the sheep hear his voice and come to him. He calls his own sheep by name and leads them out. After he has gathered his own flock, he walks ahead of them, and they follow him because they recognize his voice (NLT).

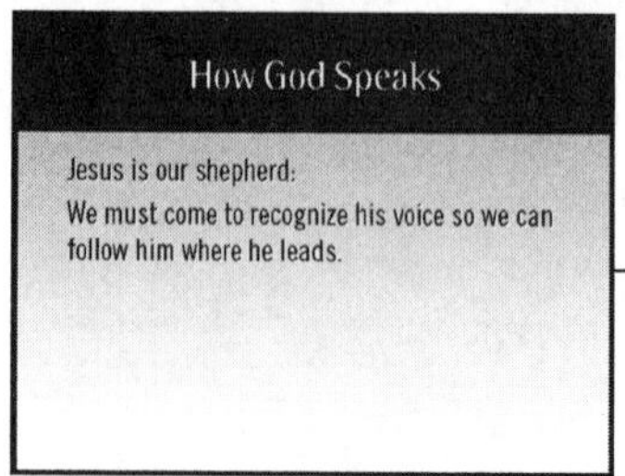

Jesus is our shepherd. Since that's true, we must come to recognize his voice so that we can follow him where he leads in the midst of the ordinary moments of our days.

6 MINUTES

VIDEO: *LEADINGS*

Now that we've seen how God speaks and gets his thoughts across to us, what might it be like to actually get a leading in an ordinary day with Jesus? We're going to watch a video that describes how simple leadings from God can affect us.

View video: *Leadings.*

Turn to page 50.

15 MINUTES

SMALL GROUP ACTIVITY: *EXPERIENCES WITH LEADINGS*

Participants Guide, page 50.

Objective
For participants to identify their own experiences and perspectives on leadings.

Let's take a few minutes to talk in small groups about our own experiences of leadings. As you share together, it's important to realize that there is a range of experiences in this area. For some of us, leadings may happen all the time. For others, they rarely if ever happen and may even seem a little strange. Whatever your experience or perspective, just be honest.

NOTES

WITH JESUS SESSION FOUR

A shepherd enters through the gate. The gatekeeper opens the gate for him, and the sheep hear his voice and come to him. He calls his own sheep by name and leads them out. After he has gathered his own flock, he walks ahead of them, and they follow him because they recognize his voice.
(John 10:2–4, NLT)

Jesus is our shepherd:

We need to recognize his voice so we can follow where he leads.

VIDEO

Leadings

Notes:

49

LEADINGS AN ORDINARY DAY

SMALL GROUP ACTIVITY

Experiences with Leadings

1. Form a group with two other people.
2. Discuss the following questions:

   Have you ever had a prompting or leading?

   If so, how did you respond? What was the outcome?

   If not, how do you imagine you'd respond if such a leading did occur?

50

Directions

1. Form a group with two other people.
2. Discuss the following questions:
   - Have you ever had a prompting or leading?
   - If so, how did you respond? What was the outcome?
   - If not, how do you imagine you'd respond if such a leading did occur?

Any questions on the directions?

You will have 15 minutes for this discussion.

Call the group back together after 15 minutes.

Now I know some of you find this strange. Some of you, if you're honest, would have to say you've rarely—or maybe never—received this kind of leading. Wherever you are with that is perfectly fine. The important thing is to be open and to realize this is worth exploring as a potential key ingredient to living ordinary days with Jesus.

10 MINUTES

Three Key Learnings about Leadings

Participant's Guide, page 51.

We want to understand what the Bible has to say about listening to God's voice and glean wisdom from those who've had practice in this area.

 Our exploration is divided into three broad areas—three key learnings about leadings.

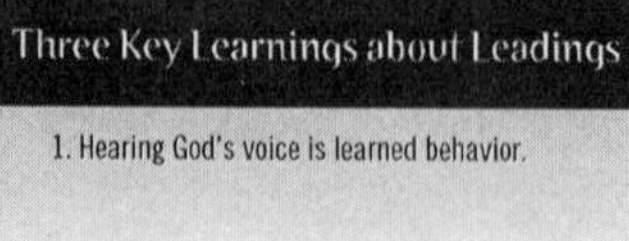

Hearing God's Voice Is Learned Behavior

 First, hearing God's voice is learned behavior—we must learn how to hear it.

People may think, "If God were speaking to me, I'd know it," but that may not be the case. We may not know it's God, we may misunderstand, we may presume it's God and find out later it wasn't.

NOTES

LEADINGS

SMALL GROUP ACTIVITY

Experiences with Leadings

1. Form a group with two other people.
2. Discuss the following questions:

Have you ever had a prompting or leading?

If so, how did you respond? What was the outcome?

If not, how do you imagine you'd respond if such a leading did occur?

Three Key Learnings about Leadings

1. Hearing God's voice is learned behavior.

The Bible teaches:

Normal, psychologically healthy people *do* hear from God.

It takes some time and ______________________ to learn how to hear God's voice.

> *Then the Lord called Samuel. Samuel answered, "Here I am." And he ran to Eli and said, "Here I am; you called me." But Eli said, "I did not call; go back and lie down." So he went and lay down. Again the Lord called, "Samuel!" And Samuel got up and went to Eli and said, "Here I am; you called me." "My son," Eli said, "I did not call; go back and lie down." Now Samuel did not yet know the Lord. The word of the Lord had not yet been revealed to him. The Lord called Samuel a third time. And then Eli realized the Lord was calling the boy. So Eli told Samuel, "Go and lie down, and if he calls you, say, 'Speak, Lord, for your servant is listening.'"*
>
> (1 Samuel 3:4–10)

A personal relationship with God is at the heart of Christianity, so ______________________ with him—and he with us—is at the heart of the relationship.

Hearing God's Voice Is Learned Behavior

The Bible teaches:

- Normal, psychologically healthy people do hear from God.
- It takes some time and TRAINING to learn how to hear God's voice.

The Bible teaches that two things are true. Number one—normal, psychologically healthy people *do* hear from God.

Optional humor:
That's especially comforting to those of us who do hear voices!

And number two—it takes some time and TRAINING to learn how to hear God's voice.

God doesn't speak in audible words that hit our eardrums—at least, that's not standard operating procedure. Instead, he speaks directly to our hearts and minds. That's why it takes training to learn to sift through all the messages we receive so we can discern his voice.

One story about God speaking directly to someone is recorded in 1 Samuel 3. It is the story of Samuel when he was a young boy training for ministry under the priest, Eli. Here's the story:

Then the Lord called Samuel. Samuel answered, "Here I am." And he ran to Eli and said, "Here I am; you called me." But Eli said, "I did not call; go back and lie down." So he went and lay down. Again the Lord called, "Samuel!" And Samuel got up and went to Eli and said, "Here I am; you called me." "My son," Eli said, "I did not call; go back and lie down." Now Samuel did not yet know the Lord. The word of the Lord had not yet been revealed to him. The Lord called Samuel a third time. And then Eli realized the Lord was calling the boy. So Eli told Samuel, "Go and lie down, and if he calls you, say, 'Speak, Lord, for your servant is listening.'"

And that's what Samuel did.

Here's what's happening. The Lord speaks to Samuel, but Samuel does not know that it's God talking to him. It is possible for God to speak to someone and for that person not to realize it's God speaking.

Some people seem to hear the Holy Sprit clearly, and for others it doesn't work that way. For most, it takes time and training to discern the voice of God, even as it took Samuel a few tries. But part of what it means to experience the reality of God in our everyday lives is to learn to hear the leadings of the Holy Spirit.

NOTES

WITH JESUS SESSION FOUR

Three Key Learnings about Leadings

1. Hearing God's voice is learned behavior.

   The Bible teaches:

   Normal, psychologically healthy people *do* hear from God.

   It takes some time and ________________________ to learn how to hear God's voice.

Then the Lord called Samuel. Samuel answered,
"Here I am." And he ran to Eli and said, "Here I am; you called me."
But Eli said, "I did not call; go back and lie down."
So he went and lay down. Again the Lord called,
"Samuel!" And Samuel got up and went to Eli and said,
"Here I am; you called me." "My son," Eli said, "I did not call;
go back and lie down." Now Samuel did not yet know the Lord.
The word of the Lord had not yet been revealed to him.
The Lord called Samuel a third time. And then Eli realized
the Lord was calling the boy. So Eli told Samuel,
"Go and lie down, and if he calls you, say,
'Speak, Lord, for your servant is listening.'"
(1 Samuel 3:4–10)

A personal relationship with God is at the heart of Christianity, so ________________________ with him—and he with us—is at the heart of the relationship.

51

Think about it in terms of a relationship you have with someone. What would that relationship be without communication? It's a monologue! If you know someone, you communicate with that person. You talk to them, they talk to you. It's a dialogue.

Optional humor:
As "theologian" Lily Tomlin said, "Why is it that when we speak to God, it's called prayer, but when God speaks to us, it's called schizophrenia?"

Hearing God's Voice Is Learned Behavior

A personal relationship with God is at the heart of Christianity, so COMMUNICATING with him—and he with us—is at the heart of the relationship.

A personal relationship with God is at the heart of Christianity, so COMMUNICATING with him—and he with us—is at the heart of the relationship.

It really couldn't be a relationship if it were any other way.

God does speak, and being able to hear God's voice is learned behavior. It can and must be developed over time.

Turn to page 52.

Participant's Guide, page 52.

Hearing God's Voice Is Learned Behavior

We can invite God to teach us with the prayer: *"Speak, Lord, for your servant is listening."*

Taking a lesson from Samuel, we can invite God to teach us with the prayer, "Speak, Lord, for your servant is listening."

Lots of ordinary moments in your day can be filled with that invitation—and filled with God's answers to that invitation.

God Can Speak to Anyone

Three Key Learnings about Leadings

1. Hearing God's voice is learned behavior.
2. God can speak to anyone.

The second key learning about leadings is that God can speak to anyone. He does not restrict his voice to Christian leaders or spiritual superstars.

Sometimes, there's an assumption that unless I'm a spiritual giant like Billy Graham or Mother Teresa, God would not speak to me. But Scripture teaches that God can speak to anyone.

NOTES

Three Key Learnings about Leadings

1. Hearing God's voice is learned behavior.

   The Bible teaches:

   Normal, psychologically healthy people *do* hear from God.

   It takes some time and ____________________ to learn how to hear God's voice.

> *Then the Lord called Samuel. Samuel answered, "Here I am." And he ran to Eli and said, "Here I am; you called me." But Eli said, "I did not call; go back and lie down." So he went and lay down. Again the Lord called, "Samuel!" And Samuel got up and went to Eli and said, "Here I am; you called me." "My son," Eli said, "I did not call; go back and lie down." Now Samuel did not yet know the Lord. The word of the Lord had not yet been revealed to him. The Lord called Samuel a third time. And then Eli realized the Lord was calling the boy. So Eli told Samuel, "Go and lie down, and if he calls you, say, 'Speak, Lord, for your servant is listening.'"*
> (1 Samuel 3:4–10)

A personal relationship with God is at the heart of Christianity, so ____________________ with him—and he with us—is at the heart of the relationship.

LEADINGS

We can invite God to teach us with the prayer: "Speak, Lord, for your servant is listening."

2. God can speak to anyone.

   He does not restrict his voice to Christian leaders or spiritual superstars.

3. God's voice has distinguishing characteristics.

   - He will always speak in ways consistent with his character.

     If you have anxious thought—it's not from God.

     We come to recognize God's promptings by:

     —Focusing on God's attributes

     —Learning from our personal experience

     —Studying his voice in Scripture

     We can learn to recognize God's voice from the way it affects our hearts.

   - Will always be consistent with ______________.
   - Will be consistent with who he made you to be.
   - Will be consistent with love.

     A simple question to ask: Is this action selfish or loving?

There is a somewhat humorous story in the Old Testament[2] about a prophet named Balaam who learns this the hard way. In the story, Balaam goes astray. He heads off to curse Israel instead of bless the nation as God instructed. God *does* intervene and speaks clearly in this situation, but not through the prophet Balaam. He speaks through the prophet's *donkey*! How high would you rate a donkey on the spiritual giant scale? So if God can speak to and through an animal, he can certainly talk to anyone!

God's Voice Has Distinguishing Characteristics

We've noted that hearing God's voice is learned behavior, and that God can speak to anyone.

 The final key learning about leadings is that God's voice has distinguishing characteristics.

People often wonder: "How can I know if it's God speaking to me and not just my imagination?"

If someone you know calls you on the phone, you recognize their voice almost immediately. How do you know who it is? Sometimes, someone will just say, "Hi, it's me." That's a sure sign it's someone who knows you well.

What are some other ways you know who is on the other end of the line?

Solicit three or four comments from the group. Be sure to repeat their answers so everyone hears the response.

Possible responses:

- *Sound or tone*
- *Familiarity*
- *Word choices or types of things the person would say*
- *Ways of addressing me*
- *Issues that are important to the person*

It all boils down to this: the one undeniable way to recognize someone's voice is through experience.

[2] Numbers 22

NOTES

AN ORDINARY DAY

LEADINGS

We can invite God to teach us with the prayer: "Speak, Lord, for your servant is listening."

2. God can speak to anyone.

   He does not restrict his voice to Christian leaders or spiritual superstars.

3. God's voice has distinguishing characteristics.

   - He will always speak in ways consistent with his character.

     If you have anxious thought—it's not from God.

     We come to recognize God's promptings by:

     —Focusing on God's attributes

     —Learning from our personal experience

     —Studying his voice in Scripture

     We can learn to recognize God's voice from the way it affects our hearts.

   - Will always be consistent with __________________.
   - Will be consistent with who he made you to be.
   - Will be consistent with love.

     A simple question to ask: Is this action selfish or loving?

52

Over time, as you listen to someone talk, you come to know the tone of their voice—whether it's warm, cold, harsh—and the kind of things they say. Then, when that person calls you on the phone, you know who it is.

This is also true in learning to listen to God. Over time, we become practiced in recognizing and understanding his voice, because God's voice is unique.

The Bible teaches that there are at least four distinguishing characteristics of God's voice.

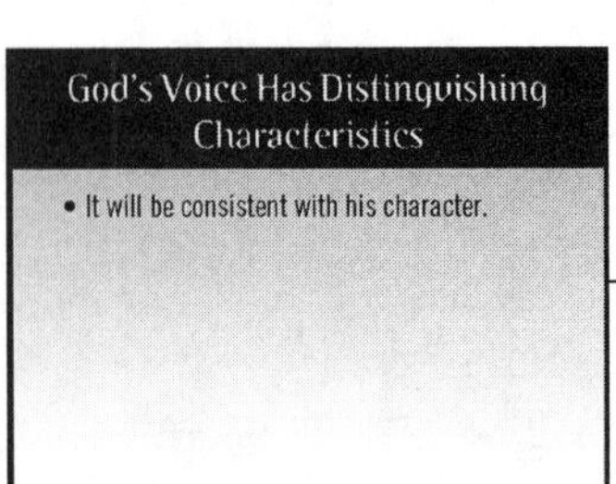

Consistent with His Character

 The first distinguishing characteristic of God's voice is that he will always speak in ways consistent with his character.

For example, God is never frantic or anxious. You'll never come across a phrase in the Bible that says, "And God was worried." So his voice—and the leadings he gives—won't be that way.

 If you're having an anxious thought, you can be sure it's not from God.

God is also good, so his voice will say good things. He is peace, so his voice will bring peace. He is above all love, so his voice will be loving.

 We come to recognize God's promptings in daily life by focusing on God's attributes, learning from our personal experience, and studying his voice in Scripture.

Luke 24:13–32 talks about an experience of two disciples walking along the road to Emmaus after the Crucifixion.

There they encountered the risen Christ, but the text says in verse 16 that "they were kept from recognizing him."

Here he was, speaking to them, guiding their thoughts—but they didn't know it! Even though he was physically present, they didn't recognize his voice.

In a similar way, God can be speaking to us, yet we don't realize who it is. Though he's not physically present, we can hear from him and still not recognize his voice.

NOTES

LEADINGS

We can invite God to teach us with the prayer: "Speak, Lord, for your servant is listening."

2. God can speak to anyone.

   He does not restrict his voice to Christian leaders or spiritual superstars.

3. God's voice has distinguishing characteristics.

   - He will always speak in ways consistent with his character.

     If you have anxious thought—it's not from God.

     We come to recognize God's promptings by:

     —Focusing on God's attributes

     —Learning from our personal experience

     —Studying his voice in Scripture

     We can learn to recognize God's voice from the way it affects our hearts.

   - Will always be consistent with ________________.

   - Will be consistent with who he made you to be.

   - Will be consistent with love.

     A simple question to ask: Is this action selfish or loving?

Later, the disciples did their own "review of the day" similar to the one we talked about in session one. When they reflected on their experience, they realized that there had been clues about who it was talking with them.

They said to each other, "Were not our hearts burning within us while he talked with us?"

That was the key that unlocked their ability to recognize him. Jesus' words had always had a certain effect on their hearts—their inner lives. When Jesus spoke, their hearts were filled with love for God. When Jesus spoke, they saw sin for the folly it truly was. When Jesus spoke, they were reminded that servanthood is the true path to greatness. He touched their best longings for all that was good. When Jesus spoke, he made the disciples' hearts feel what Dallas Willard calls "Jesus heartburn."[3]

Nobody else's words affected them quite the same way. And they admitted as much. Their conclusion was, "We should have recognized his voice from the way it affected our hearts!"

We're going to be able to say that too.

Two thousand years later, we can learn to recognize God's voice from the way it affects our hearts.

We can recognize God's voice because it is always consistent with his character. He's never worried, so his voice won't be worried. He's always good, so his voice will bring good. Above all he is love, so his voice will be loving.

Consistent with Scripture

The second distinguishing characteristic of God's voice is that his leadings will always be consistent with SCRIPTURE.

When people "feel led" to violate Scripture—for instance, to get romantically involved with someone other than their spouse—clearly this is not the Holy Spirit speaking.

[3] Dallas Willard, *Hearing God* (Downers Grove: InterVarsity Press, 1999), 222.

NOTES

LEADINGS

We can invite God to teach us with the prayer: "Speak, Lord, for your servant is listening."

2. God can speak to anyone.

   He does not restrict his voice to Christian leaders or spiritual superstars.

3. God's voice has distinguishing characteristics.

   - He will always speak in ways consistent with his character.

     If you have anxious thought—it's not from God.

     We come to recognize God's promptings by:

     —Focusing on God's attributes

     —Learning from our personal experience

     —Studying his voice in Scripture

     We can learn to recognize God's voice from the way it affects our hearts.

   - Will always be consistent with __________________.
   - Will be consistent with who he made you to be.
   - Will be consistent with love.

     A simple question to ask: Is this action selfish or loving?

Knowing that God *can* speak to us directly doesn't mean we will infallibly recognize his voice. Unfortunately, this kind of thing can be easily abused, and most of us have been around somebody who casually says, "God is telling me you should do this . . ."—but what they really want is to get their own way or to end the discussion. We must be very careful to avoid this manipulation by checking all leadings to make sure they are consistent with Scripture.

Consistent with Who God Made You to Be

The third distinguishing characteristic of God's voice is that his leadings will be consistent with who he made you to be.

Usually, God will call you to serve and work in areas where he has gifted you. After all, he's the one who made you in the first place! Surely if an inventor invents a tool, the tool is suited for the work it will do. You were made by God for the work he calls you to do. There should be a correspondence between you, your design, and where he leads you. God's leadings will always be consistent with who God made you to be.

Consistent with Love

The final distinguishing characteristic of God's voice is that his leadings will be consistent with love.

If someone says they feel led to pass along some gossip or enrich themselves at the expense of others—watch out. As a general rule, God will lead us in the direction of living the kind of servant-oriented life that Jesus modeled. The evil one will always lead us into self-service rather than servanthood, which is a key expression of love. A simple question to ask is: Is this action selfish or loving? Every leading from God will be consistent with love.

To summarize, we've seen there are at least four distinguishing characteristics of God's voice and the leadings he gives: they will always be consistent with his character, consistent with Scripture, consistent with who he made you to be, and consistent with love.

NOTES

LEADINGS

We can invite God to teach us with the prayer: "Speak, Lord, for your servant is listening."

2. God can speak to anyone.

   He does not restrict his voice to Christian leaders or spiritual superstars.

3. God's voice has distinguishing characteristics.

   - He will always speak in ways consistent with his character.

     If you have anxious thought—it's not from God.

     We come to recognize God's promptings by:

     —Focusing on God's attributes

     —Learning from our personal experience

     —Studying his voice in Scripture

     We can learn to recognize God's voice from the way it affects our hearts.

   - Will always be consistent with ________________.
   - Will be consistent with who he made you to be.
   - Will be consistent with love.

     A simple question to ask: Is this action selfish or loving?

5 MINUTES

VIDEO: *COMPETING VOICES*

Participant's Guide, page 53.

It's not enough just to know the distinguishing characteristics of God's voice. If we want to hear him speak, we must listen—but we live in a noisy world.

External voices compete for our attention all the time. Voices from advertisers are constantly trying to get us to buy something. Voices from the entertainment industry offer escape. Voices from our work beckon us to run faster, try harder, or compete against others.

Some of the conflicting voices are within us. Internal voices vie for our attention. They may be voices from our past—telling us that we're inadequate or weak. They may be angry voices, or greedy, or jealous. They might even be voices that speak inaccurate information about God that we need to sift through.

If we're going to hear God's voice, we must first learn to be still.

We're going to watch a video that shows how challenging it can be to actually do this.

View video: *Competing Voices.*

2 MINUTES

Wrap-up

What competing voices made it difficult for the characters in the video to hear God's voice?

Solicit two or three comments from the group. Be sure to repeat their answers so everyone hears the response.

Possible responses:

- *Problems at work*
- *Family pressures and responsibilities*
- *The media—all the advertisements on TV*
- *Internal voices—things they said to themselves*

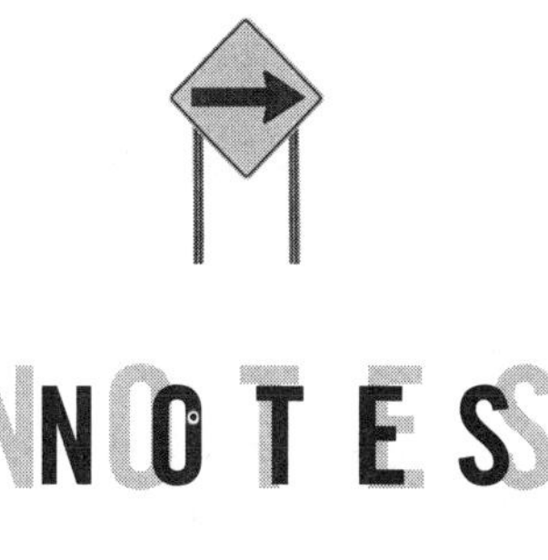

VIDEO

Competing Voices

Notes:

"The Whisper Test"

Summary

Everything changed once they were able to silence the competing voices and listen.

Let me ask you: When do you have quiet in your day to listen to the Holy Spirit like that? What keeps you from creating silence so the other voices go still for a while? It would be nice to just yell, "Stop!" But we all know it isn't that easy. In our next session, we'll learn more about how to silence competing voices so we can be quiet before God.

You and I need to hear God's voice to have a truly personal relationship with him. And obviously when we hear him, we must ruthlessly obey. Otherwise, there's no point in learning to listen. *Courage* as well as silence is required.

2 MINUTES

"The Whisper Test"

I want to conclude this session with a brief story. While this is an example of how one person's words impacted another person, it profoundly illustrates how the Holy Spirit's voice can impact us.

It may be that God wants to speak to you through this story. As I read, I'd like you to close your eyes and listen attentively. This story is called "The Whisper Test."

Pause briefly before reading to help set a more reflective tone.

I grew up knowing I was different, and I hated it. I was born with a cleft palate, and when I started school, my classmates made it clear to me how I looked to others: a little girl with a misshapen lip, crooked nose, lopsided teeth, and garbled speech.

When schoolmates asked: "What happened to your lip?" I'd tell them I'd fallen and cut it on a piece of glass. Somehow it seemed more acceptable to have suffered an accident than to have been born different. I was convinced that no one outside my family could love me.

There was, however, a teacher in the second grade who we all adored—Mrs. Leonard by name. She was short, round, happy—a sparkling lady.

[3] "The Whisper Test," quoted by Les Parrott in *High Maintenance Relationships* (Wheaton: Tyndale House Publishers, 1996), 205.

NOTES

VIDEO

Competing Voices

Notes:

"The Whisper Test"

Summary

Annually we had a hearing test. Mrs. Leonard gave the test to everyone in the class, and finally it was my turn. I knew from past years that as we stood against the door and covered one ear, the teacher sitting at her desk would whisper, and we would have to repeat it back—things like, "The sky is blue," or "Do you have new shoes?" I waited there for those words that God must have put into her mouth, those seven words that changed my life.

Mrs. Leonard said, in her whisper, "I wish you were my little girl."[3]

3 MINUTES

SUMMARY

Keep your eyes closed. What do you need to hear from God right now? While all the other voices are silenced, tell him, "Speak, Lord, your servant is listening."

Pause for 1 minute.

Maybe God is telling you he loves you. Maybe he is desiring to heal a wound. Maybe he's offering forgiveness, or guidance. Tell him now that you'll be fully responsive.

Pause for 1 minute.

Father, we're grateful for your Holy Spirit. Help us to listen to you with wise minds, to make time to shut out competing voices, and then to respond to all you say to us with obedient hearts. In Jesus' name, amen.

SOLITUDE

SESSION SNAPSHOT

Overview

Every significant human relationship needs time when the people involved give each other their undivided attention. This is also true of our relationship with God. That's why solitude—time spent alone with God—is such an important spiritual practice in the Christian life. During times of solitude we might pray, journal, reflect on Scripture, or do other activities, but the key is to get away from outside stimulus and get quiet enough to hear his voice. This session gives participants ideas about how to engage in solitude and provides them an opportunity to have some time alone with God.

Objectives

In this session, participants will:

1. Discover the importance of setting aside some time each day to give God their undivided attention
2. Learn how to enjoy God's presence in solitude
3. Experience time in solitude

SESSION OUTLINE

I. Introduction

II. Discovery

A. Solitude

Video: *Quiet Time*

B. Experiencing Solitude

1. Find a Quiet Place that Is Free of Distractions
2. Quiet Yourself in God's Presence
3. Tell God What You Need
4. Use Scripture to Listen to God
5. Be Fully Present
6. Respond to What You Hear God Saying to You through Scripture or in Prayer
7. Express Gratitude and Commitment
8. Individual Activity: *Experiencing Solitude*

III. Summary

SOLITUDE

TIME & MEDIA

CONTENTS

0 MINUTES

INTRODUCTION

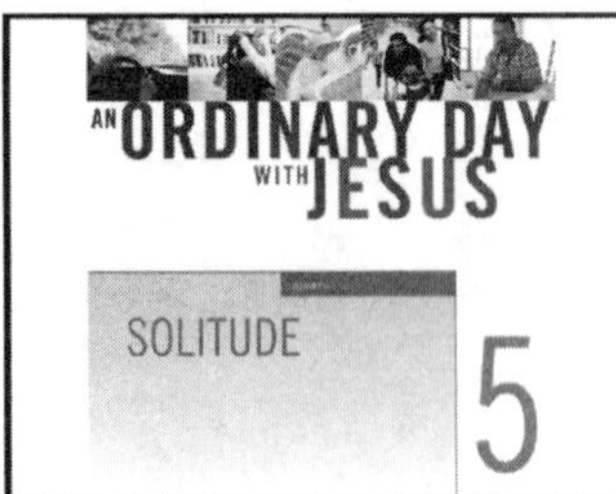

If you are teaching this course in an eight-week format rather than a weekend seminar format, you may want to begin by briefly discussing participants' experiences since the last session. Start the session as follows:

"In the last session we talked about leadings and learning to hear God's voice. Did anyone have an experience of the Holy Spirit's leading or trying to discern God's voice that you'd like to share?"

Solicit two or three comments from the group. Be sure to repeat their answers so everyone hears the response.

Possible responses:

- *I thought maybe I was getting a leading, but it was hard to be sure it wasn't just my own internal voice.*
- *I got a leading and followed through on it—it was great.*
- *This was a new adventure for me, and I'm still trying to sort out how this works.*

We've been talking about how to listen to God, and a key way to do that is to begin to spend time alone with him—spend solitude time with him so we can hear him.

NOTES

SESSION FIVE

SOLITUDE

1 MINUTE

DISCOVERY

Solitude

Participant's Guide, page 56.

Solitude

Solitude is: a time when we withdraw from the company of others in order to give God our undivided attention.

First, however, we need to be clear on what solitude *is* and what solitude is *not*.

 Solitude is a time when we withdraw from the company of others in order to give God our undivided attention.

It's not so much about what we do as it is about what we *don't* do.

 We shut out the external stimulation of our lives and allow ourselves to become quiet on the inside.

We say "stop" to all the noise and then say "I'm listening" to God. That's when we'll hear his still, small voice—in the quiet.

Has anyone ever struggled to make time to be alone with God? Raise your hand.

Pause.

Even when we take the time, we often find it difficult to make our "quiet time" time more meaningful. Spending time alone with God is a struggle for many of us.

We're going to watch a video now that I think most of us will relate to.

8 MINUTES

VIDEO: *QUIET TIME*

View video: *Quiet Time.*

NOTES

SOLITUDE

Solitude

Solitude is:

A time when we withdraw from the company of others in order to give God our undivided attention.

—Shut out external stimulation

—Allow ourselves to become quiet

VIDEO

Quiet Time

Notes:

3 MINUTES

Wrap-up

Does anyone here relate to *anything* in this video, or am I the only one?

This should be a lighthearted moment—almost everyone will be able to identify with the character in the video.

What barriers that kept Patty from experiencing connection with God do you most relate to?

Solicit three or four comments from the group. Be sure to repeat their answers so everyone hears the response.

Possible responses:

- *Distractions*
- *No plan*
- *Exhaustion*
- *Chores to do*
- *Wandering thoughts*
- *Bad timing*
- *Not authentic with God; not talking to him about her frustrations with her husband*
- *A sense of obligation instead of enjoyment of God*

One of the things you may have noticed about this woman's experience is that she viewed solitude as an obligation. Remember the first thing she said when she realized she had a few minutes to herself? She said, "I know what I *ought* to do. I *ought* to have a quiet time."

Let me ask you something: How does it feel to be with someone who feels *obligated* to be with you—like they *ought to* spend time with you? Not much fun, is it?

What about someone who really *enjoys* being with you—who *wants* to be with you? Completely different, right?

God is a real person and he desires to be with us. So which attitude in us do you think God prefers? Does he want people who show up in his presence to fulfill an obligation? Or does he want people who *enjoy* and *look forward to,* and *plan expectantly* to be with him?

NOTES

SOLITUDE

Solitude

Solitude is:

A time when we withdraw from the company of others in order to give God our undivided attention.

—Shut out external stimulation

—Allow ourselves to become quiet

VIDEO

Quiet Time

Notes:

Unfortunately, many of us approach our times with God as a duty rather than something we enjoy. We view him as someone we're *supposed* to see—like a dentist—rather than someone we *want* to see—like a best friend.

No wonder we have such a hard time with solitude. We don't just lack the time, we lack the right view of God.

Participant's Guide, page 57.

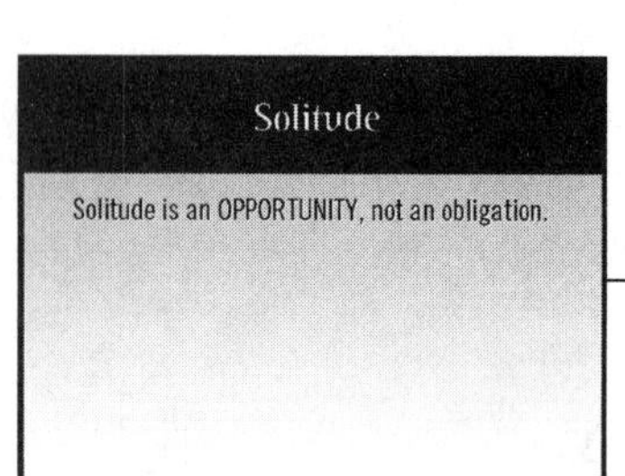

In this session, we're going to think about solitude in a new way.

Solitude is an OPPORTUNITY, not an obligation.

It is an opportunity to enjoy God—and he really is someone who is enjoyable to be with.

So the question is: How do we approach our times in solitude in such a way that we really do begin to experience them as times for enjoying God's presence rather than as a performance of a religious duty?

One way to do that is to think of how we relate to a good friend. When we anticipate times with a spouse or loved one, we usually make plans that include things we enjoy doing together. For example, we may want to go out to eat, see a movie, take a walk, or just hang out and talk. We choose our activity based on what the relationship needs at that time.

It's the same with God.

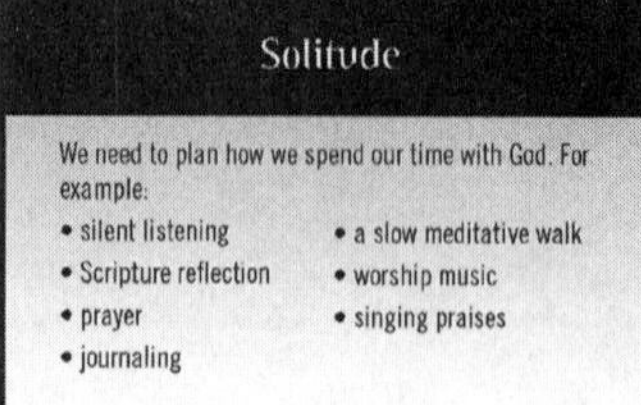

We need to plan how we spend our time with him. It might include time for silent listening, Scripture reflection, prayer, journaling, taking a slow meditative walk, listening to worship music, or singing praises to him.

Of course, it's best to hold our plan loosely so we can be responsive to God's leading in the moment, but it is good to have a plan as well.

A plan helps us to stay focused on our original intent so we don't get sidetracked by distractions.

Turn to page 58.

NOTES

Solitude is an ____________________, not an obligation.

We need to plan how we spend our time with God. For example:

silent listening

Scripture reflection

prayer

journaling

a slow meditative walk

worship music

singing praises

A plan helps us to stay focused.

5 MINUTES

Experiencing Solitude

Participant's Guide, page 58.

In just a few moments you're going to have an opportunity to spend time in solitude. On page 121 in the Appendix you'll find additional guidelines for how you can spend time alone with God. You can take a look at that later. Right now we're going to follow a simple seven-part outline.

Experiencing Solitude

1. Find a quiet place that is free of distractions.

1. Find a Quiet Place that Is Free of Distractions

First, find a quiet place that is free of distractions.

When Jesus was human here on earth, he knew the importance of finding the right place to get alone with his Father.

Mark 1:35 says:

Very early in the morning, while it was still dark, Jesus got up, left the house and went off to a solitary place, where he prayed.

In Mark 6:31-32 we read:

Then, because so many people were coming and going that they did not even have a chance to eat, [Jesus] said to [his disciples], "Come with me by yourselves to a quiet place and get some rest." So they went away by themselves in a boat to a solitary place.

Notice the common denominators in the locations Jesus chose.

They were SOLITARY and quiet.

Jesus was very careful about where he went when he needed time with God.

He shows by example that we need to pay attention to *where* we meet with God.

We need to find a place that is quiet and free of distractions.

In our session today, you can't go off into the desert. But you *will* need to find a place—either in this room or in some other area—where you won't be distracted by noise or activity.

NOTES

SOLITUDE

Experiencing Solitude

1. Find a quiet place that is free of distractions.

Very early in the morning, while it was still dark, Jesus got up, left the house and went off to a solitary place, where he prayed.
(Mark 1:35)

Then, because so many people were coming and going that they did not even have a chance to eat, [Jesus] said to [his disciples], "Come with me by yourselves to a quiet place and get some rest." So they went away by themselves in a boat to a solitary place.
(Mark 6:31-32)

The locations Jesus chose were ______________________ and quiet.

We need to pay attention to *where* we meet with God.

2. ____________________ yourself in God's presence.

   Breathe deeply

   Slow down

58

This is a good time to offer specific suggestions about where participants might go for their solitude experience at your location.

Today, although there may be people not too far from you, we want you to be alone with God. As you find your place and settle in, if others are near, give each other the gift of not interrupting each other.

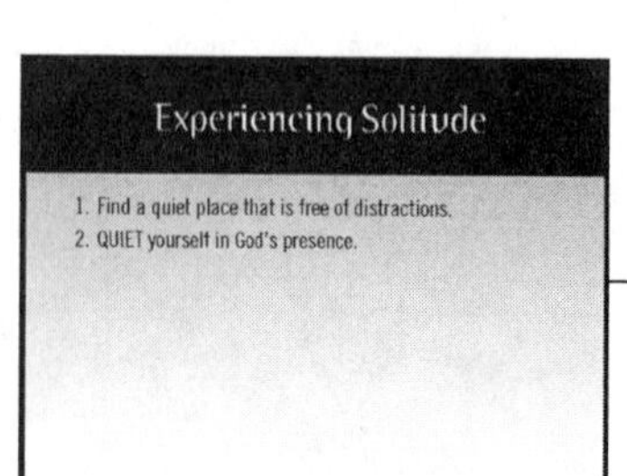

2. Quiet Yourself in God's Presence

Second, QUIET yourself in God's presence.

Too often we rush into prayer and time alone with God. We lead hurried lives and too easily fall into the habit of approaching solitude with the same frantic pace we approach everything else with.

Take a few moments as you begin your time with God to breathe deeply, to slow down, and to quiet yourself in God's presence.

3. Tell God What You Need

Participant's Guide, page 59.

Third, tell God what you need.

What would you like to receive from God?

Use a simple prayer like "God, I just want to be with you," or "God, I need your guidance," or "Lord, I want to feel your love."

Sometimes our lack of focus in prayer comes from not even knowing what we want.

Be clear about what you would like to receive from God, and tell him what you need.

4. Use Scripture to Listen to God

After finding the right place, quieting yourself in God's presence, and telling God what you need, use SCRIPTURE to listen to God.

NOTES

SOLITUDE

Experiencing Solitude

1. Find a quiet place that is free of distractions.

> *Very early in the morning, while it was still dark, Jesus got up, left the house and went off to a solitary place, where he prayed.*
> (Mark 1:35)

> *Then, because so many people were coming and going that they did not even have a chance to eat, [Jesus] said to [his disciples], "Come with me by yourselves to a quiet place and get some rest." So they went away by themselves in a boat to a solitary place.*
> (Mark 6:31-32)

The locations Jesus chose were ______________________ and quiet.

We need to pay attention to *where* we meet with God.

2. ___________________ yourself in God's presence.

   Breathe deeply

   Slow down

3. Tell God what you need.

   Use a simple prayer:

   "God, I just want to be with you."

   "God, I need your guidance."

   "Lord, I want to feel your love."

   Be clear about what you would like to receive from God.

4. Use _______________________ to listen to God.

   Read it slowly and deliberately.

   Notice the words or phrases that stand out and speak to your heart.

   What thoughts or emotions do you experience?

5. Be fully present.

   Give him your undivided attention.

   Speak to him directly about whatever you are thinking or feeling.

   Wandering thoughts:

   Aren't always a barrier to prayer

   May be a guide for prayer

For our solitude time in this session, we're going to use Psalm 23.

Read it slowly and deliberately, as though you were reading a love letter from God to you. Notice the words or phrases that stand out and speak to your heart.

Do you see yourself in any of the scenes described in the psalm?

What thoughts or emotions do you experience?

Which of the aspects of the Lord as a caring shepherd do you most need or desire at this time?

These are the kinds of questions that can help you use Scripture to listen to God.

5. Be Fully Present

Then, be fully present.

Remind yourself that you are here to be yourself, with God.

Give him your undivided attention. Being fully present with God involves speaking to him directly about whatever you are thinking or feeling—anger, gratitude, boredom, joy—or whether you feel spiritual or unspiritual.

You can tell when someone isn't really present with you. Prayer is often hard because we're not fully present with God.

Have you ever found your mind wandering in prayer? Some people feel guilty about that, but we need to learn to talk to God about whatever it is our minds wander to.

Wandering thoughts aren't always a barrier to prayer—they may actually be a guide for prayer.

Maybe my mind keeps wandering to something because it's weighing on my heart—and it's the very thing I need to talk to God about.

So be fully present with God, and speak to him directly about what is on your mind and heart.

NOTES

3. Tell God what you need.

   Use a simple prayer:

   "God, I just want to be with you."

   "God, I need your guidance."

   "Lord, I want to feel your love."

   Be clear about what you would like to receive from God.

4. Use ____________________ to listen to God.

   Read it slowly and deliberately.

   Notice the words or phrases that stand out and speak to your heart.

   What thoughts or emotions do you experience?

5. Be fully present.

   Give him your undivided attention.

   Speak to him directly about whatever you are thinking or feeling.

   Wandering thoughts:

   - Aren't always a barrier to prayer
   - May be a guide for prayer

Turn to page 60.

6. Respond to What You Hear God Saying to You through Scripture or in Prayer

Participant's Guide, page 60.

Next, respond to what you hear God saying to you through Scripture or in prayer.

You can respond verbally or by writing in a journal. If you use a journal, you could start your entry with the words, "God, what I hear you saying to me is . . . " Then fill in what you're hearing.

7. Express Gratitude and Commitment

Finally, express gratitude and commitment.

Spend a few moments at the end of your solitude time thanking God for his presence with you and expressing your commitment to respond faithfully to whatever it is that you have heard from him during this time.

INDIVIDUAL ACTIVITY: *EXPERIENCING SOLITUDE*

Participant's Guide, pages 60–62.

Objective
For participants to experience time with God in solitude.

Now we're going to take some time to experience solitude with God. You'll find directions for this activity on pages 60 to 62 in your Participant's Guide.

Before sending you out for your solitude experience, let me give you a few words of encouragement. It is impossible for you to fail at this. Your job is simply to be present with God. You don't have to manufacture a profound experience. All you have to do is show up and open up—God does the rest. And remember, he may not do anything, and that's his business. God is delighted simply because you come. It's not any more complicated than that.

NOTES

SOLITUDE

6. Respond to what you hear God saying to you through Scripture or in prayer.

   Respond verbally or by writing in a journal.

   Start with: "God, what I hear you saying to me is …."

7. Express gratitude and commitment.

INDIVIDUAL ACTIVITY

Experiencing Solitude

1. Find a quiet place that is free of distractions.

2. Quiet yourself in God's presence.
   - Begin by breathing deeply.
   - Slow down.
   - Become aware of God's presence with you.

3. Tell God what you need.
   - Use a simple prayer:
     "God, I just want to be with you."
     "God, I need your guidance."
     "Lord, I want to feel your love."

60

4. Use Scripture to listen to God.
   - Invite God to speak to you through his Word (Psalm 23 is included below).
   - Read it slowly and deliberately, as though you were reading a love letter from God to you.
   - Notice the words or phrases that stand out and speak to your heart.
   - In which of the scenes described in this psalm do you see yourself?
   - What thoughts or emotions surface as you see yourself there?
   - Which aspects of the Lord as a caring shepherd do you most need or desire at this time?

The LORD is my shepherd, I shall not be in want.
He makes me lie down in green pastures,
he leads me beside quiet waters,
he restores my soul.
He guides me in paths of righteousness
for his name's sake.
Even though I walk
through the valley of the shadow of death,
I will fear no evil,
for you are with me;
your rod and your staff,
they comfort me.
You prepare a table before me
in the presence of my enemies.
You anoint my head with oil;
my cup overflows.
Surely goodness and love will follow me
all the days of my life,
and I will dwell in the house of the LORD
forever.

(Psalm 23)

61

SOLITUDE

5. Be fully present.
   - Remind yourself that you just need to be yourself with God.
   - Give him your undivided attention.
   - Anticipate distractions by:
     —ignoring them
     —writing them down on a piece of paper for later
     —incorporating them right into your prayers.
   - Speak to him directly about whatever you are thinking or feeling—anger, gratitude, boredom, joy, sadness, need.

6. Respond to what you hear God saying to you through Scripture or in prayer.
   - Speak to God about what you have sensed and felt and heard. Do this verbally or by writing.
   - You could start your journal entry with the words, "God, what I hear you saying to me is …" Then fill in what you're hearing. Follow up with, "This makes me feel …"

7. Express gratitude and commitment.
   - Spend a few minutes thanking God for his presence with you.
   - Express your commitment to respond faithfully to whatever it is you have heard from him during this time.

62

INDIVIDUAL ACTIVITY

Experiencing Solitude

Notes:

63

Feel free to leave the room and find a quiet place where you won't be distracted.

Any questions?

You have 30 minutes. Meet back here at _____. Let me pray for you. When I finish praying, leave in silence.

You may wish to substitute your own prayer for the prayer below.

Heavenly Father, each of us is here because we have a hunger for you. We long to be with you. We want to hear from you. We want to talk to you. We all have barriers, and sometimes we feel like we don't know what we're doing. We have mixed motivations and desires. But we give this time to you. We do this, not because we're supposed to, *but because we* want to. *We open ourselves to whatever you want to do or say. Our prayer now is Samuel's prayer: "Speak, Lord, your servant is listening." In Jesus' name, amen.*

2 MINUTES

Wrap-up

Call the group back together after 30 minutes.

You look peaceful!

So, how did things go for you? What was it like to spend time alone with God in solitude?

Solicit two or three responses from the group. Be sure to repeat their answers so everyone hears the response.

Possible responses:

- *This was great! I feel very peaceful.*
- *I really enjoyed it, although at times my mind jumped around.*
- *I am definitely going to do this more often.*

NOTES

6. Respond to what you hear God saying to you through Scripture or in prayer.

   Respond verbally or by writing in a journal.

   Start with: "God, what I hear you saying to me is . . . ."

7. Express gratitude and commitment.

INDIVIDUAL ACTIVITY

Experiencing Solitude

1. Find a quiet place that is free of distractions.

2. Quiet yourself in God's presence.
   - Begin by breathing deeply.
   - Slow down.
   - Become aware of God's presence with you.

3. Tell God what you need.
   - Use a simple prayer:
     "God, I just want to be with you."
     "God, I need your guidance."
     "Lord, I want to feel your love."

4. Use Scripture to listen to God.
   - Invite God to speak to you through his Word (Psalm 23 is included below).
   - Read it slowly and deliberately, as though you were reading a love letter from God to you.
   - Notice the words or phrases that stand out and speak to your heart.
   - In which of the scenes described in this psalm do you see yourself?
   - What thoughts or emotions surface as you see yourself there?
   - Which aspects of the Lord as a caring shepherd do you most need or desire at this time?

> The LORD is my shepherd, I shall not be in want.
> He makes me lie down in green pastures,
> he leads me beside quiet waters,
> he restores my soul.
> He guides me in paths of righteousness
> for his name's sake.
> Even though I walk
> through the valley of the shadow of death,
> I will fear no evil,
> for you are with me;
> your rod and your staff,
> they comfort me.
> You prepare a table before me
> in the presence of my enemies.
> You anoint my head with oil;
> my cup overflows.
> Surely goodness and love will follow me
> all the days of my life,
> and I will dwell in the house of the LORD
> forever.
> (Psalm 23)

5. Be fully present.
   - Remind yourself that you just need to be yourself with God.
   - Give him your undivided attention.
   - Anticipate distractions by:
     —ignoring them
     —writing them down on a piece of paper for later
     —incorporating them right into your prayers.
   - Speak to him directly about whatever you are thinking or feeling—anger, gratitude, boredom, joy, sadness, need.

6. Respond to what you hear God saying to you through Scripture or in prayer.
   - Speak to God about what you have sensed and felt and heard. Do this verbally or by writing.
   - You could start your journal entry with the words, "God, what I hear you saying to me is . . ." Then fill in what you're hearing. Follow up with, "This makes me feel . . ."

7. Express gratitude and commitment.
   - Spend a few minutes thanking God for his presence with you.
   - Express your commitment to respond faithfully to whatever it is you have heard from him during this time.

INDIVIDUAL ACTIVITY

Experiencing Solitude

Notes:

What was most meaningful?

Solicit two or three responses from the group. Be sure to repeat their answers so everyone hears the response.

Possible responses:

- *I enjoyed the quiet.*
- *The Scripture really came to life when I pondered it in silence like this.*
- *I really felt like God was speaking right to me.*

What was most challenging or difficult?

Solicit two or three responses from the group. Be sure to repeat their answers so everyone hears the response.

Possible responses:

- *My mind wandered.*
- *I was really sleepy and had a hard time staying awake.*
- *At times, I found myself worrying about my upcoming week instead of focusing on God.*

Turn to page 64.

1 MINUTE

SUMMARY

Summary

- Listen and speak to God in times of solitude.
- Your relationship with God will grow significantly deeper.

Participant's Guide, page 64.

We've seen in this session how important it is to listen and speak to God in times of solitude. Jesus used this practice, and as we engage in it, our relationship with God will grow significantly deeper.

Let's close with prayer.

NOTES

SOLITUDE

Summary

Listen and speak to God in times of solitude.

Your relationship with God will grow significantly deeper.

64

You may wish to substitute your own prayer for the prayer below.

Lord, we are so grateful you invite us to spend time with you and that you make yourself available to us. We pray you would help us set aside the time we need to in order to meet with you regularly, and we commit ourselves to doing life in your name, in your presence. In Jesus' name we pray, amen.

If you are teaching this course in the weekend seminar format, this is a good time to break for lunch. Rather than dispersing, consider providing a simple lunch for a modest fee so participants can relax and spend time with each other. Encourage them to eat together at their tables and to continue discussing their solitude experiences with one another.

Another way to handle this session is to serve lunch as participants come back in the room after their solitude time. They can then discuss in small groups the two questions, "What was most meaningful?" and "What was most challenging or difficult?" while they eat. Then, when you call them back, just begin the next session.

SPIRITUAL PATHWAYS

SESSION SNAPSHOT

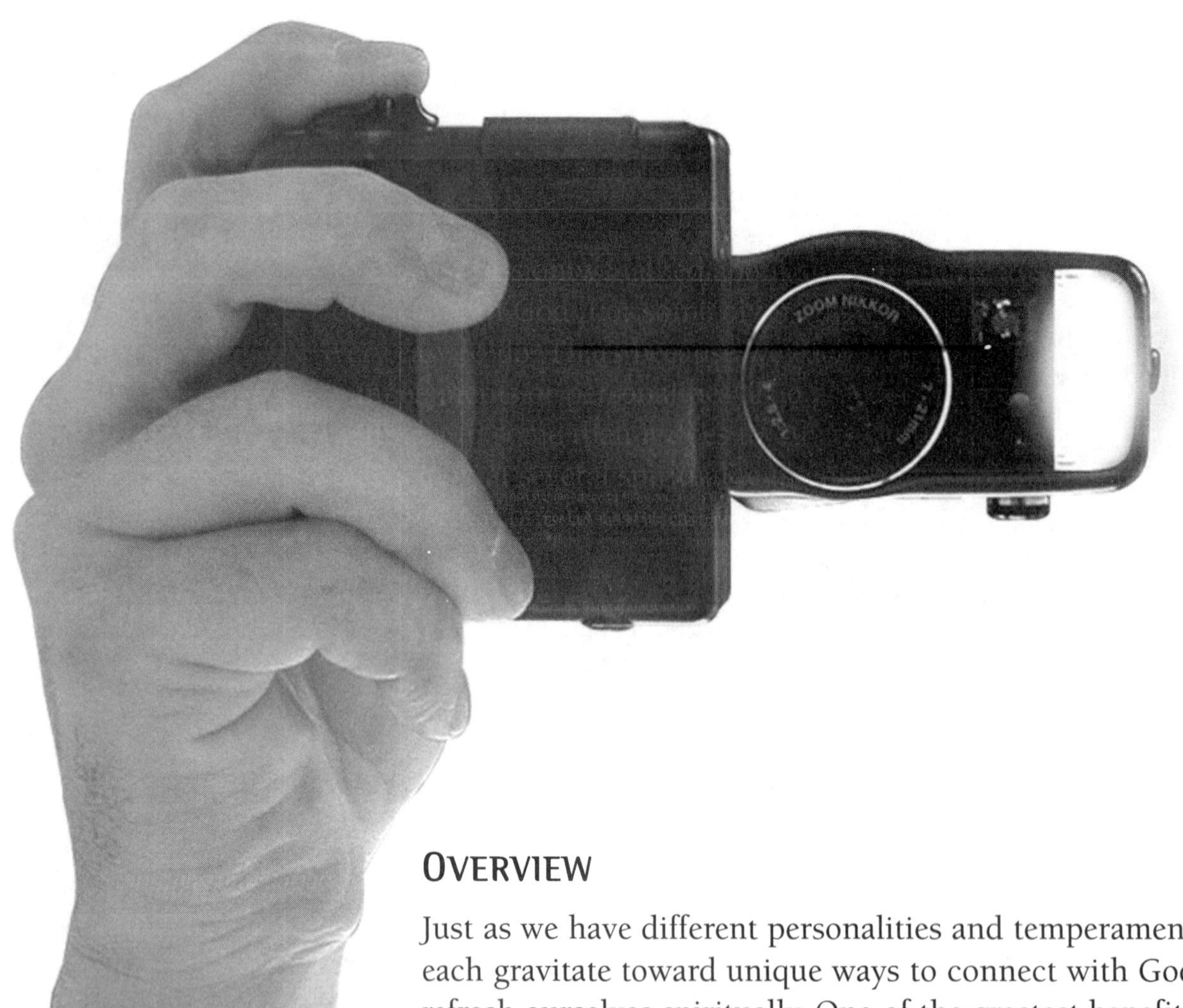

Overview

Just as we have different personalities and temperaments, we each gravitate toward unique ways to connect with God and refresh ourselves spiritually. One of the greatest benefits of knowing our spiritual temperament is the ability to build on that strength without feeling guilty for our weaknesses. Conversely, we need to be stretched in some areas to keep in balance. This session helps participants appreciate the varied ways God has given us to renew our life with him, and frees them to build on the ways that work best for them.

Objectives

In this session, participants will:

1. Discover seven spiritual pathways to connect with God
2. Identify their own preferred spiritual pathway
3. Discuss ways to develop their spiritual pathway

SESSION OUTLINE

I. Introduction

II. Discovery

A. What Is a Spiritual Pathway?

Individual Activity: *Spiritual Pathway Assessment*

B. Seven Spiritual Pathways

1. Intellectual
2. Relational
3. Serving
4. Worship
5. Activist
6. Contemplative
7. Creation

C. Individual Activity: *Developing My Spiritual Pathway*

D. Making the Most of Your Spiritual Pathway

III. Summary

SPIRITUAL PATHWAYS

TIME & MEDIA

CONTENTS

INTRODUCTION

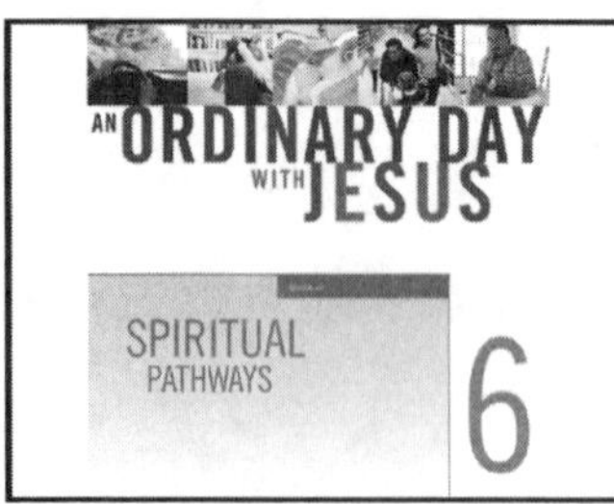

If you are teaching this course in an eight-week format rather than a weekend seminar format, you may want to begin by briefly discussing participants' experiences since the last session. Start the session as follows:

"In the last session we talked about spending time in solitude as a way to connect with God. Did anyone have an experience with a solitude time you'd like to share?"

Solicit two or three comments from the group. Be sure to repeat their answers so everyone hears the response.

Possible responses:

- *It was great; why haven't I done more of this!*
- *I tried but kept getting distracted; it seems harder to do on my own.*
- *I wasn't sure what to do but enjoyed it anyway.*

NOTES

SESSION SIX

SPIRITUAL PATHWAYS

In the last session we talked about spending time in solitude as a way to connect with God. For some of us, this was a challenge; for others it was very easy to do. That's because we each have unique spiritual temperaments or personalities. The practice of solitude comes more naturally to some than it does to others. In this session, we're going to take a look at several spiritual temperaments or pathways and how we can use each one to connect with God.

2 MINUTES

DISCOVERY

Let's do a little survey to get started. The question is this: When you have some time and you want to experience renewal or recreation, what do you do?

Solicit several comments from the group. Be sure to repeat their answers so everyone hears the response.

Possible responses:

- *Go to the beach or the woods*
- *Spend time alone*
- *Read*
- *Play a game on the computer*
- *Shop*
- *Take a nap*
- *Get together with a friend*
- *Visit a museum*
- *Go fishing*

What happens when you go too long without this activity?

Solicit two or three comments from the group. Be sure to repeat their answers so everyone hears the response.

Possible responses:

- *Fatigue*
- *Irritability*
- *Poor judgment*
- *Sadness or even depression*
- *Lack of direction or focus*

NOTES

SESSION SIX

SPIRITUAL PATHWAYS

I want you to notice something. We all have *different* ways to refresh ourselves. Some like to do a mental activity, yet others prefer little or no brain use. Some of us are refreshed by physical involvement, yet for others the last thing we want to do is exert our bodies. Some of us are refreshed by being alone, but others of us go nuts unless we can hang out with at least one other person—and preferably a whole crowd.

What Is a Spiritual Pathway?

Participant's Guide, page 66.

This reality about our differences underscores a very important truth when it comes to spiritual growth and transformation. God made each of us unique.

This means that, just as we enjoy a variety of ways to refresh ourselves physically and mentally, God has also given us a variety of ways to refresh ourselves spiritually and to connect with him. These ways of connecting with God are called "spiritual pathways."[1]

What Is a Spiritual Pathway?

- A spiritual pathway is the way we most naturally connect with God and grow spiritually.

Here's a simple definition: a spiritual pathway is the way we most naturally connect with God and grow spiritually.

Each of us has a preferred spiritual pathway, and we naturally gravitate to that way of connecting with God.

Most of us don't use just one, but we do tend to prefer one or two main pathways.

There's also usually at least one pathway that is very unnatural for us, and it takes some stretching for us to experiment using that pathway.

Here's why this is so important.

What Is a Spiritual Pathway?

- The goal is for you to feel great FREEDOM and joy using it.

Once you've discovered your pathway, the goal is for you to feel great FREEDOM and joy in using it. If you don't identify and develop your spiritual pathway, it will be very difficult to experience God's presence with you in an ordinary day.

[1] For a complete discussion of these and other spiritual pathways, see Gary Thomas, *Sacred Pathways* (Grand Rapids: Zondervan, 2000).

NOTES

SPIRITUAL PATHWAYS

What Is a Spiritual Pathway?

A spiritual pathway is the way we most naturally connect with God and grow spiritually.

We tend to favor one or two main pathways.

There is usually at least one pathway that is very unnatural for us.

The goal is for you to feel great ________________________ and joy in using it.

If you don't identify and develop your spiritual pathway, it will be very difficult to experience God's presence with you in an ordinary day.

You will likely feel stuck and spiritually defeated. It may be that you feel that way now, and finding out about spiritual pathways is going to open up a whole new level of connection between you and God.

To help us discover the unique ways we connect to God, we're going to use a Spiritual Pathway Assessment.

Individual Activity: *Spiritual Pathway Assessment*

Participant's Guide, pages 67–72.

Objective
For participants to identify their preferred spiritual pathway.

Directions

1. Respond to each statement below according to the following scale:
   3 = Consistently/definitely true of me
   2 = Often/usually true of me
   1 = Once in a while/sometimes true of me
   0 = Not at all/never true of me

   Put the number in the blank before each statement.
2. Transfer the numbers you gave for each assessment statement to the grid on page 71.
3. Total each column. The highest number identifies your preferred spiritual pathway; the next highest number, your secondary pathway.

Any questions on the directions?

You will have 10 minutes to do this.

Refer to page 325 in the Appendix to see the Spiritual Pathway Assessment.

After 5 minutes, inform participants that they have 5 minutes left.

Call the group back together after 10 minutes.

NOTES

INDIVIDUAL ACTIVITY

Spiritual Pathway Assessment

1. Respond to each statement below according to the following scale:
   3 = Consistently/definitely true of me
   2 = Often/usually true of me
   1 = Once in a while/sometimes true of me
   0 = Not at all/never true of me

   Put the number in the blank before each statement.
2. Transfer the numbers you gave for each assessment statement to the grid on page 71.
3. Total each column. The highest number identifies your preferred spiritual pathway; the next highest number, your secondary pathway.

1. When I have a problem, I'd rather pray with people than pray alone.
2. In a church service, I most look forward to the teaching.
3. People who know me would describe me as enthusiastic during worship times.
4. No matter how tired I get, I usually come alive when a challenge is placed before me.
5. Spiritual reality sometimes feels more real to me than the physical world.

6. I get distracted in meetings or services if I notice details in the surroundings that haven't been attended to.
7. A beautiful sunset can give me a spiritual high that temporarily blocks out everything bothering me.
8. It makes me feel better about myself to hang out with people I know and like.
9. I've never understood why people don't love to study the Bible in depth.
10. God touches me every time I gather with other believers for praise.
11. People around me know how passionate I feel about the causes I'm involved in.
12. I experience a deep inner joy when I am in a quiet place, free from distractions.
13. Helping others is easy for me, even when I have problems.
14. When faced with a difficult decision, I am drawn to walk in the woods, on the beach, or in some other outdoor setting.
15. When I am alone too much, I tend to lose energy or get a little depressed.
16. People seek me out when they need answers to biblical questions.
17. Even when I'm tired, I look forward to going to a church service.
18. I sense the presence of God most when I'm doing his work.
19. I don't understand how Christians can be so busy and still think they're hearing from God.
20. I love being able to serve behind the scenes, out of the spotlight.
21. I experience God in nature so powerfully I'm sometimes tempted not to bother with church.

22. I experience God most tangibly in fellowship with a few others.
23. When I need to be refreshed, a stimulating book is just the thing.
24. I am happiest when I praise God together with others.
25. "When the going gets tough, the tough get going"—that's true about me!
26. My family and friends sometimes tease me about being such a hermit.
27. People around me sometimes tell me they admire my compassion.
28. Things in nature often teach me valuable lessons about God.
29. I don't understand people who have a hard time revealing personal things about themselves.
30. Sometimes I spend too much time learning about an issue rather than dealing with it.
31. I don't think there's any good excuse for missing a worship time.
32. I get tremendous satisfaction from seeing people working together to achieve a goal.
33. When I face a difficulty, being alone feels most helpful.
34. Even when I'm tired, I find I have the energy and desire to care for people's problems.
35. God is so real when I'm in a beautiful, natural setting.
36. When I'm tired, there's nothing better than going out with friends to refresh me.
37. I worship best in response to theological truth clearly explained.
38. I like how all the world's problems—including mine—seem unimportant when I'm praising God at church.

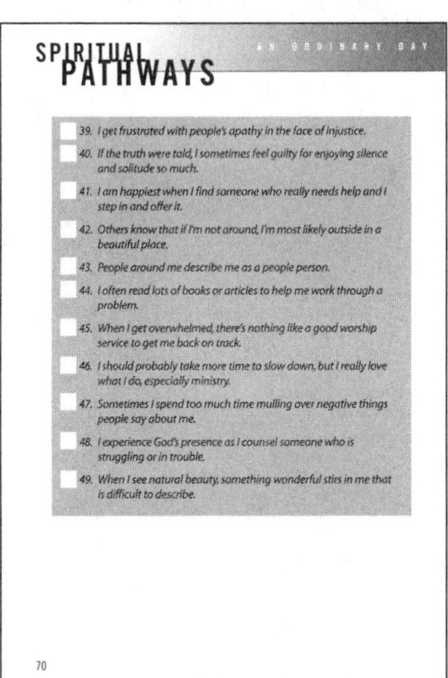

39. I get frustrated with people's apathy in the face of injustice.
40. If the truth were told, I sometimes feel guilty for enjoying silence and solitude so much.
41. I am happiest when I find someone who really needs help and I step in and offer it.
42. Others know that if I'm not around, I'm most likely outside in a beautiful place.
43. People around me describe me as a people person.
44. I often read lots of books or articles to help me work through a problem.
45. When I get overwhelmed, there's nothing like a good worship service to get me back on track.
46. I should probably take more time to slow down, but I really love what I do, especially ministry.
47. Sometimes I spend too much time mulling over negative things people say about me.
48. I experience God's presence as I counsel someone who is struggling or in trouble.
49. When I see natural beauty, something wonderful stirs in me that is difficult to describe.

Spiritual Pathway Assessment Scoring

Spiritual Pathway Scoring

Transfer the numbers from the assessment to this grid, and total each column.

1.	2.	3.	4.	5.	6.	7.
8.	9.	10.	11.	12.	13.	14.
15.	16.	17.	18.	19.	20.	21.
22.	23.	24.	25.	26.	27.	28.
29.	30.	31.	32.	33.	34.	35.
36.	37.	38.	39.	40.	41.	42.
43.	44.	45.	46.	47.	48.	49.
Total	Total	Total	Total	Total	Total	Total
A Relational	B Intellectual	C Worship	D Activist	E Contem-plative	F Serving	G Creation

Relational—I connect best to God when I am with others. A
Intellectual—I connect best to God when I learn. B
Worship—I connect best to God when I worship. C
Activist—I connect best to God when doing great things. D
Contemplative—I connect best to God in silence. E
Serving—I connect best to God while completing Kingdom tasks. F
Creation—I connect best to God in nature. G

1 MINUTE

Wrap-up

What were your reactions to doing this? Any surprises?

Solicit three or four comments from the group. Be sure to repeat their answers so everyone hears the response.

Possible responses:

- *I enjoyed this exercise.*
- *I ended up pretty much where I thought I would be.*
- *I seem to straddle two pathways; is that a problem?*

28 MINUTES

Seven Spiritual Pathways

Participant's Guide, page 73.

In order to cover the material in this session in 50 minutes, you will need maintain a brisk pace in presenting each of the seven spiritual pathways. If time allows, it's best to allow at least 60 minutes to complete the entire session.

Now that we've discovered our spiritual pathways, let's take a closer look at each one.

We can find examples of at least seven different spiritual pathways in the Bible. There may be more, but most people usually relate well to one or more of these seven spiritual pathways:

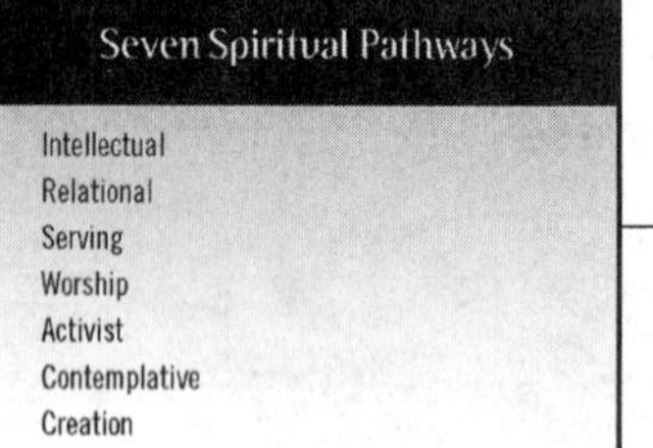

Intellectual
Relational
Serving
Worship
Activist
Contemplative
Creation

Turn to page 74.

NOTES

Seven Spiritual Pathways*

- *Intellectual*
- *Relational*
- *Serving*
- *Worship*
- *Activist*
- *Contemplative*
- *Creation*

* For a complete discussion of these and other spiritual pathways, see Gary Thomas, *Sacred Pathways* (Grand Rapids: Zondervan, 2000).

If you are familiar with the *Becoming a Contagious Christian* evangelism course, you may note that three spiritual pathways—Intellectual, Relational, and Serving—have the same name as three of the evangelism styles. Those evangelism styles and these pathways do not *necessarily* correlate (though they may).

INTELLECTUAL

Participant's Guide, page 74.

 First, the intellectual pathway.

Characteristics

Intellectual: *Characteristics*

- You draw close to God as you're able to learn more about him.
- The study of SCRIPTURE and theology comes naturally.

 If this is you, you draw close to God as you're able to learn more about him.

The study of SCRIPTURE and theology comes naturally.

When you go into a Christian bookstore, you're not likely to come out until your picture ends up on a milk carton!

Intellectual: *Characteristics*

- You have little patience for emotional approaches to faith.
- You are a thinker.
- When you face problems or spiritual challenges, you go into problem-solving mode.

 You have little patience for emotional approaches to faith.

During worship, you sometimes find yourself marking time until the message starts. In a small group, you're concerned that those relational types just swap ignorance when they get together.

 You are a thinker.

You may have a feeling occasionally, but you've found that if you wait, it usually passes!

 When you face problems or spiritual challenges, you go into problem-solving mode.

Biblical Example

Intellectual: *Biblical Example*

The Apostle Paul

 The Apostle Paul is an example of someone in the Bible who had an intellectual pathway.

NOTES

SPIRITUAL PATHWAYS

Intellectual

Characteristics

You draw close to God as you're able to learn more about him.

The study of ______________________ and theology comes naturally.

You have little patience for emotional approaches to faith.

You are a thinker.

When you face problems or spiritual challenges, you go into problem-solving mode.

Biblical Example

The Apostle Paul

Other Example

____

Strengths

Read great books that challenge you.

Expose yourself to lots of teaching.

Find like-minded people with whom you can learn.

Even before his conversion, he tells us that he studied at the feet of Gamaliel (Gah-māy-lē-el), one of the great Jewish scholars of his day. After his conversion, Paul went into the synagogues and reasoned from Scripture. He also went to Athens and talked with the philosophers.

If you're like Paul, the road to your heart usually leads through your head. You hear God best as you learn. When you're deeply immersed in great books, classes, deep thought, and new learning, you come to life. Many of your moments of decision or repentance flow out of discovery and insight as you learn.

Other Example

With this and the remaining spiritual pathways, be sure to mention local examples of people participants know and respect. If time permits, describe how these individuals use their pathway to connect with God. Also, be sure to share your own spiritual pathway with participants when you come to it.

Intellectual: *Other Example*

C. S. LEWIS

Cambridge professor and author C.S. LEWIS, who wrote *Mere Christianity,* is a good recent example of this pathway. That book—and many of Lewis' other books—contained a well-reasoned defense of the Christian faith.

If time permits, you may wish to mention these other examples:

- Chuck Colson, author and former White House staff member, founder of Prison Fellowship ministry
- Dorothy Sayers, a British author and educator
- Lee Strobel, a former atheist and author of *The Case for Christ* and *The Case for Faith*

Anyone think you have an intellectual pathway? Raise your hand.

Pause.

Strengths

Intellectual pathway people need to build on their strength: the discipline of study. If they quit learning, they grow stagnant.

NOTES

Intellectual

Characteristics

You draw close to God as you're able to learn more about him.

The study of ________________________ and theology comes naturally.

You have little patience for emotional approaches to faith.

You are a thinker.

When you face problems or spiritual challenges, you go into problem-solving mode.

Biblical Example

The Apostle Paul

Other Example

____

Strengths

Read great books that challenge you.

Expose yourself to lots of teaching.

Find like-minded people with whom you can learn.

Intellectual: *Strengths*

- Read great books that challenge you.
- Expose yourself to lots of teaching.
- Find like-minded people with whom you can learn.

 If this is your pathway, you need to read great books that challenge you.

Expose yourself to lots of teaching, maybe through seminary or message tapes that feed your mind.

Find some like-minded people with whom you can learn.

Cautions

Participant's Guide, page 75.

Intellectual: *Cautions*

- Guard against becoming all head and no heart

 If you're on this pathway, a caution for you is to guard against becoming all head and no heart.

You love to be right, and that can be dangerous.

 Dallas Willard once observed:

One of the hardest things in the world is to be right and not to hurt anybody with it.

Isn't it remarkable that Jesus was always right and never hurt anybody with being right?

 Another caution: don't confuse being smart with being spiritually mature.

As we noted in session two, the right gauge of spiritual health and maturity is love, not intelligence.

Ways to Stretch

Intellectual: *Ways to Stretch*

- Devote yourself to corporate worship and to private adoration and prayer.
- If your learning doesn't lead to WORSHIP, it will get dangerous.
- Engage in self-examination to assess whether or not you are being loving.

 One way you can stretch is to devote yourself to corporate worship and to private adoration and prayer.

This may not come naturally, but your learning needs to lead to WORSHIP; otherwise it will get dangerous. In 1 Corinthians 8:1, Paul warns, "Knowledge puffs up, but love builds up."

Another way to stretch is to engage in self-examination to assess whether or not you are being loving as you interact with others in sharing your knowledge.

NOTES

SPIRITUAL PATHWAYS — AN ORDINARY DAY

Intellectual

Characteristics

You draw close to God as you're able to learn more about him.

The study of ______________ and theology comes naturally.

You have little patience for emotional approaches to faith.

You are a thinker.

When you face problems or spiritual challenges, you go into problem-solving mode.

Biblical Example

The Apostle Paul

Other Example

____

Strengths

Read great books that challenge you.

Expose yourself to lots of teaching.

Find like-minded people with whom you can learn.

74

WITH JESUS — SESSION SIX

Cautions

Guard against becoming all head and no heart.

> *One of the hardest things in the world is to be right and not to hurt anybody with it.*
> Dallas Willard

Don't confuse being smart with being spiritually mature.

Ways to Stretch

Devote yourself to corporate worship and to private adoration and prayer.

Your learning needs to lead to ______________; otherwise it will get dangerous.

> *Knowledge puffs up, but love builds up.*
> (1 Corinthians 8:1b)

Engage in self-examination to assess whether or not you are being loving.

75

Turn to page 76.

RELATIONAL

Participant's Guide, page 76.

 Next is the relational pathway.

Characteristics

Relational: *Characteristics*

- Spiritual growth comes most naturally when you're involved in significant RELATIONSHIPS
- Small groups and other community life experiences are key.

 If this is your preferred pathway, spiritual growth comes most naturally when you're involved in significant RELATIONSHIPS. Small groups and other community life experiences are key.

In fact, people with a relational pathway are small group junkies. You start small groups in your neighborhood, at work, during plane trips, on long elevator rides.

Relational: *Characteristics*

- Your life is an open book.
- Being alone can drive you crazy.
- In key times of growth, God will often speak to you through people.

 Your life is an open book, and you're surprised that it's difficult for others to be open.

Salespeople call you up to refinance your home, and you ask them, "How are you doing, *really?*"

 Being alone can drive you crazy.

"Solitude wouldn't be so bad," you think, "if I could just bring a few friends along." Being with people energizes you—the more people, the better.

 In key times of growth—like confronting sin, guidance for decisions, accountability for actions, expressions of love—God will often speak to you through people.

Biblical Example

Relational: *Biblical Example*

The Apostle Peter

 An example of someone in the Bible with a relational pathway is the Apostle Peter.

NOTES

Relational

Characteristics

Spiritual growth comes most naturally when you're involved in significant ______________________.

Small groups and other community life experiences are key.

Your life is an open book.

Being alone can drive you crazy.

In key times of growth, God will often speak to you through people.

Biblical Example

The Apostle Peter

Other Example

____

Strengths

You need a relationally rich life.

Use your spiritual gift to serve others.

Pray with others in community.

Learn in a class with other people or in a small group.

Use your network of contacts to further God's kingdom.

Peter came to Jesus *with* others. He was part of that inner circle along with James and John and Jesus. In John 21, after the Crucifixion, Peter gathered others together with him and went fishing. The defining moments of his life—his choice to follow Christ, his confession of Jesus as Messiah, his denial of Christ, his restoration—all took place in a relational context.

Relational: *Other Example*

JOHN WESLEY

Other Example

Although he lived over 200 years ago, JOHN WESLEY, the founder of Methodism, is a good example of this pathway.

Wesley was radically committed to relationships and had a passion for getting believers to meet together in small groups, which is how Methodism started.

If time permits, you may wish to mention these other examples:

- Bill McCartney, founder of Promise Keepers men's ministry
- Corrie ten Boom, whose family hid Jews during World War II in Holland and who survived imprisonment in the Nazi concentration camp at Auschwitz

Anyone here think you have a relational pathway? Raise your hand.

Pause.

Relational: *Strengths*

- You need a relationally rich life
- Use your spiritual gift to serve others
- Pray with others in community

Relational: *Strengths*

- Learn in a class with other people or in a small group
- Use your network of contacts to further God's kingdom

Strengths

If this is you, you need a relationally rich life.

Use your spiritual gift to serve others, and pray with others in community.

You'll probably learn best in a class with other people, or in a small group.

You'll tend to have lots of relationships, and you can use your network of contacts to further God's kingdom.

NOTES

SPIRITUAL PATHWAYS

Relational

Characteristics

Spiritual growth comes most naturally when you're involved in significant ____________________.

Small groups and other community life experiences are key.

Your life is an open book.

Being alone can drive you crazy.

In key times of growth, God will often speak to you through people.

Biblical Example

The Apostle Peter

Other Example

____

Strengths

You need a relationally rich life.

Use your spiritual gift to serve others.

Pray with others in community.

Learn in a class with other people or in a small group.

Use your network of contacts to further God's kingdom.

Cautions

Participant's Guide, page 77.

Relational: *Cautions*

- Guard against superficiality

Here are two cautions for those who have a relational pathway.

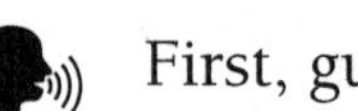

First, guard against superficiality.

You need to be sure you have a few *deep* relationships in your life—people who get past your external self and who love you, challenge you, encourage you, and give you wise counsel.

Second, you can grow DEPENDENT on others and become a spiritual chameleon.

Peter had this problem. In the beginning of Galatians, Paul talks about how Peter had to be confronted. When Peter was with people from different ethnic backgrounds, he initially reached out to them and made no distinction between himself and them. But when some legalistic Jewish believers came along, Peter started acting aloof as they did.

Ways to Stretch

Relational: *Ways to Stretch*

- Develop a capacity for SILENCE
- Keep some of your experiences with God secret
- Study Scripture for yourself
- Invite close friends to speak truth to you

Here are a few ways to stretch.

Develop a capacity for SILENCE so you can learn to speak and listen to God when you are alone.

Keep some of your experiences with God secret so you don't get addicted to what other people think.

Study Scripture for yourself so you are grounded in God's Word rather than in others' opinions.

Finally, be intentional about inviting one or two close friends to speak truth to you so that your relationship is more than just social.

Turn to page 78.

NOTES

Cautions

Guard against superficiality.

You can grow ______________________ on others and become a spiritual chameleon.

Ways to Stretch

Develop a capacity for ______________________ .

Keep some of your experiences with God secret so you don't get addicted to what other people think.

Study Scripture for yourself so you are grounded in God's Word rather than in others' opinions.

Invite close friends to speak truth to you so that your relationship is more than just social.

SERVING

Participant's Guide, page 78.

 The next pathway is serving.

Serving: *Characteristics*

- God's presence seems most tangible when you're involved in helping others
- You're often uncomfortable in a setting where you don't have a role
- You constantly look for acts of SERVICE you can engage in

Characteristics

 If this is you, God's presence seems most tangible when you're involved in helping others.

You're often uncomfortable in a setting where you don't have a role. But if you have a role—as simple as setting up chairs, serving coffee, or offering some kind of care—then you sense God's presence and delight.

You constantly look for acts of SERVICE you can engage in, and often don't even need to be asked.

Serving: *Biblical Example*

Dorcas in the Book of Acts

Biblical Example

 An example of someone in the Bible with this pathway is a woman named Dorcas.

The Book of Acts describes her as someone well known for a life of good deeds. Her name became synonymous with acts of servanthood and caring for the poor.

Other Example

Who would be a modern-day example of the serving pathway?

Pause.

Serving: *Other Example*

MOTHER TERESA

 MOTHER TERESA, the nun who served those who were homeless and dying in the streets of Calcutta, India, is an example of someone in our lifetime who had this pathway.

She said the reason she lived life the way she did was for the joy it brought her. She saw the face of Christ in the people she served, and it motivated her for a lifetime.

NOTES

SPIRITUAL PATHWAYS

Serving

Characteristics

God's presence seems most tangible when you're involved in helping others.

You're often uncomfortable in a setting where you don't have a role. If you have a role, then you sense God's presence and delight.

You constantly look for acts of ____________________ you can engage in and often don't even need to be asked.

Biblical Example

Dorcas in the Book of Acts

Other Example

____

Strengths

Get plugged into a ____________________so you have opportunities for meaningful service to offer God.

Look for glimpses of God's presence in the people you serve and in the execution of your tasks.

Prepare to serve first by praying so your service is genuinely spiritual service.

Serving: *Strengths*

- Get plugged into a COMMUNITY
- Look for glimpses of God's presence in the people you serve, and in the execution of your tasks
- Prepare to serve first by praying so your service is genuinely spiritual service

Serving: *Cautions*

- Be careful not to resent other people who don't serve as much as you do
- Remember that God loves you not because you are so faithful in serving him, but because you are his CHILD
- Don't confuse serving with earning God's love.

If time permits, you may wish to mention this other example:

Jimmy Carter, former U.S. President and now active with Habitat for Humanity, an organization that builds homes for low-income families

Anyone think you have a serving pathway? Raise your hand.

Pause.

Strengths

If this is you, you connect with God when you're helping. So you need to build on this strength.

 Get plugged into a COMMUNITY so you have opportunities for meaningful service to offer God.

If you're just attending church but you have nowhere to serve, your connection to God will begin to feel distant.

 Look for glimpses of God's presence in the people you serve and in the execution of your tasks.

Cultivate an awareness of those moments when you sense God with you as you serve.

 Prepare to serve first by praying so your service is genuinely spiritual service.

Cautions

Participant's Guide, page 79.

Here are a couple of cautions.

 First, be careful not to resent other people who don't serve as much as you do.

Second, remember that God loves you, not because you are so faithful in serving him, but because you are his CHILD. Don't confuse serving with earning God's love.

NOTES

Serving

Characteristics

God's presence seems most tangible when you're involved in helping others.

You're often uncomfortable in a setting where you don't have a role. If you have a role, then you sense God's presence and delight.

You constantly look for acts of ________________________ you can engage in and often don't even need to be asked.

Biblical Example

Dorcas in the Book of Acts

Other Example

____

Strengths

Get plugged into a ________________________ so you have opportunities for meaningful service to offer God.

Look for glimpses of God's presence in the people you serve and in the execution of your tasks.

Prepare to serve first by praying so your service is genuinely spiritual service.

Cautions

Be careful not to resent other people who don't serve as much as you do.

Remember that God loves you, not because you are so faithful in serving him, but because you are his _______________.

Don't confuse serving with earning God's love.

Ways to Stretch

Balance your service with small group and community life.

Learn how to receive love even when you're not being productive.

Practice expressing love through ________________________ as well as actions.

Serving: *Ways to Stretch*

- Balance your service with small group and community life.
- Learn to receive love even when you're not being productive.
- Practice expressing love through WORDS as well as actions.

Ways to Stretch

A way for you to stretch is to balance your service with small group and community life.

Learn how to receive love even when you're not being productive.

Practice expressing love through WORDS as well as actions.

That way, your pathway will help you feel liberated by service rather than confined by it.

Turn to page 80.

WORSHIP

Participant's Guide, page 80.

Next is the worship pathway.

Worship: *Characteristics*

- You have a deep love of corporate praise and a natural inclination toward celebration.
- In difficult periods of life, worship is one of the most healing activities you engage in.

Characteristics

If you have a worship pathway, you love Psalm 122:1, which says:

I rejoiced with those who said to me, "Let us go to the house of the LORD."

You have a deep love of corporate praise and a natural inclination toward celebration.

In difficult periods of life, worship is one of the most healing activities you engage in.

When you worship at church, you hope it will go on for hours. While the intellectual types are looking at their watches, waiting for the message to start, you're shouting, "Sing it again!"

Sometimes you are naturally outgoing, but often people on this pathway are not demonstrative or expressive.

Worship: *Characteristics*

- In worship, your HEART opens up and you come alive and enthusiastically participate.

Yet in worship, your HEART opens up, and you come alive and enthusiastically participate.

NOTES

Cautions

Be careful not to resent other people who don't serve as much as you do.

Remember that God loves you, not because you are so faithful in serving him, but because you are his ______________.

Don't confuse serving with earning God's love.

Ways to Stretch

Balance your service with small group and community life.

Learn how to receive love even when you're not being productive.

Practice expressing love through ______________________ as well as actions.

Worship

> *I rejoiced with those who said to me, "Let us go to the house of the Lord."*
> (Psalm 122:1)

Characteristics

You have a deep love of corporate praise and a natural inclination toward celebration.

In difficult periods of life, worship is one of the most healing activities you engage in.

In worship, your ______________________ opens up, and you come alive and enthusiastically participate.

Biblical Example

King David

Other Example

____

Worship: *Biblical Example*

King David

Biblical Example

 King David is an example in the Bible of someone who had a worship pathway.

David danced before the Lord with all of his heart. He wrote psalms and poetry to God. He played his lyre and expressed his love for God through music.

Worship: *Other Example*

DARLENE ZSCHECH

Other Example

 DARLENE ZSCHECH (pronounced "check"), a worship leader and songwriter from Australia, is one of the many worship leaders in our day who exemplifies this pathway.

If time permits, you may wish to mention these other examples:

- Jack Hayford, pastor and author of worship songs like "Majesty"
- Tommy Walker, worship leader and songwriter
- Cliff Barrows, long-time worship leader at Billy Graham crusades

Who thinks this might be your pathway?

Pause.

Strengths

Participant's Guide, page 81.

Worship: *Strengths*

- Experience great worship on a regular basis.
- Use worship tapes or CDs and make your car a private sanctuary.
- Learn about other worship traditions, and incorporate what you learn into your personal worship time

Here are some ways to build on your strengths.

 Experience great worship on a regular basis.

When the body of Christ gathers, be there.

 Use worship tapes or CDs and make your car a private sanctuary.

Don't worry that we're all staring at you as you go down the road, singing your lungs out. It doesn't matter because this is how you connect to God.

NOTES

Worship

> *I rejoiced with those who said to me, "Let us go to the house of the Lord."*
> (Psalm 122:1)

Characteristics

You have a deep love of corporate praise and a natural inclination toward celebration.

In difficult periods of life, worship is one of the most healing activities you engage in.

In worship, your ________________________ opens up, and you come alive and enthusiastically participate.

Biblical Example

King David

Other Example

____

Strengths

Experience great worship on a regular basis.

Use worship tapes or CDs and make your car a private sanctuary.

Learn about other worship traditions, and incorporate what you learn into your personal worship time.

Cautions

Be careful not to judge those who aren't as expressive in worship.

Guard against an experience-based spirituality that always has you looking for the next worship "high."

This is what C.S. Lewis called "the fatal sin of saying 'encore!'"

> *The danger in finding a way to God is that people grow to love the way more than they love God.*
> Meister Eckhart

Ways to Stretch

Engage in the discipline of ________________________.

Serve God in concrete ways as an extension of your worship.

Remain committed to your church even when worship isn't all you would like it to be.

 Learn about other worship traditions, and incorporate what you learn into your personal worship time.

Cautions

Worship: *Cautions*

- Be careful not to judge those who aren't as expressive in worship

Here are a couple of cautions.

 Be careful not to judge those who aren't as expressive in worship.

Don't assume they don't love God as much or aren't experiencing the work of the Holy Spirit. Some people are consumed by love and joy and peace—the Spirit's true fruit—but in their tradition, nobody even lifts a finger, let alone a hand, in a worship service.

 Guard against an experience-based spirituality that has you always looking for the next worship "high."

This is what C. S. Lewis called "the fatal sin of saying 'encore!'" by demanding that God reproduce an experience or an emotion.

Meister Eckhart says, "The danger in finding a way to God is that people grow to love the way more than they love God."

You'll need to watch out for this.

Ways to Stretch

Worship: *Ways to Stretch*

- Engage in the discipline of STUDY
- Serve God in concrete ways as an extension of your worship
- Remain committed to your community of faith

 To stretch, engage in the discipline of STUDY.

You need to make sure that your mind is filled with the knowledge of God and to keep that area growing so your heart and emotions are solidly rooted.

 Serve God in concrete ways as an extension of your worship.

Serving gets you into people's lives and provides a practical outlet for the exuberance you feel in worship.

 Remain committed to your church even when worship isn't all you would like it to be.

NOTES

Strengths

Experience great worship on a regular basis.

Use worship tapes or CDs and make your car a private sanctuary.

Learn about other worship traditions, and incorporate what you learn into your personal worship time.

Cautions

Be careful not to judge those who aren't as expressive in worship.

Guard against an experience-based spirituality that always has you looking for the next worship "high."

This is what C.S. Lewis called "the fatal sin of saying 'encore!'"

> *The danger in finding a way to God is that people grow to love the way more than they love God.*
>
> Meister Eckhart

Ways to Stretch

Engage in the discipline of ______________________.

Serve God in concrete ways as an extension of your worship.

Remain committed to your church even when worship isn't all you would like it to be.

Be part of the solution by staying faithful and bringing your best contribution to making worship a meaningful experience for your church.

Turn to page 82.

ACTIVIST

Participant's Guide, page 82.

 Next is the activist pathway.

Characteristics

> **Activist:** ***Characteristics***
>
> - You have a single-minded zeal and a very strong sense of VISION.
> - You have a passion to build the church; a passion to work for justice.
> - Challenges don't discourage you.

 If you have an activist pathway, you have a single-minded zeal and a very strong sense of VISION.

You have a passion to build the church and to work for justice.

Challenges don't discourage you.

They energize you. You thrive on opposition. You love it when somebody says to you, "This can't be done." You smile and say: "Watch me!"

> **Activist:** ***Characteristics***
>
> - You do everything you can to bring out the POTENTIAL God has placed in other people.
> - You love a high-paced, problem-filled, complex, strenuous way of life.

 You do everything you can to bring out the POTENTIAL God has placed in other people.

You love a fast-paced, problem-filled, complex, strenuous way of life.

At the end of the day, those with the activist pathway want to say, "I ran really hard. I used every ounce of effort and zeal at my disposal, God, and it's all for you." An activist wants to run with everything he or she has got between now and the day they die—which will probably be in their early fifties of a heart attack!

Biblical Example

> **Activist:** ***Biblical Example***
>
> Nehemiah

 One example of an activist in the Bible is Nehemiah.

When Nehemiah hears about the condition of Jerusalem—that the capital city of his people has fallen into disrepair—he is upset and wants to take action.

NOTES

SPIRITUAL PATHWAYS

Activist

Description

You have a single-minded zeal and a very strong sense of ______________________.

You have a passion to build the church and to work for justice.

Challenges don't discourage you.

You do everything you can to bring out the ________________ God has placed in other people.

You love a fast-paced, problem-filled, complex, strenuous way of life.

Biblical Example

Nehemiah

> *I prayed to the God of heaven, and I answered the king.*
> (Nehemiah 2:4b-5a)

Prayer and action go hand in hand for the activist.

Other Example

____

82

There's a little line in the story that you could easily overlook. It's a simple phrase that captures the essence of the activist.

Nehemiah says, "I prayed to the God of heaven, and I answered the king."

He then makes his proposal for action. Prayer and action go hand in hand for the activist. Nehemiah prays, and then he talks to the authorities to get the ball rolling. That's the activist.

Activist: *Other Example*

WILLIAM AND CATHERINE BOOTH

Other Example

In the 1800s, WILLIAM AND CATHERINE BOOTH, the founders of the Salvation Army, exemplified this spiritual pathway.

Their ministry began as they saw the suffering of impoverished people in the city, and they determined to reach "into hell" to bring them back.

If time permits, you may wish to mention these other examples:

- John Perkins, an author, pastor, activist, founder of Voice of Calvary Ministries and Harambee Christian Family Center
- Ron Sider, head of Evangelicals for Social Action
- Jim Wallis, a leader of Call to Renewal and cofounder of *Sojourners* Magazine

Anyone think this is your pathway?

Pause.

Strengths

Activist: *Strengths*

- Create a sense of CHALLENGE in your life.
- Find a team of people you can invest in and work with to accomplish big goals.

Participant's Guide, page 83.

To build on your strengths, create a sense of CHALLENGE in your life by immersing yourself in tasks that demand the best you have to offer. If you aren't moving, you get frustrated and stagnant. Like Eric Liddel, the Olympic athlete featured in the movie *Chariots of Fire,* said, "When I run, I feel God's pleasure."

NOTES

Activist

Description

You have a single-minded zeal and a very strong sense of ____________________.

You have a passion to build the church and to work for justice.

Challenges don't discourage you.

You do everything you can to bring out the ________________ God has placed in other people.

You love a fast-paced, problem-filled, complex, strenuous way of life.

Biblical Example

Nehemiah

> *I prayed to the God of heaven, and I answered the king.*
> (Nehemiah 2:4b-5a)

Prayer and action go hand in hand for the activist.

Other Example

____

Strengths

Create a sense of ____________________ in your life by immersing yourself in tasks that call out the best you have to offer.

> *When I run, I feel God's pleasure.*
> Eric Liddel, *Chariots of Fire*

Find a team of people you can invest in and work with to accomplish big goals.

Cautions

You may run over people or use them because you get so focused on achieving the goal.

Guard against going too long without pausing to reflect on what you're doing.

You can end up not even knowing your own ________________, spiritual condition, or emotional state.

Ways to Stretch

Spend time in solitude and silence.

Cultivate a reflective discipline like journaling. (It is an *action.)*

Develop close spiritual friendships with one or two other people.

Invite them to:

—regularly ask you questions.

—speak to you about what God is doing *in* you, not just *through* you.

These relationships must be focused on you, not on tasks.

Activist: *Cautions*

- You may run over people or use them
- Guard against going too long without pausing to reflect on what you're doing
- You can end up not even knowing your own MOTIVES, spiritual condition, or emotional state

Activist: *Ways to Stretch*

- Spend time in solitude and silence
- Cultivate a reflective discipline like journaling
- Develop close spiritual friendships with one or two other people

 Find a team of people you can invest in and work with to accomplish big goals.

Cautions

 A caution for you is to be aware that you may run over people or use them because you get so focused on achieving the goal.

Also, guard against going too long without pausing to reflect on what you're doing; otherwise you can end up not even knowing your own MOTIVES, spiritual condition, or emotional state.

Ways to Stretch

Here are some ways to stretch.

 Create a balance to your activism by spending time in solitude and silence.

This will help you to become increasingly aware of your motives so you can respond to God's purposes rather than your own.

 Cultivate a reflective discipline like journaling.

Journal writing can be helpful because it's an *action*—and you like action—but it requires you to slow down long enough to reflect on your interior world.

 Develop close spiritual friendships with one or two other people. Invite them to regularly ask you questions and speak to you about what God is doing *in* you, not just *through* you. These relationships must be focused on you, not on tasks.

Turn to page 84.

CONTEMPLATIVE

Participant's Guide, page 84.

 The next pathway is the contemplative pathway.

NOTES

Strengths

Create a sense of ______________________ in your life by immersing yourself in tasks that call out the best you have to offer.

> *When I run, I feel God's pleasure.*
> Eric Liddel, *Chariots of Fire*

Find a team of people you can invest in and work with to accomplish big goals.

Cautions

You may run over people or use them because you get so focused on achieving the goal.

Guard against going too long without pausing to reflect on what you're doing.

You can end up not even knowing your own __________________, spiritual condition, or emotional state.

Ways to Stretch

Spend time in solitude and silence.

Cultivate a reflective discipline like journaling. (It is an *action.)*

Develop close spiritual friendships with one or two other people.

Invite them to:

—regularly ask you questions.

—speak to you about what God is doing *in* you, not just *through* you.

These relationships must be focused on you, not on tasks.

Contemplative

Characteristics

You love uninterrupted ____________________.

Reflection comes naturally to you.

You have a large capacity for prayer.

If you get busy or spend a lot of time with people, you feel drained and yearn for times of solitude.

Biblical Example

Mary, Martha's sister (Luke 10:38-42)

Other Example

____

Strengths

(Note: You have *permission* to build on your strengths!)

You need regular, protected, intense times of solitude and stillness.

Faithfully follow the intuitions and leadings that come in your times alone with God.

Act on what you hear from God in the silence.

Contemplative: *Characteristics*

- You love uninterrupted TIME ALONE
- Reflection comes naturally to you
- You have a large capacity for prayer
- If you get busy or spend a lot of time with people, you feel drained and yearn for times of solitude

Characteristics

If you have a contemplative pathway, you love uninterrupted TIME ALONE.

Reflection comes naturally to you.

The presence of God is most real when all distractions are removed.

You have a large capacity for prayer.

If you get busy or spend a lot of time with people, you feel drained and yearn for times of solitude.

Contemplative: *Biblical Example*

Mary, Martha's sister

Biblical Example

Someone in the Bible who fits this profile was Mary, Martha's sister in the story of Mary and Martha recorded in Luke 10:38–42.

Mary sat at Jesus' feet while Martha was preparing a meal. If you're like her, you love to just sit at Jesus' feet. You'd rather be with him, in quiet, than be busy with tasks.

In a noisy world like ours, this can pose challenges. What happens when a quiet, contemplative type meets a chatty, relational type? They get married—and drive each other crazy! The contemplative says, "Don't you have any depth at all? You just want to socialize!" And the relational type says, "Don't you care about people? You just want to navel-gaze all the time!"

Optional humor:
Let me point out an interesting comparison here between the activist and the contemplative. When an activist says, "I'll call you back," that means, "I'll call you back when I get home—probably even before then because I've got a cell phone with me at all times." When a contemplative says, "I'll call you back," it means, "I'll call you back before I die."

Contemplative: *Other Example*

HENRI NOUWEN

Other Example

Author HENRI NOUWEN is a recent example of someone with this pathway.

NOTES

Contemplative

Characteristics

You love uninterrupted ______________________.

Reflection comes naturally to you.

You have a large capacity for prayer.

If you get busy or spend a lot of time with people, you feel drained and yearn for times of solitude.

Biblical Example

Mary, Martha's sister (Luke 10:38-42)

Other Example

____

Strengths

(Note: You have *permission* to build on your strengths!)

You need regular, protected, intense times of solitude and stillness.

Faithfully follow the intuitions and leadings that come in your times alone with God.

Act on what you hear from God in the silence.

He thought deeply about many aspects of the Christian life, and his insights and writings—rooted in times of quiet reflection and solitude—provide much needed wisdom for our journey with God and each other.

If time permits, you may wish to mention these other examples:

- Ken Gire, author of *Intimate Moments with the Savior* and *Windows of the Soul*
- Dallas Willard, professor and author of *The Spirit of the Disciplines.*

Who thinks they have a contemplative pathway? Raise your hand.

Pause.

Strengths

 If you're a contemplative, you probably need to hear this: you have *permission* to build on your strengths.

Contemplative: *Strengths*

- You need regular, protected, intense times of solitude and stillness.
- Faithfully follow the intuitions and leadings that come in your times alone with God.
- Act on what you hear from God in the silence.

Don't criticize yourself for what you're not. You have what Gordon MacDonald calls "a large interior world."

 You need regular, protected, intense times of solitude and stillness.

Making time to listen to God is vital to the health of your soul. The Holy Spirit will often use your intuitions, and you will probably feel things deeply.

 Faithfully follow your intuitions and the leadings that come in your times alone with God.

Act on what you hear from God in the silence.

Cautions

Participant's Guide, page 85.

Contemplative: *Cautions*

- You have a tendency to avoid the demands of the real world.
- Be careful not to retreat to your inner world when friends, family, or society disappoint you.
- Resist the temptation to consider your times of private prayer and solitude as less important than the more public acts of ministry performed by others.

Here are a few cautions.

 You have a tendency to avoid the demands of the real world because it doesn't live up to your ideals.

NOTES

Contemplative

Characteristics

You love uninterrupted ______________________.

Reflection comes naturally to you.

You have a large capacity for prayer.

If you get busy or spend a lot of time with people, you feel drained and yearn for times of solitude.

Biblical Example

Mary, Martha's sister (Luke 10:38-42)

Other Example

____

Strengths

(Note: You have *permission* to build on your strengths!)

You need regular, protected, intense times of solitude and stillness.

Faithfully follow the intuitions and leadings that come in your times alone with God.

Act on what you hear from God in the silence.

Cautions

You have a tendency to avoid the demands of the real world because it doesn't live up to your ideals.

Be careful not to retreat to your inner world when friends, family, or society disappoint you.

Resist the temptation to consider your times of private prayer and solitude as less important than the more public acts of ministry performed by others.

Ways to Stretch

Choose a regular place of active service.

Stay relationally connected, even when those relationships become difficult or challenging.

Connect with those who have an activist pathway.

—Pray for them.

—Consider getting involved in some aspect of their ministry activities.

 Be careful not to retreat to your inner world when friends, family, or society disappoint you.

Resist the temptation to consider your times of private prayer and solitude as less important than the more public acts of ministry performed by others.

Contemplative: *Ways to Stretch*

- Choose a regular place of active service.
- Stay relationally connected, even when those relationships become difficult or challenging.
- Connect with those who have an activist pathway.

Ways to Stretch

 To stretch, choose a regular place of active service.

That way your deep insights and learning will be useful to more people, and you'll be able to "show [your] faith by what [you] do," as the Apostle James urged.[5]

 Stay relationally connected, even when those relationships become difficult or challenging.

Connect with those who have an activist pathway. Pray for them and consider getting involved in some aspect of their ministry activities.

Turn to page 86.

CREATION

Participant's Guide, page 86.

 The final pathway is the creation pathway.

Creation: *Characteristics*

- You respond deeply to God through your experience of NATURE.
- Being outdoors replenishes you.

Characteristics

 If this is you, you respond deeply to God through your experience of NATURE.

Being outdoors replenishes you.

It moves your heart, opens your soul, and strengthens your faith. You relate to the words of the artist Vincent van Gogh:

> *All nature seems to speak. As for me, I cannot understand why everybody does not see it or feel it.*[6]

[5] James 2:18

[6] Vincent van Gogh, *The Complete Letters of Vincent van Gogh, Vol. 1* (Boston: Little, Brown and Company, 1958), 495.

NOTES

Cautions

You have a tendency to avoid the demands of the real world because it doesn't live up to your ideals.

Be careful not to retreat to your inner world when friends, family, or society disappoint you.

Resist the temptation to consider your times of private prayer and solitude as less important than the more public acts of ministry performed by others.

Ways to Stretch

Choose a regular place of active service.

Stay relationally connected, even when those relationships become difficult or challenging.

Connect with those who have an activist pathway.

—Pray for them.

—Consider getting involved in some aspect of their ministry activities.

Creation

Characteristics

You respond deeply to God through your experience of ____________________.

Being outdoors replenishes you.

You're highly aware of your physical senses, and often art, or symbols, or ritual will help you grow.

You tend to be creative.

Biblical Example

Jesus

Other Example

____

Strengths

Spend time ____________________.

Find a location for getaways.

Make beauty a part of your spiritual life.

Creation: *Characteristics*

- You're highly aware of your physical senses, and often art, or symbols, or ritual will help you grow.
- You tend to be creative.

And John Muir, the great naturalist, may have captured your perspective when he called nature "the manuscripts of God."[7]

You're highly aware of your physical senses, and often art, or symbols, or ritual will help you grow.

Because you have an appreciation for God's creation, you tend to be creative yourself.

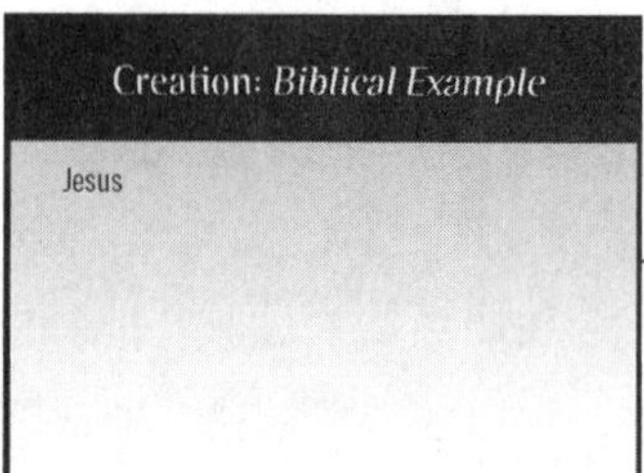

Biblical Example

The biblical example here is Jesus.

Of course, Jesus lived in continual connection with his Father and can be said to exemplify all the pathways. However, the Bible portrays him as being especially drawn to nature. He often withdrew from others to be outdoors—to go to a lake or the mountains—to be with his Father. He always wanted to be in creation, which is not surprising because he created it!

Creation: *Other Example*

GEORGE WASHINGTON CARVER

Other Example

GEORGE WASHINGTON CARVER is an example from the previous century who exemplifies this pathway.

He was an African-American chemist who invented hundreds of uses for peanut by-products. It is claimed he prayed, "God show me the secrets of the universe," and God responded, "The universe is too big for you; I'll show you what is in the peanut!"[8]

If time permits, you may wish to mention this additional example: Paul Brand, a physician, who, with Philip Yancey wrote *Fearfully and Wonderfully Made*—a book that captures the marvels of the human body and how it exhibits divine design as well as lessons about the Body of Christ

Who thinks this might be your pathway?

Pause.

[7] Quoted by Ken Gire in *Windows of the Soul* (Grand Rapids: Zondervan, 1996), 205.

[8] Quoted by Ray Stedman in "Opening the Books," a sermon given on January 25, 1970.

NOTES

SPIRITUAL PATHWAYS

AN ORDINARY DAY

Creation

Characteristics

You respond deeply to God through your experience of

______________________.

Being outdoors replenishes you.

You're highly aware of your physical senses, and often art, or symbols, or ritual will help you grow.

You tend to be creative.

Biblical Example

Jesus

Other Example

____

Strengths

Spend time ______________________.

Find a location for getaways.

Make beauty a part of your spiritual life.

86

Strengths

Creation: *Strengths*

- Spend time OUTDOORS.
- Find a location for getaways.
- Make beauty a part of your spiritual life.

The Psalmist says, "The heavens declare the glory of God."[9] If you're on this pathway, you hear that message all the time.

To build on your strengths, you need to spend time OUTDOORS.

In Jesus' day, this happened quite naturally—people were outdoors most of the time. In our day, it doesn't.

Find a location for getaways.

Make beauty a part of your spiritual life.

When you pray, you may need to have some beauty near you—maybe art, or flowers, or candles that create soft lighting.

Cautions

Participant's Guide, page 87.

Creation: *Cautions*

- You may be tempted to use beauty or nature to escape.
- You will find that people are sometimes disappointing.
- Guard against the temptation to avoid church.

Here are a few cautions for you.

You may be tempted to use beauty or nature to escape.

You will find that people are sometimes disappointing.

Guard against the temptation to avoid church because you think to yourself, "I can worship God in nature, on my own."

Yes, you were made for God's beauty, but you also need to learn to see beauty in people and allow God to speak to you through them. Otherwise, you're missing an important aspect of how he works.

Ways to Stretch

Creation: *Ways to Stretch*

- Stay involved in a worshipping community.
- Be willing to help out in less-than-beautiful settings.
- Take Scripture with you into nature and meditate on God's Word.

A way you can stretch is to stay involved in a worshiping community.

You need people, because, after all, they're part of God's wonderful creation too!

[9] Psalm 19:1

NOTES

Creation

Characteristics

You respond deeply to God through your experience of ______________.

Being outdoors replenishes you.

You're highly aware of your physical senses, and often art, or symbols, or ritual will help you grow.

You tend to be creative.

Biblical Example

Jesus

Other Example

____

Strengths

Spend time ______________.

Find a location for getaways.

Make beauty a part of your spiritual life.

Cautions

You may be tempted to use beauty or nature to escape.

You will find that people are sometimes disappointing.

Guard against the temptation to avoid church because you think to yourself, "I can worship God in nature, on my own."

Ways to Stretch

Stay involved in a worshiping community.

Be willing to help out in less-than-beautiful settings.

Take Scripture with you into nature, and meditate on God's Word as you enjoy his creation.

From time to time, be willing to help out in less-than-beautiful settings.

The ugliness of the fallen world may be repulsive, but God's love has to reach into every dark corner, and you can help bring it there.

Take Scripture with you into nature, and meditate on God's Word as you enjoy his creation.

Turn to page 88.

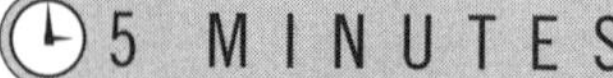

INDIVIDUAL ACTIVITY: *DEVELOPING MY SPIRITUAL PATHWAY*

Participant's Guide, page 88.

Objectives

For participants to:

- Identify activities that help them use their spiritual pathway to connect with God
- Identify a pathway that is a stretch but would help them connect to God in new ways.

Now that we've described all the pathways, we're going to take a few minutes to look at this on a more personal level.

Directions

Based on what you've learned about your preferred spiritual pathway, answer the following questions:

- What are one or two activities you need to engage in regularly to stay connected with God?
- How might you incorporate these activities into your daily or weekly routine?
- Which pathway is a stretch for you but might help you connect with God in new ways?

Any questions on the directions?

You will have 4 minutes.

NOTES

Cautions

You may be tempted to use beauty or nature to escape.

You will find that people are sometimes disappointing.

Guard against the temptation to avoid church because you think to yourself, "I can worship God in nature, on my own."

Ways to Stretch

Stay involved in a worshiping community.

Be willing to help out in less-than-beautiful settings.

Take Scripture with you into nature, and meditate on God's Word as you enjoy his creation.

Developing My Spiritual Pathway

Based on what you've learned about your preferred spiritual pathway, answer the following questions:

What are one or two activities you need to engage in regularly to stay connected with God?

How might you incorporate these activities into your daily or weekly routine?

Which pathway is a stretch for you but might help you connect with God in new ways?

Call the group back together after 4 minutes.

1 MINUTE

Wrap-up

What are some activities you identified to help you stay connected to God?

Solicit three or four comments from the group. Be sure to repeat their answers so everyone hears the response.

Possible responses:

- *I am going to start journaling.*
- *I am going to set aside time every week to get outside for a prayer walk.*
- *I need to get into a study group to encourage my growth.*

1 MINUTE

Making the Most of Your Spiritual Pathway

Participant's Guide, page 89.

Making the Most of Your Spiritual Pathway

- Give yourself permission to be who you are in God.
- Be willing to engage in activities that move you out of your comfort zone.

I'd like to close with a few ideas about how to make the most of your spiritual pathway.

First, give yourself permission to be who you are in God. Celebrate the pathway God has given you, and enjoy it.

Next, be willing to engage in activities that move you out of your comfort zone and force you to stretch a little.

As we discovered, every pathway has strengths and cautions. It's easy to default only toward our strengths and forget that we need to grow in other areas as well.

For example, you might fall into the trap of saying, "Oh I'm a relational type. Good, I'm off the hook with solitude—I don't have to do that at all." Because one of the cautions for those who have a relational pathway is to guard against being overly influenced by others, solitude is an important stretching experience—even though it may never come naturally. For each pathway, the cautions or temptations will tell you where you need to stretch.

NOTES

SPIRITUAL PATHWAYS

AN ORDINARY DAY

INDIVIDUAL ACTIVITY

Developing My Spiritual Pathway

Based on what you've learned about your preferred spiritual pathway, answer the following questions:

What are one or two activities you need to engage in regularly to stay connected with God?

How might you incorporate these activities into your daily or weekly routine?

Which pathway is a stretch for you but might help you connect with God in new ways?

88

WITH JESUS

SESSION SIX

Making the Most of Your Spiritual Pathway

Give yourself permission to be who you are in God. Celebrate it!

Engage in activities that move you out of your comfort zone.

Be careful not to envy someone else's pathway.

Beware the temptation to ______________________ someone else because of his or her pathway.

Explore and develop the other pathways.

89

Making the Most of Your Spiritual Pathway

- Be careful not to envy someone else's pathway.

Be careful not to envy someone else's pathway.

For example, it may be easy to think, "The activists are the ones who really get things done in this world. I'm not like that, so I guess I'll always be second-class." Embrace the unique person God made *you* to be.

On the other hand, beware the temptation to JUDGE someone else because of his or her pathway.

For instance, a contemplative may be tempted to think of an activist, "What's the matter with them? Why can't they pray for long periods like I can? Don't they have any depth?" Part of growing in community means we learn to neither envy nor judge each other, but help and learn from one another.

Finally, explore and develop the other pathways.

Most people can relate easily to more than one. You may find several of them very important to your spiritual growth—but at some point every one of them can be useful to you.

To make the most of our pathways, we need to give ourselves permission to be who we are in God, be willing to stretch, beware of envy or judging, and explore all the pathways.

Turn to page 90.

1 MINUTE

SUMMARY

Participant's Guide, page 90.

Summary

- Each of us has one or two preferred spiritual pathways.
- It's good to explore *all* the spiritual pathways.

In this session we've discovered seven spiritual pathways— intellectual, relational, serving, worship, activist, contemplative, and creation.

Each of us has one or two preferred spiritual pathways, and we need to lean into those and enjoy them. At the same time, it's good to explore all the spiritual pathways for the blessings they are from God.

If you are teaching this course in an eight-week format rather than a

NOTES

WITH JESUS SESSION SIX

Making the Most of Your Spiritual Pathway

Give yourself permission to be who you are in God. Celebrate it!

Engage in activities that move you out of your comfort zone.

Be careful not to envy someone else's pathway.

Beware the temptation to ________________________ someone else because of his or her pathway.

Explore and develop the other pathways.

89

SPIRITUAL PATHWAYS AN ORDINARY DAY

Summary

Each of us has one or two preferred spiritual pathways.

It's good to explore *all* the spiritual pathways.

90

weekend seminar format, you may close the session with the following prayer or substitute your own prayer.

Lord, thank you for making us all different, and thank you for giving us different ways to connect with you. May we find times in our ordinary days to use these pathways to make a fresh connection with you. We look forward to a deeper walk with you, because of these gifts. In Jesus' name, amen.

PACE OF
LIFE

SESSION SNAPSHOT

Overview

This session is about the disease of our culture called "Hurry Sickness." We all are infected in some measure. The cure is not just to resolve to change but to engage in practices that will train us away from our ingrained habits. Several areas of life will be discussed where we can make changes so we can live in Jesus' name in that area.

Objectives

In this session, participants will:

1. Consider the price of Hurry Sickness in their own life
2. Discover the two big illusions behind Hurry Sickness
3. Note the difference between being busy and being hurried
4. Learn five training activities they can use to simplify their life

SESSION OUTLINE

THE BIG PICTURE

I. Introduction

II. Discovery

A. Hurry Sickness

1. Guided Individual Activity: *Do You Have Hurry Sickness?*

2. Individual Activity: *The Price of Hurry Sickness*

B. Two Big Illusions

1. Time: "Someday, Things Will Settle Down"

2. Stuff: "Someday, 'More' Will Be Enough"

C. Five Training Activities

1. Slowing

2. Saying No

3. Keep the Sabbath

4. De-clutter

5. Use Leisure Time in Life-giving Ways

D. Guided Individual Activity: *Letting God Speak*

III. Summary

SESSION SEVEN

PACE OF LIFE

TIME & MEDIA | CONTENTS

1 MINUTE

INTRODUCTION

If you are teaching this course in an eight-week format rather than a weekend seminar format, you may want to begin by briefly discussing participants' experiences since the last session. Start the session as follows:

"In the last session we talked about seven different spiritual pathways to help us stay connected to God. Did anyone have a chance to use their preferred pathway or to stretch by using a different pathway? What was that like for you?"

Solicit two or three comments from the group. Be sure to repeat their answers so everyone hears the response.

Possible responses:

- *I didn't do anything different, but I really enjoyed knowing it "counted" to use my pathway.*
- *I tried a different pathway that wouldn't have even occurred to me had I not been in last week's session; it was great.*
- *I realized that I need to schedule in these times—they won't happen otherwise.*

In this session, we're going to talk about pace of life issues.

NOTES

SESSION SEVEN

PACE OF LIFE

Turn to page 92. Hurry! We don't have much time for this!

Just kidding!

Who *doesn't* wrestle with hurry?

As we've gone through each session in this course, you may have felt tension between what you're hearing in this course and the reality of your life. When we've looked at things like spending time with God, giving authentic love, or enjoying spiritual pathways, you may have been feeling like your life is just too crowded right now to actually do these things.

You've come face-to-face with the fact that the biggest barrier between you and spending an ordinary day with Jesus is your frantic pace of life.

2 MINUTES

DISCOVERY

Hurry Sickness

Participant's Guide, page 92.

The pressure to cram more and more activities into fewer and fewer hours impacts many aspects of an ordinary day. Take driving, for example. A recent study revealed the three most dangerous things people do while driving. In reverse order they are:

- Third most dangerous: talking on a cell phone.
- Second most dangerous: putting on make-up—you know who you are!

And what do you think is the *most* dangerous thing people do while driving?

Pause briefly for participants' responses.

- Reading the newspaper.

People actually try to *read* while they drive!

NOTES

PACE OF LIFE

Hurry Sickness

GUIDED INDIVIDUAL ACTIVITY

Do You Have Hurry Sickness?

1. You go through your day with a constant sense of urgency.

   Not at all like me — Like me sometimes — Describes me most of the time

2. You notice underlying tension in close relationships.

   Not at all like me — Like me sometimes — Describes me most of the time

3. You have a preoccupation with escaping.

   Not at all like me — Like me sometimes — Describes me most of the time

4. You often feel frustrated because you're not getting things done.

   Not at all like me — Like me sometimes — Describes me most of the time

A man named E. Myer Friedman has coined the term "hurry sickness."[1] It describes this tendency we have to do too many things at once. So we're going to do a mass confession about our hurry sickness.

This is not a serious activity. Have fun with it.

I'm going to read a short list. When I'm done reading, if you suffer from hurry sickness, I'm going to ask you to raise your hand. If you're *really* guilty, I want you to stand up—maybe even on your chair—just to get it off your chest.

Here's the first one: When you come to a stoplight and there are two lanes ahead of you with one car in each lane, you find yourself guessing—based on the make and model—which car will pull away the quickest.

Pause. Some people will respond immediately with hand raises or by standing up. If that happens, you can have fun with their reaction by saying:

"No, not yet! This is exactly what I was talking about. Some of you are in a hurry to confess your hurry!"

Second one: If you're ready to check out at the grocery store, you find yourself counting how many people are in each line and multiplying it by how many items are in each cart so you know which line will go the quickest.

Pause.

If you've really got a bad case of hurry sickness, you keep track of the *other* line you might have gotten into, just to see if you picked the faster one. And if you get out before the person you would have been behind in the other line, you feel happy! But if the person who would have been you gets out first, you're a little depressed the rest of the day.

Okay, now it's time for mass confession. How many of you suffer from hurry sickness?

Pause for participants to raise their hands or stand up.

[1] Meyer Friedman, M.D., and Diane Ulner, R.N., M.S., *Treating Type A Behavior and Your Heart* (New York: FawcettCrest, 1984), 39.

NOTES

Hurry Sickness

GUIDED INDIVIDUAL ACTIVITY

Do You Have Hurry Sickness?

1. You go through your day with a constant sense of urgency.

   Not at all like me — Like me sometimes — Describes me most of the time

2. You notice underlying tension in close relationships.

   Not at all like me — Like me sometimes — Describes me most of the time

3. You have a preoccupation with escaping.

   Not at all like me — Like me sometimes — Describes me most of the time

4. You often feel frustrated because you're not getting things done.

   Not at all like me — Like me sometimes — Describes me most of the time

INDIVIDUAL ACTIVITY

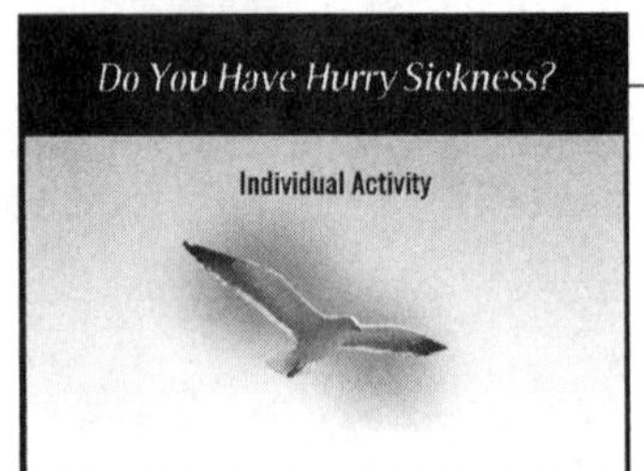

Confession is good for the soul!

If any participants are standing, tell them they may sit back down.

GUIDED INDIVIDUAL ACTIVITY: *DO YOU HAVE HURRY SICKNESS?*

Participant's Guide, pages 92–93.

Let's get a little more serious. On pages 92 and 93 is a tool to help us assess whether or not we are inclined toward hurry sickness. As I read through each of the ten statements, place an "X" on the continuum that best describes your response: "Not at all like me," "Like me sometimes," or "Describes me most of the time."

1. You go through your day with a constant sense of urgency—no time to relax or just let down. Put an X that describes where you are.

Pause.

2. You notice underlying tension in close relationships. There are a lot of sharp words, quarrels over insignificant things, or frequent misunderstandings. Same thing—mark where you are on the line.

Pause.

3. You have a preoccupation with escaping. You tend to seek time to be alone, to tinker with things around the house or garage primarily so you won't have to deal with people. You watch a lot of TV because you just want to "check out" from everything.

Pause.

4. You often feel frustrated because you're not getting things done. You frequently find yourself thinking, "I'm just not disciplined enough."

Pause.

NOTES

Hurry Sickness

GUIDED INDIVIDUAL ACTIVITY

Do You Have Hurry Sickness?

1. You go through your day with a constant sense of urgency.

   Not at all like me — Like me sometimes — Describes me most of the time

2. You notice underlying tension in close relationships.

   Not at all like me — Like me sometimes — Describes me most of the time

3. You have a preoccupation with escaping.

   Not at all like me — Like me sometimes — Describes me most of the time

4. You often feel frustrated because you're not getting things done.

   Not at all like me — Like me sometimes — Describes me most of the time

5. You sense that time is passing too quickly without you getting what you really want out of life.

   Not at all like me — Like me sometimes — Describes me most of the time

6. You have a persistent desire for a simpler life.

   Not at all like me — Like me sometimes — Describes me most of the time

7. You have little time for love.

   Not at all like me — Like me sometimes — Describes me most of the time

8. You find that you're often trying to do many things at once.

   Not at all like me — Like me sometimes — Describes me most of the time

9. You have lost a sense of gratitude and wonder about life.

   Not at all like me — Like me sometimes — Describes me most of the time

10. You sometimes have a gnawing feeling that *there has to be more to life than this.*

    Not at all like me — Like me sometimes — Describes me most of the time

5. You sense that time is passing too quickly—that your children are growing up too fast or your life is passing by without you getting what you really want out of it.

Pause.

6. You have a persistent desire for a simpler life. You imagine moving to the country or changing jobs. When you see photos of people living at a much slower pace, you try to picture yourself in the image because you want that so much.

Pause.

7. You have little time for love—for doing caring, thoughtful things. You get ideas for how to be helpful, or kind, but find yourself backing away because you're afraid of how much time it would take. If you're married, you find you don't take the time for romance or sexual intimacy.

Pause.

8. You find that you're often trying to do many things at once—that you slip into frequent multi-tasking. A car ride is a time for talking on the phone, putting on make-up, and flipping around to different radio stations—simultaneously. In fact, you're probably making a "to do" list while you take this test!

Pause.

9. You've lost a sense of gratitude and wonder about life. Maybe you know it intellectually, but you've lost the *feeling* of life being good and the desire to thank God for all you have.

Pause.

10. When it gets really quiet, you sometimes have a gnawing feeling that *there has to be more to life than this.*

NOTES

Hurry Sickness

GUIDED INDIVIDUAL ACTIVITY

Do You Have Hurry Sickness?

1. You go through your day with a constant sense of urgency.

   Not at all like me — Like me sometimes — Describes me most of the time

2. You notice underlying tension in close relationships.

   Not at all like me — Like me sometimes — Describes me most of the time

3. You have a preoccupation with escaping.

   Not at all like me — Like me sometimes — Describes me most of the time

4. You often feel frustrated because you're not getting things done.

   Not at all like me — Like me sometimes — Describes me most of the time

5. You sense that time is passing too quickly without you getting what you really want out of life.

   Not at all like me — Like me sometimes — Describes me most of the time

6. You have a persistent desire for a simpler life.

   Not at all like me — Like me sometimes — Describes me most of the time

7. You have little time for love.

   Not at all like me — Like me sometimes — Describes me most of the time

8. You find that you're often trying to do many things at once.

   Not at all like me — Like me sometimes — Describes me most of the time

9. You have lost a sense of gratitude and wonder about life.

   Not at all like me — Like me sometimes — Describes me most of the time

10. You sometimes have a gnawing feeling that *there has to be more to life than this.*

    Not at all like me — Like me sometimes — Describes me most of the time

Pause.

There is no scorecard for this inventory—it's designed to simply help you see if you're *inclined* toward hurry sickness.

You can sense it in the room—we all wrestle with this.

Let's look at the impact hurry sickness has on our lives. We're going to do this as an individual activity.

Turn to page 94.

6 MINUTES

INDIVIDUAL ACTIVITY

Individual Activity: *The Price of Hurry Sickness*

Participant's Guide, page 94.

Objective
For participants to assess the negative impact hurry has on them.

Directions

1. Review your responses to the ten questions on the Hurry Sickness Inventory on pages 92–93. Which question and response has the greatest "ouch" factor for you? Circle that one.
2. Reflect on the following questions and then write your responses in the spaces below.
   - What problems arise—or affect those you love—because you are hurried?
   - What price are you paying for hurry sickness?

You have 5 minutes.

Call the group back together after 5 minutes.

2 MINUTES

Wrap-up

What are some of the problems hurry sickness causes in your life?

NOTES

INDIVIDUAL ACTIVITY

The Price of Hurry Sickness

1. Review your responses to the ten questions on the Hurry Sickness Inventory on pages 92–93. Which question and response has the greatest "ouch" factor for you? Circle that one.

2. Reflect on the following questions and then write your responses in the spaces below.

   What problems arise—or affect those you love—because you are hurried?

   What price are you paying for hurry sickness?

Solicit two or three comments from the group. Be sure to repeat their answers so everyone hears the response.

Possible responses:

- *It strains family relationships.*
- *I'm in such a hurry I don't have time to be courteous.*
- *My kids are complaining about my unavailability because I'm constantly going from one thing to the next.*
- *Not getting to the really important things in life; caught up in the urgent things instead.*
- *I am physically drained and even sick because of the pace of my life.*

5 MINUTES

Two Big Illusions

Participant's Guide, page 95.

People with hurry sickness tend to fall for two illusions. One has to do with time; the other has to do with money.

Two Big Illusions

1. Time: "Someday, things will settle down."

TIME: "SOMEDAY, THINGS WILL SETTLE DOWN"

Hurry sickness is driven, first of all by an illusion having to do with time—that, "Someday, things will settle down."

We think, "*When things settle down,* I will get around to it." "*When things settle down,* I will live my priorities." "*When things settle down,* I'll get around to what matters." Ever find yourself saying or thinking those things?

Here's when things will settle down: when you *die!* You'll be amazed at how life slows down then. Until that time, things will probably never settle down.

Two Big Illusions

- You must ruthlessly eliminate HURRY from your life.
- Hurry is the great enemy of spiritual life.

That's why some of the wisest spiritual advice you will ever hear is contained in these words: You must ruthlessly eliminate HURRY from your life.

Hurry is the great enemy of spiritual life in our day.

NOTES

Two Big Illusions

1. Time: "Someday, things will settle down."

   You must ruthlessly eliminate ____________________ from your life.

   Hurry is the great enemy of spiritual life.

   The difference between being *busy* and being *hurried:*

   Busy has to do with our outward condition.

   Hurry:

   —has to do with the state of our ____________________.

   —is an inward condition that results from having too many competing priorities in any given moment.

   Jesus was often ____________________, but he was never hurried.

2. Stuff: "Someday, 'more' will be enough."

   The distance between more and enough is an unbridgeable chasm.

> *To be content is . . . not to have all you want, but to want only what you have.*
>
> Mike Bellah

Almost nothing that has to do with life in the Kingdom can be done in a hurried fashion. You can't receive love from God in a hurry. You can't listen to somebody in a hurry. You can't love somebody in a hurry.

Here is a vital distinction.

Two Big Illusions

- Busy has to do with our outward condition.
- Hurry:
  —has to do with the state of our SOULS.
  —is an inward condition that results from having too many competing priorities in any given moment.
- Jesus was often BUSY but he was never hurried.

 There is a difference between being *busy* and being *hurried.*

Busy has to do with our outward condition. But *hurry* has to do with the state of our SOULS.

Hurry is an inward condition that results from having too many competing priorities in any given moment.

Jesus was often BUSY, but he was never *hurried.*

He was always free to receive love from the Father, and free to give it to those in need. Hurry is the great enemy of spiritual life. Things will never settle down, so you must ruthlessly eliminate hurry from your life.

That's the first illusion: "Someday, things will settle down."

STUFF: "SOMEDAY, 'MORE' WILL BE ENOUGH"

Two Big Illusions

1. Time: "Someday, things will settle down."
2. Stuff: "Someday, 'more' will be enough."

 The second illusion has to do with our stuff. This illusion is, "Someday, 'more' will be enough."

Have you ever found yourself thinking this way: "If I just buy this one outfit, I will finally have enough clothes." Or, "If we just replace this carpeting, our house will be complete." Or, "If I can just buy this car or this house, I'll be satisfied."

We live in a world that often says we're just a collection of appetites to be satisfied. We're surrounded by billboards and ads for products that say: "Use me, buy me, wear me, drink me, drive me, own me, put me in your hair—and you will be content."

But we're not content.

NOTES

Two Big Illusions

1. Time: "Someday, things will settle down."

   You must ruthlessly eliminate ____________________ from your life.

   Hurry is the great enemy of spiritual life.

The difference between being *busy* and being *hurried:*

Busy has to do with our outward condition.

Hurry:

—has to do with the state of our ____________________.

—is an inward condition that results from having too many competing priorities in any given moment.

Jesus was often ____________________, but he was never hurried.

2. Stuff: "Someday, 'more' will be enough."

   The distance between more and enough is an unbridgeable chasm.

> *To be content is . . . not to have all you want, but to want only what you have.*
>
> Mike Bellah

Two Big Illusions

Between more and enough is an unbridgeable chasm.

The distance between *more* and *enough* is an unbridgeable chasm.

Author Mike Bellah put it this way:

To be content is . . . not to have all you want, but to want only what you have.[2]

Optional humor:
Think about it for a moment; who's more content—the person with $10 million or the person with ten children? Answer: the person with ten children—because he doesn't want any more!

Let's try an experiment. Pull out your wallet and pass it to the person next to you.

Pause briefly to allow participants to retrieve their wallets.

I bet you're feeling a little uncomfortable, aren't you? But don't worry. All we're going to do is take an offering.

Pause.

And now is the time to give like you've always wanted to give!

Pause.

No, we're not going to do that. You can pass the wallets back now.

Pause briefly to allow participants to return the wallets.

Notice how nervous you were? The truth is, we're all pretty attached to our stuff. Maybe it's because we think *more* equals happiness and *less* equals unhappiness.

[2] Mike Bellah, *Baby Boom Believers* (Wheaton: Tyndale House Publishers, 1988), 49.

NOTES

Two Big Illusions

1. Time: "Someday, things will settle down."

   You must ruthlessly eliminate ____________________ from your life.

   Hurry is the great enemy of spiritual life.

   The difference between being *busy* and being *hurried:*

   Busy has to do with our outward condition.

   Hurry:

   —has to do with the state of our ____________________.

   —is an inward condition that results from having too many competing priorities in any given moment.

   Jesus was often ____________________, but he was never hurried.

2. Stuff: "Someday, 'more' will be enough."

   The distance between more and enough is an unbridgeable chasm.

> *To be content is . . . not to have all you want, but to want only what you have.*
> Mike Bellah

"Someday, things will settle down," and "Someday, 'more' will be enough." How do we break the spell these illusions have over us? We know the truth is things *will not* settle down, and more *will not* be enough. So how can we slow down the frantic pace of our lives and live the way we want to?

Turn to page 96.

Five Training Activities

Participant's Guide, page 96.

Let's look at some practical ways to ruthlessly eliminate hurry.

These are five training activities you can do during ordinary days to simplify your life and align yourself with God's priorities.

Over time, these training activities will enable you to do eventually what you cannot do now by direct effort alone.

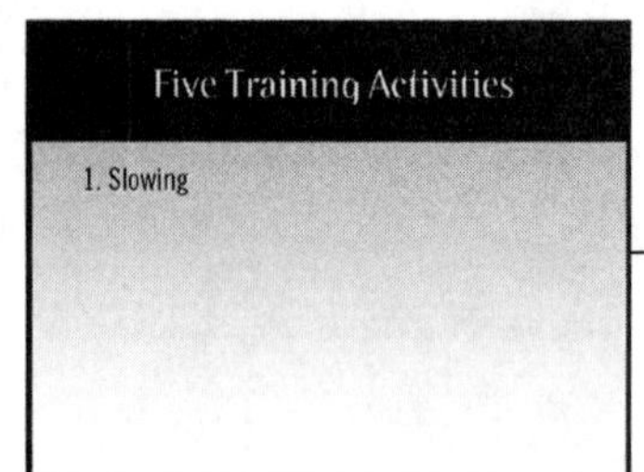

1. Slowing

 First is slowing.

One very simple way we can break the hold of a frantic pace of life is to deliberately slow down.

 We can use techniques such as walking more slowly, actually chewing our food, remembering to breathe deeply, or getting down at eye level with children in order to really listen to them.

E. Myer Friedman, whom we quoted before, works with Type A personalities. These are people who are constantly driven to do and achieve more.

 In his work, Friedman suggests simple training exercises such as deliberately driving in the slow lane for a week to keep these aggressive folks from self-destructing.

That sounds almost like torture, doesn't it? The truth is, what it really means is that you'll arrive maybe two minutes later. That two minutes will train you to go more slowly and to learn patience.

NOTES

Five Training Activities

Five training activities you can do during ordinary days to simplify your life and align yourself with God's priorities:

1. Slowing

    Walk more slowly.

    Chew your food.

    Breathe deeply.

    Really listen to children.

    Drive in the slow lane.

    Get in the longest line at the grocery store.

2. Saying no

    Every commitment is a decision that helps or hinders our ability to love God and others.

    Every time we say yes to one thing, we are saying no to something else.

Another suggestion is to deliberately get in the longest line at the grocery store, only this time, don't keep track of who gets checked out quicker than you. Just enjoy the wait.

These are a few examples of activities you can use to train in slowing.

2. Saying No

The second training activity is saying no.

Some of us need to become more realistic about the fact that every commitment we make—large or small—is a decision that helps or hinders our ability to love God and others. The hard truth is that every time we say yes to one thing, we are saying no to something else.

Here are some examples of how this works. Making the commitment to chair another committee means that I am away from my family one or two additional times a month. Scheduling early morning breakfasts means I don't spend any time alone with God that day because I'm just too tired by the evening. Packing my schedule too full means I race around and end up being rude or feeling irritable.

Just because we *can* squeeze in one more thing does not mean that we *should.* We need to set appropriate boundaries by learning to say no.

3. Keep the Sabbath

Participant's Guide, page 97.

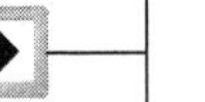

Third, keep the SABBATH.

Educator Dorothy Bass observes that while we're liable to break any of the Ten Commandments, the fourth, "Remember the Sabbath to keep it holy," is the only one we *brag* about breaking.[3] That's because we tend to associate busyness with importance—and too much free time is proof we're not needed.

[3] Dorothy C. Bass, *Receiving the Day: Christian Practices for Opening the Gift of Time* (San Francisco: Jossey-Bass, 1999), 45–46.

NOTES

PACE OF LIFE — AN ORDINARY DAY

Five Training Activities

Five training activities you can do during ordinary days to simplify your life and align yourself with God's priorities:

1. Slowing

    Walk more slowly.

    Chew your food.

    Breathe deeply.

    Really listen to children.

    Drive in the slow lane.

    Get in the longest line at the grocery store.

2. Saying no

    Every commitment is a decision that helps or hinders our ability to love God and others.

    Every time we say yes to one thing, we are saying no to something else.

96

WITH JESUS — SESSION SEVEN

3. Keep the __________________________.

    Commit to one day a week when you rest and do no work.

    Take a long walk.

    Read a spiritually enriching book.

    Have an unhurried conversation.

    Avoid certain activities (reading advertisements or checking e-mail).

    Thank God for the gift of a Sabbath.

    Engage in activities that are restful and renewing.

4. De-clutter

    The more stuff we have, the more time and energy are required to maintain it.

    What could you live without in order to simplify your life?

    Go through your closet, basement, and garage—give things away.

5. Use leisure time in ____________________ ways.

    Choose activities that refresh.

    Incorporate your spiritual pathway into your schedule.

97

Though we whine about it, many of us secretly love it when we're called upon to work extra hours. As C. S. Lewis wrote:

> *It is tiring and unhealthy to lose your Saturday afternoons* [going into the office]; *but to have them free because you don't matter, that is much worse.*[4]

Some of us are in desperate need of a sane rhythm of work and rest.

We need to acknowledge our limitations by choosing and committing to one day a week when we rest and do no work.

On that day, we can do at least one thing that is quite out of the ordinary, such as taking a long walk or reading a spiritually enriching book or having an unhurried conversation with a friend or loved one. We can also avoid certain activities we usually do, such as reading advertisements or checking e-mail.

We could get some extra sleep. And perhaps most important, we could create a time for prayer and solitude within the day.

Whatever we do, we need to consciously remember to thank God for the gift of a Sabbath, and to keep the Sabbath by engaging in activities that are restful and renewing for us.

4. De-Clutter

Fourth, we need to de-clutter.

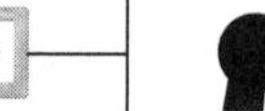

The more stuff we have, the more time and energy are required to maintain it. What could you live without in order to simplify your life? Perhaps you could also increase your generosity by going through your closet, basement, and garage and giving some things away.

[4] C.S. Lewis, "The Inner Ring," in *The Weight of Glory* (San Francisco: HarperCollins, 2001), 59.

NOTES

3. Keep the ______________________.

 Commit to one day a week when you rest and do no work.

 Take a long walk.

 Read a spiritually enriching book.

 Have an unhurried conversation.

 Avoid certain activities (reading advertisements or checking e-mail).

 Thank God for the gift of a Sabbath.

 Engage in activities that are restful and renewing.

4. De-clutter

 The more stuff we have, the more time and energy are required to maintain it.

 What could you live without in order to simplify your life?

 Go through your closet, basement, and garage—give things away.

5. Use leisure time in ________________ ways.

 Choose activities that refresh.

 Incorporate your spiritual pathway into your schedule.

Paul Pearsall writes:

> *You may need help with this assignment because many people cannot seem to bring themselves to get rid of any of their "stuff." You may require a "closet exorcist." A trusted friend can also prevent the "restuffing phenomenon." Restuffing happens when, in the process of cleaning out closets and drawers, we are somehow stimulated to acquire new stuff. Beware of the stuff co-addicts, who may see a closet cleaning as a chance to acquire stuff for themselves from your stuff, supply. Such friends are likely to go with you on a restuffing expedition.*[5]

Resist the urge to restuff, and discover the freedom that comes from de-cluttering your life.

5. Use Leisure Time in Life-giving Ways

 Finally, after slowing, saying no, keeping a Sabbath, and de-cluttering, we can use leisure time in LIFE-GIVING ways.

Because we're so hurried, when we actually do take a break we often pursue escapist activities such as watching television, shopping when we don't need anything, or eating just to eat even though we aren't hungry. We look for the least demanding way to avert boredom. Yet often these activities aren't life giving. For example, after a night spent in front of the TV, do you have more energy or less?

Pause.

 We need to choose those activities that really do refresh us. These are the times to incorporate our spiritual pathway into our schedule and do other things that leave us energized and full of joy.

We're not talking about less leisure, but rather using leisure effectively, so it does what it's supposed to do in us—which is to give us life.

[5] Paul Pearsall, *Super Joy: Learning to Celebrate Everyday Life* (New York: Doubleday Publishers, 1988), 134–135.

NOTES

3. Keep the ______________________.

   Commit to one day a week when you rest and do no work.

   Take a long walk.

   Read a spiritually enriching book.

   Have an unhurried conversation.

   Avoid certain activities (reading advertisements or checking e-mail).

   Thank God for the gift of a Sabbath.

   Engage in activities that are restful and renewing.

4. De-clutter

   The more stuff we have, the more time and energy are required to maintain it.

   What could you live without in order to simplify your life?

   Go through your closet, basement, and garage—give things away.

5. Use leisure time in ________________ ways.

   Choose activities that refresh.

   Incorporate your spiritual pathway into your schedule.

INDIVIDUAL ACTIVITY

Letting God Speak

Summary

Use these five training activities—slowing, saying no, keeping a Sabbath, de-cluttering, and using leisure time in life-giving ways—to simplify your life and cure you of hurry sickness. You'll be a healthier person, in more ways than one! If you would like some more ideas, later you can review page 125 in the Appendix.

Turn to page 98.

20 MINUTES

GUIDED INDIVIDUAL ACTIVITY: *LETTING GOD SPEAK*

INDIVIDUAL ACTIVITY

Participant's Guide, page 98.

Now we want to give God a chance to speak to us directly about these matters. We're going to engage in a slow and unhurried reading of Scripture.

We're going to ask God to help us make choices that will enable us to live consistently with our desire to eliminate hurry and spend each ordinary day with him.

This slow, meditative reading of Scripture is based on an ancient practice called *lectio divina,* which means "divine reading." It has been used widely for centuries by Christians, going back to the time of Benedict, a fifth-century Italian monk. He was most famous for his "Rule of Life," which he wrote to help structure the rhythms of work, rest, and worship within the monastic community.

This practice is rooted in the belief that through the presence of the Holy Spirit, the Scriptures are indeed alive and active as we engage them for spiritual transformation (Hebrews 4:12). It is a great way to thoughtfully and prayerfully allow the Word to "dwell in us richly" (Colossians 3:16).

Lectio divina is not Bible study per se, but can be used as a powerful follow-up to more traditional Bible study methods. It can help people make specific, memorable application for their lives.

Additional information about this practice can be found in *Contemplative Bible Reading* by Richard Peace.

NOTES

PACE OF LIFE

AN ORDINARY DAY

INDIVIDUAL ACTIVITY

Letting God Speak

Summary

98

To prepare yourself for this reading, put down your pen, close your Participant's Guide, and settle into a comfortable position in your chair. If you have a watch, take it off, and put it where you won't see it. Let go of whatever tension you're carrying as best you can. You might even want to close your eyes and breathe deeply as a way of settling into a listening mode before God.

To create a more meditative atmosphere, it is recommended that you dim the lights in the room at this point.

In the quietness of these moments, invite God to speak to you through his Word. Pray the phrase from the book of Samuel, "Speak, Lord, for your servant is listening." I'm going to give you a moment of silence right now for you to do that.

Call the group back together after 30 seconds. As you resume speaking, let your voice be softer and slower in anticipation of the reflective Scripture reading below.

Now I am going to read a passage from Luke 10 three times. Between readings, you will have brief interactions with those seated at your table. If you prefer not to speak, simply say, "I pass."

As I read the passage for the first time, listen for the word or the phrase that strikes you.

Read the passage below slowly, with pauses. As you read, remember that there is value in silence. A music composer once commented that creating the rests between notes was as much a part of the music as the notes themselves. As teachers, we tend to think what we say is the most important part of the lesson. But for the following section, pauses and silence are as important as words. The passage is Luke 10:38-42.

> *As Jesus and his disciples were on their way, he came to a village where a woman named Martha opened her home to him.*

Pause.

NOTES

PACE OF LIFE

AN ORDINARY DAY

INDIVIDUAL ACTIVITY

Letting God Speak

Summary

98

She had a sister called Mary, who sat at the Lord's feet listening to what he said.

Pause.

But Martha was distracted by all the preparations that had to be made. She came to him and asked, "Lord, don't you care that my sister has left me to do the work by myself? Tell her to help me!"

Pause.

"Martha, Martha," the Lord answered, "you are worried and upset about many things, but only one thing is needed.

Pause.

"Mary has chosen what is better, and it will not be taken away from her."

Pause for 1 minute of silence.

This may seem somewhat unusual, but I want to ask you to go around your circle and share the one word or the phrase that struck you. Say only that one word or phrase; no discussion, no comment or elaboration.

Pause for 1 minute, or until all the groups have finished.

Now I am going to read the passage a second time. This time, listen for the way in which the word or phrase you just said connects with your life right now.

Ask yourself, "What aspect of my life does this word or phrase speak to? What attitude, or habit, or aspect of my lifestyle does God want to address through this passage?" In the silence that follows, listen to God for the connection between this word and your life.

NOTES

PACE OF LIFE

INDIVIDUAL ACTIVITY

Letting God Speak

Summary

98

As Jesus and his disciples were on their way, he came to a village where a woman named Martha opened her home to him.

Pause.

She had a sister called Mary, who sat at the Lord's feet listening to what he said.

Pause.

But Martha was distracted by all the preparations that had to be made. She came to him and asked, "Lord, don't you care that my sister has left me to do the work by myself? Tell her to help me!"

Pause.

"Martha, Martha," the Lord answered, "you are worried and upset about many things, but only one thing is needed.

Pause.

"Mary has chosen what is better, and it will not be taken away from her."

Pause for 1 minute of silence.

In just one sentence or phrase, briefly share around your table the way in which you are sensing that this word connects with your life. When everyone in your group has shared their one sentence, sit quietly until I continue with the final reading.

Pause for 1 or 2 minutes while the groups share around their tables. Continue when the room is silent.

Now I will read the Scripture one last time. This may feel strange. We usually move so fast that we just skim over things. But it's very good to be unhurried and silent before God's Word.

NOTES

INDIVIDUAL ACTIVITY

Letting God Speak

Summary

During this reading, listen for God's call to action. Is there anything God is asking you to do in response to what you have heard? In the silence that follows this time, listen to God's invitation to you, and talk to him about what you are hearing.

> *As Jesus and his disciples were on their way, he came to a village where a woman named Martha opened her home to him.*

Pause.

> *She had a sister called Mary, who sat at the Lord's feet listening to what he said.*

Pause.

> *But Martha was distracted by all the preparations that had to be made. She came to him and asked, "Lord, don't you care that my sister has left me to do the work by myself? Tell her to help me!"*

Pause.

> *"Martha, Martha," the Lord answered, "you are worried and upset about many things, but only one thing is needed.*

Pause.

> *"Mary has chosen what is better, and it will not be taken away from her."*

Pause.

We're going to take three minutes for silence. Listen to God's invitation to you, and talk to him about what it is that you are hearing. As honestly as you can, let him know what you are thinking and feeling. Express any concerns or questions you might have silently in prayer.

Call the group back together after 3 minutes.

NOTES

INDIVIDUAL ACTIVITY

Letting God Speak

Summary

98

You are invited now to go around your circle and share with each other what you believe God is calling you to do based on the word or phrase you have received from him today. Share simply and briefly without elaboration. Then again settle into silence after the last person finishes sharing. Don't let this time develop into a discussion; keep the focus on a simple statement about what God is calling you to do.

Allow groups to do this. Continue when the room falls silent.

Now I'd like you to pair up with one other person. Briefly pray for each other according to what each of you just shared. A few sentences each is enough.

Call the group back together after 2 minutes.

1 MINUTE

SUMMARY

Let's stay in a posture of prayer together.

You may wish to substitute your own prayer for the prayer below.

Dear God, thank you that your Word has been alive and active in our lives during this session. I pray for every person in this room, that you will help each one to respond faithfully to what they have heard from you. Keep us from going through life worried and distracted. Help us choose what is better. In Jesus' name, amen.

Break.

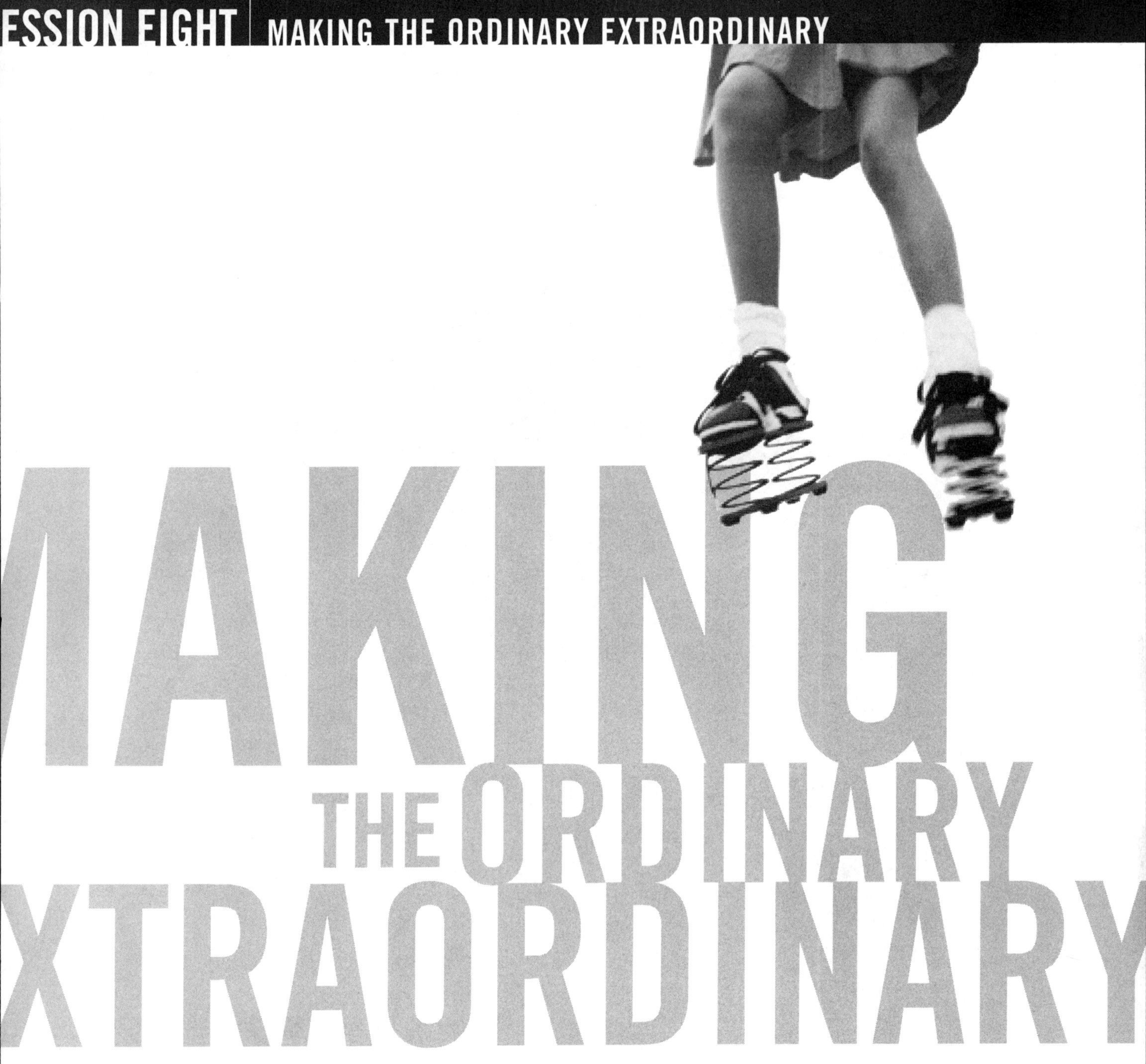

MAKING THE ORDINARY EXTRAORDINARY

SESSION SNAPSHOT

Overview

This session is the culmination of the course. We need to believe what we've been taught. Next, we need to desire it for our lives. Finally, we need to decide to make it happen. We also need a written plan and a written statement of our desires in prayer form to God. By the end of this session, everyone will have these things in hand—and everyone will be challenged to live one day in Jesus' name. It's an experiment that could become habit-forming!

Objectives

In this session, participants will:

1. Address three preliminary issues and key questions to prepare themselves to plan and commit to spending an ordinary day with Jesus
2. Plan and commit to spending an ordinary day with Jesus

SESSION OUTLINE

I. Introduction

II. Discovery

  A. Three Issues

    1. Belief

    2. Desire

    3. Decision

  B. Guided Individual Activity: *My Ordinary Day with Jesus*

  C. Two Things to Keep in Mind

  D. Video: *An Ordinary Day with Jesus*

  E. Individual Activity: *Letter to God*

III. Course Summary

MAKING THE ORDINARY EXTRAORDINARY

TIME & MEDIA

CONTENTS

INTRODUCTION

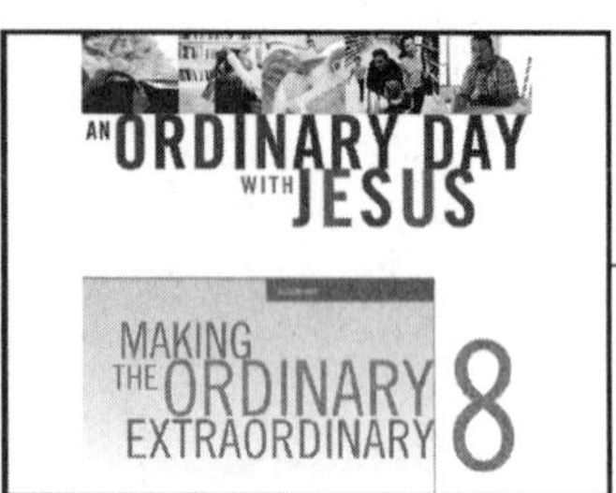

If you are teaching this course in an eight-week format rather than a weekend seminar format, you may want to begin by briefly discussing participants' experiences since the last session. Start the session as follows:

"In the last session we talked about hurry sickness and five training activities we could use to simplify our lives. Did anyone experiment with any of the training activities such as slowing, saying no, keeping the Sabbath, de-cluttering, or leisure activities that are life giving?"

Solicit two or three comments from the group. Be sure to repeat their answers so everyone hears the response.

Possible responses:

- *I took a Sabbath; it was great.*
- *My husband/wife and I de-cluttered our basement; we realized what pack-rats we have become.*
- *I tried driving in the slow lane—it was really hard!*

NOTES

SESSION EIGHT

MAKING THE ORDINARY EXTRAORDINARY

We began this course with the good news that Jesus wants to join with us in the ordinary moments of life. It's based on the simple but profound truth that if we learn how to spend one ordinary day with Jesus, we can spend every day with Jesus one day at a time. So that's what we have to do. "Whether in word or deed, [we] do it all in the name of the Lord Jesus" (Colossians 3:17).

In this session, we're going to draw on everything we've learned so far and use it to actually plan an ordinary day with Jesus.

4 MINUTES

DISCOVERY

Three Issues

Participant's Guide, page 100.

We need to consider three issues to help us not only to make that plan, but to commit to following through on it as well.

Belief

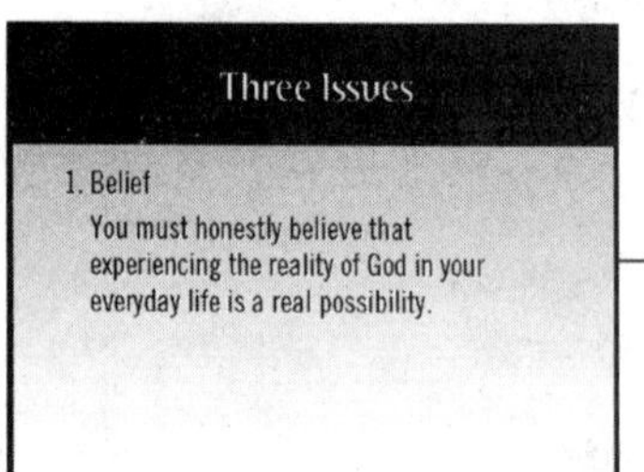

The first issue is belief. You must honestly believe that experiencing the reality of God in your everyday life is a real possibility.

You might be thinking: "Maybe God showed up in times past for biblical characters like Jacob or Moses, but who am I?"

If you struggle with believing that God will show up for you, talk to God about it.

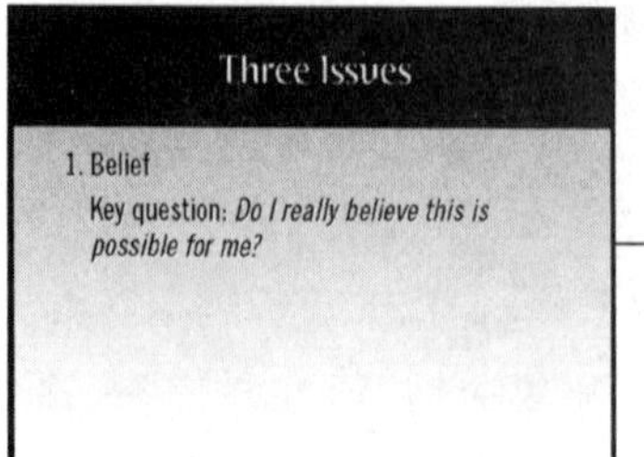

Ask yourself this key question: Do I really believe this is possible for *me?*

This is what is promised in the gospel—the good news proclaimed by Jesus: "The kingdom of God is near." Believe it!

So let me ask you again: Do you believe this offer is for you?

Pause.

NOTES

MAKING THE ORDINARY EXTRAORDINARY

Three Issues

1. Belief

You must honestly believe that experiencing the reality of God in your everyday life is a real possibility.

Key question: Do I really believe this is possible for *me?*

> *The kingdom of God is near.*
> (Mark 1:15)

Believe it!

2. Desire

We must grow in our desire for this kind of life.

> *We must journey to find the life we prize*
> *and the guide we have been given*
> *is the desire set deep within.*
> John Eldredge

Key question: Do I really want Jesus to accompany me through every moment of my day?

The truth about us never scares Jesus.

If you do not believe Jesus wants to be with you in every moment throughout your day, it should come as no surprise that you don't see his activity there. But if you do believe it is possible—and the Bible overwhelmingly affirms it is—you can experience it. And if you still have doubts, talk to God honestly about them.

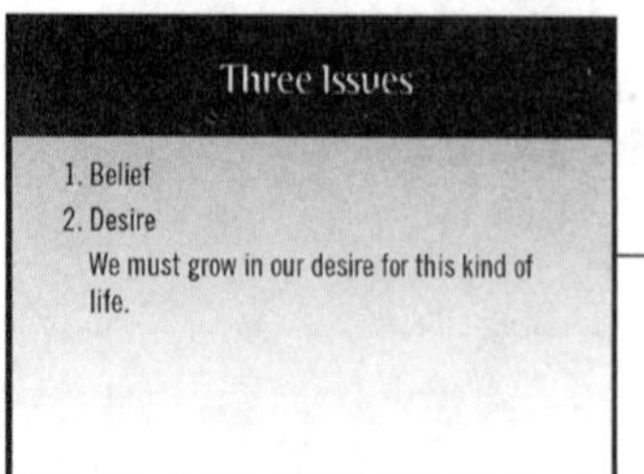

DESIRE

Once we believe this is possible, we must grow in our desire for this kind of life.

John Eldredge, author of *The Journey of Desire,* writes:

We must journey to find the life we prize. And the guide we have been given is the desire set deep within.[1]

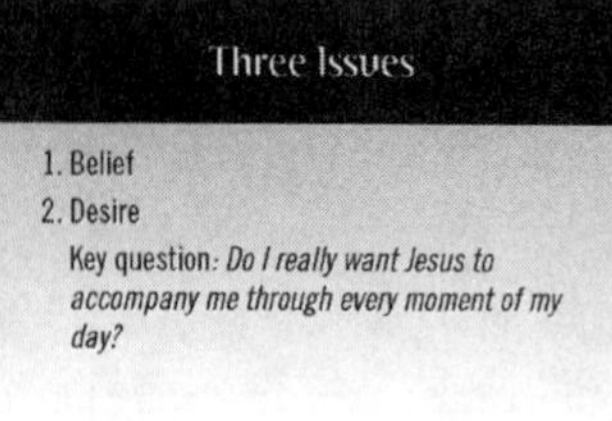

But the key question we need to ask ourselves is, Do I really want Jesus to accompany me through every moment of my day?

Imagine yourself in a dark alley, with large, menacing people following you. You would be thrilled to see a police officer in that situation, wouldn't you? But are there ever times in your life when you *don't* want to see a police officer?

Pause.

In the same way, there might be times and places in our lives when we don't want Jesus to be with us. There might be certain kinds of activities we're fairly attached to and we're pretty sure Jesus doesn't approve of them. Or perhaps we harbor destructive thought patterns and behaviors we would rather keep hidden. Maybe we are afraid that if we invite Jesus to be with us in every moment, he might demand more of us than we feel prepared to give. Or perhaps—if we are really honest—there are things in our lives that we want more than Jesus, such as money, success, or the security of a relationship.

The truth about us never scares Jesus, even if we don't want to face it.

The Bible says that one of the things God wants most from us is "truth in the inner parts."[2]

[1] John Eldredge, *The Journey of Desire* (Nashville: Thomas Nelson, 2000), 2.
[2] Psalm 51:6

NOTES

MAKING THE ORDINARY EXTRAORDINARY

Three Issues

1. Belief

You must honestly believe that experiencing the reality of God in your everyday life is a real possibility.

Key question: Do I really believe this is possible for *me?*

> *The kingdom of God is near.*
> (Mark 1:15)

Believe it!

2. Desire

We must grow in our desire for this kind of life.

> *We must journey to find the life we prize*
> *and the guide we have been given*
> *is the desire set deep within.*
> John Eldredge

Key question: Do I really want Jesus to accompany me through every moment of my day?

The truth about us never scares Jesus.

Maybe the most truthful thing you could say right now is, "Jesus, spending my ordinary days with you sounds great. But there are a couple of areas that I'm not sure I want you to mess with." Then name those areas and keep listening for guidance on how you and Jesus will work these things out.

If you're struggling to settle the issue of desire, an appropriate prayer for you might be, "Jesus, this is a struggle, but I want to be made willing."

Decision

Three Issues

1. Belief
2. Desire
3. Decision
There is a big difference between desiring to do something and actually doing it. The difference is a decision.

Three Issues

1. Belief
2. Desire
3. Decision
Key question: *What am I willing to do so my desires come to pass?*

Participant's Guide, page 101.

There is a big difference between desiring to *do* something and actually doing it. The difference is a decision.

The key question to answer is, What am I willing to do so my desires come to pass?

For example, we might desire to exercise and be more physically fit, but when it comes right down to it, we never quite make it to the gym. We might desire to save money for something in the future, but when we are faced with the choice, we end up spending our money now. We might want to have a cleaner house, but when it comes down to actually doing the work, we choose to sit and watch TV or read a magazine.

The same is true of our spiritual lives. We might say we want to spend our ordinary days with Jesus, but if our day-to-day decisions work against our desire, our good intentions will fail.

This is a time to decide—not necessarily about every day; but to decide you will spend one ordinary day in the not-too-distant future doing everything in Jesus' name.

Decision is the final issue we need to settle by answering the question, What am I willing to do so my desires come to pass?

Now let's get specific.

Turn to page 102 in your Participant's Guide.

NOTES

Three Issues

1. Belief

    You must honestly believe that experiencing the reality of God in your everyday life is a real possibility.

    Key question: Do I really believe this is possible for *me?*

    > *The kingdom of God is near.*
    > (Mark 1:15)

    Believe it!

2. Desire

    We must grow in our desire for this kind of life.

    > *We must journey to find the life we prize*
    > *and the guide we have been given*
    > *is the desire set deep within.*
    > John Eldredge

    Key question: Do I really want Jesus to accompany me through every moment of my day?

    The truth about us never scares Jesus.

3. Decision

    There is a big difference between desiring to do something and actually doing it. The difference is a decision.

    Key question: What am I willing to *do* so my desires come to pass?

18 MINUTES

INDIVIDUAL ACTIVITY

GUIDED INDIVIDUAL ACTIVITY: *MY ORDINARY DAY WITH JESUS*

Participant's Guide, pages 102–103.

Objective
For participants to identify what it would mean to do every part of their day in Jesus' name.

We're going to begin this activity by walking through part of it together, and then I'll give you time to complete it on your own.

For many of us, the next ordinary or routine day in our schedule will be next Monday, __________.

Insert the date of the next Monday.

If you're ready, write the date at the top of the chart. If you're not sure, you can leave it blank—don't allow yourself to feel pressured into something you're not ready to do. But if you *are* ready to commit to making next Monday your first ordinary day with Jesus, write that date at the top of your chart.

Let's begin to go through the day. Your primary goal is to think about how to spend each portion of the day with Jesus.

Remember, this is not "self-improvement day." This is not the time to go on a tofu diet, or memorize Leviticus, or start flossing. Don't try to impress Jesus. He already knows the real you anyhow.

Plan to do what you would normally do—but do it with him.

The Night Before

Let's start—as the biblical day does—with the night before. When do you want to go to sleep? What do you need to do to get adequate rest so you don't have to spend a sleep-deprived day with Jesus?

NOTES

102

MY ORDINARY DAY

date:

PART OF THE DAY	HOW I WANT TO DO THIS IN JESUS' NAME	EXAMPLES FROM THE COURSE
The Night Before		• Get enough sleep. • Resolve conflicts before going to bed. • Invite Jesus to be with you when you wake. • Review the day with God.
Waking Up		• Renew your invitation to Jesus. • Speak to Jesus about any anxieties or concerns you feel. • Acknowledge your dependence on Jesus.
Morning Routine/Breakfast		• Greet members of your household differently. • See *Using Meal Times as Mini-Breaks*, page 118.
During the Workday (remember, everyone works!)		**WORKING** • Show up on time. • Greet coworkers (or children) differently. • Take a moment to pray. **BREAKS** • Take mini-breaks. • Take a short walk. • Take five to ten minutes to be quiet and focus on God. **LUNCH** • See *Using Meal Times as Mini-Breaks*, page 118. **EVERYDAY RELATIONSHIPS** • Listen. Use the phrase "Tell me more." • Use touch. • Speak words of love. • Look for opportunities to do simple acts of service. • Learn from difficult people. • Receive feedback well. **MISCELLANEOUS** • Place symbols or reminders of God's presence in your work setting. • Make sure your work setting is well ordered.
During the Workday (continued)		• Walk more slowly. • Breathe deeply. • Drive in the slow lane. • Stand in the longest line at the grocery store. **ENDING THE WORKDAY** • Focus on what you have done and declare it good. • End your day honestly. Ask God for help to work diligently the next day.
Dinner/ Evening Routine		• See *Using Meal Times as Mini-Breaks*, page 118. • See *"Everyday Relationships"* above.
Miscellaneous		**LEADINGS** • Listen for God's leadings and follow them. **SOLITUDE** • Schedule a time to be alone with God. **SPIRITUAL PATHWAYS** • Use your strenghts; incorporate activities that help you stay connected with God. • Be willing to stretch; incorporate activities that move you out of your comfort zone. **PACE OF LIFE** • Declutter; Clean out your closet, basement, or garage and give things away. • Use leisure time in life-giving ways. • Set appropriate boundaries by saying no to some things so you can say yes to others.
Sabbath Day		• Keep the Sabbath: Choose and commit to one day a week to rest and do no work. • Take a long walk. • Get extra sleep. • Read a spiritually enriching book. • Have an unhurried conversation. • Create time for prayer and solitude. • Avoid certain activities: checking e-mail, reading advertisements, etc.

WITH JESUS

103

Let me suggest you do a review of your day that evening—it will help get you focused. Remember that you will find some gifts he gave you that day—so express thanks. Take the opportunity to hand him any burdens or concerns while you sleep—he'll be up all night anyway! Jot down how you want to enter sleep in Jesus' name.

Pause briefly to allow participants to write their response. Continue when you see that almost everyone is finished.

Waking Up

How about waking up? What time do you want to get up? It's probably a good idea *not* to change your wake-up time by too much, if at all. But you might jot down a reminder to let God have the first few moments and renew your invitation for Jesus to be with you.

What frame of mind do you want to have? Peaceful? Enthusiastic? Do you need to be more open to surprises? More focused and self-disciplined? Ask God what he wants for you.

Pause to allow participants to write their response. Continue when you see almost everyone is finished.

Morning Routine

Let's talk about your morning routine. Who will you be likely to greet first thing in the morning? You may want to write their names. How would you like to greet them? Don't try to be too spiritual. Remember Proverbs 27:14: "If you shout a pleasant greeting to your neighbor too early in the morning, it will be counted as a curse!" (NLT).

What's your breakfast routine? If you typically read the newspaper during breakfast, go ahead as usual—only this time read it with Jesus. Speak to him about things that interest you, as you would with a friend.

This gives you an idea of how to proceed. Don't try to do everything you've learned in this course—one day simply isn't enough time. Instead, pick a few ideas that you honestly think you can do, and note those. You can look back over your notes from previous sessions, or use the brief summaries listed on the chart if you need specific ideas.

Now continue planning the rest of your ordinary day with Jesus.

NOTES

102

MY ORDINARY DAY date:

PART OF THE DAY	HOW I WANT TO DO THIS IN JESUS' NAME	EXAMPLES FROM THE COURSE
The Night Before		• Get enough sleep. • Resolve conflicts before going to bed. • Invite Jesus to be with you when you wake. • Review the day with God.
Waking Up		• Renew your invitation to Jesus. • Speak to Jesus about any anxieties or concerns you feel. • Acknowledge your dependence on Jesus.
Morning Routine/Breakfast		• Greet members of your household differently. • See *Using Meal Times as Mini-Breaks*, page 118.
During the Workday (remember, everyone works!)		**WORKING** • Show up on time. • Greet coworkers (or children) differently. • Take a moment to pray. **BREAKS** • Take mini-breaks. • Take a short walk. • Take five to ten minutes to be quiet and focus on God. **LUNCH** • See *Using Meal Times as Mini-Breaks*, page 118. **EVERYDAY RELATIONSHIPS** • Listen. Use the phrase "Tell me more." • Use touch. • Speak words of love. • Look for opportunities to do simple acts of service. • Learn from difficult people. • Receive feedback well. **MISCELLANEOUS** • Place symbols or reminders of God's presence in your work setting. • Make sure your work setting is well ordered.
During the Workday (continued)		• Walk more slowly. • Breathe deeply. • Drive in the slow lane. • Stand in the longest line at the grocery store. **ENDING THE WORKDAY** • Focus on what you have done and declare it good. • End your day honestly. Ask God for help to work diligently the next day.
Dinner/ Evening Routine		• See *Using Meal Times as Mini-Breaks*, page 118. • See *"Everyday Relationships"* above.
Miscellaneous		**LEADINGS** • Listen for God's leadings and follow them. **SOLITUDE** • Schedule a time to be alone with God. **SPIRITUAL PATHWAYS** • Use your strenghts; incorporate activities that help you stay connected with God. • Be willing to stretch; incorporate activities that move you out of your comfort zone. **PACE OF LIFE** • Declutter; Clean out your closet, basement, or garage and give things away. • Use leisure time in life-giving ways. • Set appropriate boundaries by saying no to some things so you can say yes to others.
Sabbath Day		• Keep the Sabbath: Choose and commit to one day a week to rest and do no work. • Take a long walk. • Get extra sleep. • Read a spiritually enriching book. • Have an unhurried conversation. • Create time for prayer and solitude. • Avoid certain activities: checking e-mail, reading advertisements, etc.

WITH JESUS

103

Any questions?

You'll have 15 minutes to complete your plan.

Call the group back together after 15 minutes.

2 MINUTES

Wrap-up

So what are your reactions to planning this day? Are you excited? Fearful? What are you thinking and feeling?

Solicit three or four comments from the group. Be sure to repeat their answers so everyone hears the response.

Possible responses:

- *I felt sad, realizing how much Jesus has been lost in my ordinary days.*
- *I'm really looking forward to this.*
- *This is hard; I don't know what's going to happen, and it's difficult to plan.*
- *The day isn't long enough to do all I want to do.*
- *It's scary—I'm not sure God is going to like how this will turn out.*
- *What if I blow it? This could be a setup for disappointment.*

Turn to page 104.

2 MINUTES

Two Things to Keep in Mind

Participant's Guide, page 104.

Two Things to Keep in Mind

1. Don't be defeated by "failure."

As you anticipate and plan for your ordinary day with Jesus, there are two things to keep in mind.

First, don't be defeated by "failure."

Many times throughout the day you will forget about Jesus altogether, or not do something you had planned on, or make mistakes.

NOTES

MY ORDINARY DAY

date:

PART OF THE DAY	HOW I WANT TO DO THIS IN JESUS' NAME	EXAMPLES FROM THE COURSE
The Night Before		• Get enough sleep. • Resolve conflicts before going to bed. • Invite Jesus to be with you when you wake. • Review the day with God.
Waking Up		• Renew your invitation to Jesus. • Speak to Jesus about any anxieties or concerns you feel. • Acknowledge your dependence on Jesus.
Morning Routine/Breakfast		• Greet members of your household differently. • See *Using Meal Times as Mini-Breaks*, page 118.
During the Workday (remember, everyone works!)		**WORKING** • Show up on time. • Greet coworkers (or children) differently. • Take a moment to pray. **BREAKS** • Take mini-breaks. • Take a short walk. • Take five to ten minutes to be quiet and focus on God. **LUNCH** • See *Using Meal Times as Mini-Breaks*, page 118. **EVERYDAY RELATIONSHIPS** • Listen. Use the phrase "Tell me more." • Use touch. • Speak words of love. • Look for opportunities to do simple acts of service. • Learn from difficult people. • Receive feedback well. **MISCELLANEOUS** • Place symbols or reminders of God's presence in your work setting. • Make sure your work setting is well ordered.

102

During the Workday (continued)		• Walk more slowly. • Breathe deeply. • Drive in the slow lane. • Stand in the longest line at the grocery store. **ENDING THE WORKDAY** • Focus on what you have done and declare it good. • End your day honestly. Ask God for help to work diligently the next day.
Dinner/ Evening Routine		• See *Using Meal Times as Mini-Breaks*, page 118. • See *"Everyday Relationships"* above.
Miscellaneous		**LEADINGS** • Listen for God's leadings and follow them. **SOLITUDE** • Schedule a time to be alone with God. **SPIRITUAL PATHWAYS** • Use your strenghts; incorporate activities that help you stay connected with God. • Be willing to stretch; incorporate activities that move you out of your comfort zone. **PACE OF LIFE** • Declutter; Clean out your closet, basement, or garage and give things away. • Use leisure time in life-giving ways. • Set appropriate boundaries by saying no to some things so you can say yes to others.
Sabbath Day		• Keep the Sabbath: Choose and commit to one day a week to rest and do no work. • Take a long walk. • Get extra sleep. • Read a spiritually enriching book. • Have an unhurried conversation. • Create time for prayer and solitude. • Avoid certain activities: checking e-mail, reading advertisements, etc.

WITH JESUS

103

MAKING THE ORDINARY EXTRAORDINARY

AN ORDINARY DAY

Two Things to Keep in Mind

1. Don't be defeated by "failure."

   Don't worry about a missed moment—there's another one coming right after it.

2. Don't forget to look for "burning bushes."

   Be ready to turn aside and notice when God does unexpected things in your day.

VIDEO

An Ordinary Day with Jesus

Notes:

104

Don't worry about it. Jesus doesn't. Just talk to him about those things, receive grace, and move forward. Remember: this is not about trying really hard—it's about *training!*

Every moment is a chance to be with Jesus, whatever the moment contains.

Don't worry about a missed moment—there's another one coming right after it. They're all chances to be with Jesus.

Make a covenant with yourself: I will not allow myself to be defeated by failure.

You really can do this.

Second, don't forget to look for "burning bushes."

God appeared to Moses in the desert when he was doing his everyday work—tending sheep. All of a sudden there was a bush that was on fire, but it didn't burn up. On this ordinary day, God showed up, and he wanted Moses to turn aside and notice this unusual event in what was otherwise a very ordinary setting.

Part of your ordinary day with Jesus is planning, but the other part is being ready to turn aside and notice when God does unexpected things in your day.

He may speak to you through a friend. He may bring reassurance or love from an unexpected source. He may have some task for you to do. Like the character in the *Where's Waldo?* books, remember that God is always present and he wants to be noticed. Keep watching and looking for him.

So, don't be defeated by failure, and don't forget to look for burning bushes. Remember—you're not the one ultimately setting the agenda for your day. God is still very much in control.

VIDEO: *AN ORDINARY DAY WITH JESUS*

Now we're going to watch a video and listen to people like you and me talk about the impact living an ordinary day with Jesus has had on their lives.

NOTES

MAKING THE ORDINARY EXTRAORDINARY

Two Things to Keep in Mind

1. Don't be defeated by "failure."

   Don't worry about a missed moment—there's another one coming right after it.

2. Don't forget to look for "burning bushes."

   Be ready to turn aside and notice when God does unexpected things in your day.

VIDEO

An Ordinary Day with Jesus

Notes:

View video: *An Ordinary Day with Jesus.*

1 MINUTE

Wrap-up

What's your reaction to what we just saw?

Solicit two or three comments from the group. Be sure to repeat their answers so everyone hears the response.

Possible responses:

- *It's so encouraging to know that such simple things can make such a big difference.*
- *For the first time, I feel like I might actually be able to do this.*
- *I really want to experience what the people on the video experienced.*
- *I finally believe it's possible to experience God with me every day.*

You really can experience God's presence with you in an ordinary day, just like the people on the video described.

That's what it's like to live an ordinary day with Jesus. It's being pulled into an awareness that something far greater than you is at work in the midst of your ordinary life. That's what's possible.

7 MINUTES

INDIVIDUAL ACTIVITY: *LETTER TO GOD*

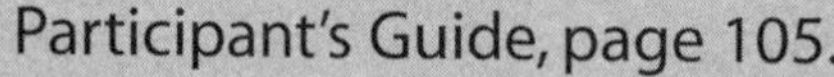

Participant's Guide, page 105.

Can you feel a desire for this welling up inside you? If so, I invite you to "get it in writing," so to speak.

Objective

For participants to express their belief, desire, and decision to spend an ordinary day with Jesus.

NOTES

Two Things to Keep in Mind

1. Don't be defeated by "failure."

   Don't worry about a missed moment—there's another one coming right after it.

2. Don't forget to look for "burning bushes."

   Be ready to turn aside and notice when God does unexpected things in your day.

VIDEO

An Ordinary Day with Jesus

Notes:

INDIVIDUAL ACTIVITY

Letter to God

1. Reflect on the ways in which God has spoken to you throughout this course.
   - Do you really believe it is possible for you to spend an ordinary day with Jesus?
   - Do you really want Jesus to accompany you through every moment of the day?
   - What are you willing to do so your desires come to pass?
2. In the space on the next page, write a letter to God expressing your belief, desire, and decision, as well as any questions or fears. Be completely honest.
3. Commit your ordinary day plan to him.
4. Close your letter with an expression of gratitude for God's presence with you now and in the days to come.

Directions

1. Reflect on the ways in which God has spoken to you throughout this course. Do you really believe it is possible for you to spend an ordinary day with Jesus? Do you really want Jesus to accompany you through every moment of the day? What are you willing to do so your desires come to pass?
2. In the space on page 106, write a letter to God expressing your belief, desire, and decision, as well as any questions or fears. Be completely honest.
3. Commit your ordinary day plan to him.
4. Close your letter with an expression of gratitude for God's presence with you now and in the days to come.

Any questions on the directions?

You will have 6 minutes to do this.

If you have audio equipment, you can create a more reflective atmosphere during this activity by playing soft instrumental music—no words—quietly in the background.

0 MINUTES

Wrap-up

It's a good thing to pour your heart out to God honestly. Your words to God will bring you closer to him and draw you toward the reality of your ordinary day with him that's coming.

4 MINUTES

COURSE SUMMARY

Participant's Guide, page 107.

Participants may have questions about their experience or portions of the course. If time allows, you may want to invite them to ask those questions now. Be sure to call attention to the list of Additional Resources on pages 128–129.

NOTES

INDIVIDUAL ACTIVITY

Letter to God

1. Reflect on the ways in which God has spoken to you throughout this course.
   - Do you really believe it is possible for you to spend an ordinary day with Jesus?
   - Do you really want Jesus to accompany you through every moment of the day?
   - What are you willing to do so your desires come to pass?
2. In the space on the next page, write a letter to God expressing your belief, desire, and decision, as well as any questions or fears. Be completely honest.
3. Commit your ordinary day plan to him.
4. Close your letter with an expression of gratitude for God's presence with you now and in the days to come.

Letter to God

Course Summary

- God calls us to the challenge and privilege to do all of life in Jesus' name.
- It's not a matter of *trying* harder, but of *training* to become like Christ.

Course Summary

- He invites us to join with him throughout the day.
- He invites us to listen to him for leadings, and to spend time alone with him.

Course Summary

- He gives each of us at least one unique spiritual pathway to connect with him.
- He calls us to let go of the illusions that *someday* we'll have time for him or *someday*, we'll have the stuff we need to be happy.

Course Summary

- Instead he says now—in our ordinary days—that this is the time and place for us to know and enjoy him.
- Remember, there is no failure.

Through this course, we've seen the great adventure God calls us to: the challenge and privilege to do all of life in Jesus' name.

It's not a matter of *trying* harder but of *training* to become like Christ.

He invites us to join with him throughout the day—how we begin it, how we relate to those we encounter, and how we do our work.

He invites us to listen to his leadings and to spend time alone with him.

He gives each of us at least one unique spiritual pathway to connect with him, and he encourages us to use our pathway with freedom and joy.

He calls us to let go of the illusions that *someday* we'll have time for him or *someday* we'll have the stuff we need to be happy.

Instead he says now—in our ordinary days—that *this* is the time and place for us to know and enjoy him.

And remember, there is no failure.

He invites us to spend our day with him knowing that he is always with us whatever the day may bring.

I'm excited for the day you're going to have!

Before we close together in prayer, I'd like you to take your letter and read it silently to God as a prayer. Express to him the belief, desire, and decision you've made. If you want to, you can kneel to demonstrate your submission to him. When you're finished praying your letter, stand up to honor whatever decision you've made.

Pray that now, and in a minute, I'll close in prayer.

Kneel for 1 or 2 minutes to model what you've invited participants to do. Allow them to prayerfully read their letters. Then stand up to indicate you're about to close the session. Use your own prayer or the prayer below.

NOTES

Course Summary

God calls us to the challenge and privilege to do all of life in Jesus' name.

It's not a matter of *trying* harder but of *training* to become like Christ.

He invites us to join with him throughout the day.

He invites us to listen for his leadings and to spend time alone with him.

He gives each of us at least one unique spiritual pathway to connect with him.

He calls us to let go of the illusions that *someday* we'll have time for him or *someday* we'll have the stuff we need to be happy.

Instead he says now—in our ordinary days—that *this* is the time and place for us to know and enjoy him.

Remember, there is no failure.

Heavenly Father, in ordinary places—in an office, in a busy home, at a desk, in a classroom, in a shop, in a factory, in a car—you're right there with us. Please help us to grasp the great opportunity we have to be with you in ordinary moments. As we have a meal, as we lie down to sleep, as we wake up, help us to experience the reality of your presence and power.

Whatever fears we might have, help us lean into love and trust. May we be surprised by the ways you meet us. Help us to order our lives so we can be connected to you and the wonderful reality that the spiritual life is lived in ordinary moments—here and now. It is the best opportunity we've ever been given, and we accept. Thank you for the invitation. In Jesus' name, amen.

An Ordinary Day with Jesus

Enjoy your upcoming day with him!

God's blessing on you as you live your ordinary day in Jesus' name.

Course Evaluation

1. To what extent did this course meet your expectations?

5	4	3	2	1
Went beyond expectations		Met expectations		Less than expected

2. How much learning did you experience during this course?

5	4	3	2	1
Significant		Moderate		Little

3. How relevant is what you learned to your daily life?

5	4	3	2	1
Highly relevant		Somewhat relevant		Not relevant

4. Would you recommend that others attend this course?

5	4	3	2	1
Yes, definitely		Possibly		Definitely not

5. What aspects of this course were *most* useful and/or meaningful?

6. What aspects of this course were *least* useful and/or meaningful?

7. What, if anything, would you like to change about this course?

8. To what extent did the instructor demonstrate depth of understanding and credibility with regard to the material?

5	4	3	2	1
To a very great extent		To some extent		To little or no extent

9. To what extent did the instructor have a motivating effect, contributing to your learning?

5	4	3	2	1
To a very great extent		To some extent		To little or no extent

10. Additional comments:

APPENDIX

Steps to Grow through Conflict

We all experience relational conflict. To be alive means to be in conflict. Sometimes we'd rather pretend conflict doesn't exist or that a lack of conflict is a sign of spiritual maturity. *But conflict is normal.* Everybody experiences it. Maturity is shown in how you deal with it.

Jesus gives very clear council on steps to take through conflict. He says in Matthew 18:15: "If another believer sins against you, go privately and point out the fault. If the other person listens and confesses it, you have won that person back" (NLT).

Notice the steps. If there is conflict:

- You go . . .
- to the person . . .
- privately . . .
- discuss the problem . . .
- for the purpose of reconciliation.

We can summarize Jesus' instructions in a single phrase: *go and tell.* The odd thing is, we don't do it—this may be one of the most violated of all Jesus' commands. At each step, we're faced with a crossroads accompanied by powerful reasons to ignore his instructions and go the other way.

Step One: You Go

Jesus identifies the first step. He says, *you go.* The implication is clear: *You* take the initiative.

The truth is, we don't want to take initiative. Too often we think, "Let the other person come to *me!* It's not fair that I should have to be the one to take the first step."

If you have been wronged, Jesus puts the burden on you to take the initiative to make it right. If someone has something against you, you take action; if someone has done something to you, Jesus says, *you go.* Be direct, don't avoid the other person in hopes that things will somehow get better on their own.

At this point, it's tempting to balk. "But I don't want to go! I want to stay and stew. I'd rather just be mad. Besides, if I go it may get ugly." The root of the problem is this: We're afraid.

One man was thinking about a confrontation he needed to engage in, and told his wife: "Every time I think about having this confrontation, my palms get sweaty." A little later he said, "Now every time I think about it, my mouth gets dry." So his wife proposed a solution: "Why don't you lick your palms?"

Sweaty palms or dry mouth, we need to address conflict head-on.

Step Two: To the Person

Step two is, *to the person.* Jesus said go directly to the person—no third parties.

We often think to ourselves, "I don't want to go to the person I'm having conflict with. That's the *last* person I want to go to. I want to go to someone else and say, 'Don't you share my concerns about this sister or brother in Christ—who is a deeply disturbed psychopath?'"

Or we spiritualize our gossip: "I'm only telling you this because I want you to be able to pray more *intelligently.*"

But Jesus says go *to the person,* not someone else.

Step Three: Privately

Step three is, *privately.* This means when the two of you are alone. You have to say no to the temptation to embarrass somebody in front of others. Often, we rationalize that there's "safety in numbers"—it's easier to say something hard in a group setting rather than one-on-one. But don't do it. First go *privately.*

Step Four: Discuss the Problem

Step four is to point out the fault, which means *discuss the problem.* Use direct communication. Sometimes, in an effort to soften the blow, we end up addressing the problem indirectly.

For instance, sometimes we make a statement that covers up our real feelings. We say, "It's too bad we missed the start of the concert," but what we really mean is, "I'm really angry that you weren't ready when you said you would be—and that made us late!" In the same vein we may say, "You must have really been busy," but we're actually angry that the person consistently fails to be punctual.

A better way is to be honest about our emotions: "I'm really feeling angry right now!" Then ask for what you want and invite a response: "I want you to do what you say you will or next time I'll leave without you. If you've got a better idea, I'm open to it, but I'm not going to allow your delays to spoil my evening." That way the person knows how you feel, what to expect from you, and what options are still open.

Paul echoes this teaching in Ephesians 4:15 when he says to speak the truth in love. He says to be loving—but be sure to speak the truth!

Step Five: For the Purpose of Reconciliation

Step five is to win the person back, which means the confrontation is *for the purpose of reconciliation*. Be clear on the goal: to win back the other person and to restore the relationship. It's not just about dumping on the other person, or making them feel bad. It's about moving toward each other.

Conclusion

As you work through these five steps, remember that Jesus taught we should always have a humble spirit, and be keenly aware of the log in our own eye, not just the speck in someone else's (Matthew 7:3-5). We are all flawed, capable of spiritual blindness and pride. We must always look for ways we have contributed to the problem even as we try to help the other person own their part. Keep praying, "God, what do you want to teach me about my shortcomings?"

The next time you need to address conflict, follow these five steps. See if Jesus' way of handling conflict doesn't give you better results than the gossipy, roundabout way our culture tends to do it.

Using Mealtimes as Mini-Breaks

Mealtimes are not just physically nourishing; they can be spiritually nourishing too. Here are some simple ideas for using mealtimes to refresh yourself and those with whom you are eating.

Before eating, take a moment to be genuinely grateful.

If sharing your meal with others, prior to eating ask them how you can pray for them.

Be creative when you pray before eating. Many of us were brought up to think that if we didn't close our eyes during prayer it wouldn't count, but of course that's not true. If you're eating with a spouse or good friend, look right at them as you pray for God to bless them.

Pay attention to the flavor of the food you're eating.

When you eat, slow down. Chew.

If you're with others, seek to bring joy to them. Jesus did this all the time with some pretty unsavory characters—and often got in trouble for it! If you're alone, pray for someone you care about and bring them joy secretly.

Feed on Scripture. Jesus said we don't live by bread alone "but by every word that proceeds from the mouth of God" (Luke 4:4). Select a phrase from Scripture such as "the Lord is my shepherd." As your body feeds on food from God, let your mind feed on the Word of God.

What to Do If You're in a Wrong Job Fit

Discerning a calling or our true vocation often requires time and patience—and most of us have bills that must be paid in the meantime. What can we do while we're still searching for the right job fit? The truth is, there are no easy answers, and virtually all solutions unfold gradually. This is hard news for those of us who want to microwave everything, including our vocations. We may be tempted to jump into—or out of—commitments too rashly.

Author Bob Buford suggests initiating what he calls a "low-cost probe" (see his book *Halftime*). The idea is to keep your day job but test the waters of a new calling. Begin to explore your skills and abilities in the area where you feel God may be calling. In Buford's case, the low-cost probe meant retaining his CEO position while pulling together a group of pastors to see if they could benefit from the organizational expertise he'd acquired in his business career. What he discovered led to a new calling for the second half of his life. But the cost was low enough that, had it been a dead end, he could easily have turned his search elsewhere. Had he impulsively quit his job and taken a staff position at a church, he might have missed his calling and jeopardized his ability to keep searching.

Maybe for you a low-cost probe would involve a short-term mission trip, taking on a commitment to teach at your church, volunteering, or working somewhere part-time. There's actually biblical precedent for this type of two-track career exploration. Amos transitioned into the prophecy business but still had his shepherding position to fall back on. The Apostle Paul apparently kept his tent-making business while he simultaneously went into church planting.

In his book *In Time of Choice,* author Gordon Smith notes that God often honors our previous decisions and commitments. God is a careful worker and, like any other careful worker, he's not likely to waste any resources. The competencies and skills you've acquired to this point in your life matter to him, and may be squandered if you make a rash decision to leave your current situation. So while God may have a new direction for you, consider how he might "recycle" the training and expertise you've accumulated so far.

A Simple Plan for Solitude

Solitude is not a complicated practice. In fact, if you make it complicated, you work against the very simplicity and quietness it is intended to foster. Here are a few simple steps to help you eliminate unwanted distractions, and plan your solitude time for maximum effectiveness.

1. Find a quiet place that is free of distractions

Remember the video, shown early in the session, where the woman was trying to pray in the midst of her hectic day? One of the problems she faced was giving God her undivided attention in a setting filled with distractions:

- toys and clothing that begged to be picked up
- a phone waiting to interrupt her
- a TV crying to be turned on
- a dryer buzzer screaming to be attended to

She also hadn't clearly set apart the time for her and God, so she felt pulled by her desire to use the time in other ways.

Although we might not always be able to find the perfect setting, solitude requires getting away from the normal distractions of our lives. It requires a time frame in which we can be with God in an unhurried way. You will need to identify a time in the context of your ordinary day when you can give God your undivided attention on a regular basis.

People often find it helpful to identify what they might call a "sacred space"—a place set apart for meeting with God and God alone. It is important that you bring very little with you into this space—perhaps just a Bible and a journal. You may even want to personalize this space by incorporating a symbol that reminds you of God's presence with you. You could use a special Scripture verse or poem, a lit candle to remind you of the presence of the Holy Spirit, a cross or a thorn to remind you of Christ's sacrificial love for you.

Your space needs to be relatively free of distractions so you can give God your undivided attention—a special chair, a corner of your office or bedroom, a spot on your porch or in your backyard (if weather permits). Depending on your stage of life, you might have to resort to a closet or your car!

As much as possible, make this a nonnegotiable time in your schedule. You may need to communicate this to others in your household so they will be able to honor those times when you are alone with God.

2. Quiet yourself in God's presence

Interpersonal interactions rarely develop into meaningful communication when we rush in breathless and distracted. We need some time at the beginning to slow down.

Take a few moments to quiet yourself by breathing deeply, giving yourself a chance to slow down and become aware of God's presence with you. If you are distracted, make a list of your concerns and then set it aside so you can be fully present with God.

3. Tell God what you need

Tell God what you would like to receive from him during your time together. It may be that you need encouragement, to feel his forgiveness, wisdom for a decision, reassurance of his love. Be yourself. Let God know what is on your heart and invite him to give you what he already knows you need. You may find it helpful to use a brief prayer such as, "Here I am," or "Jesus Christ, have mercy on me," or "Come, Lord Jesus," to express your openness to God and your desire to receive whatever he has to give.

4. Use Scripture to listen to God

Approach Scripture prayerfully, inviting God to speak to you. You might begin with the prayer that the little boy Samuel prayed: "Speak, Lord, for your servant is listening." Read slowly and deliberately, listening for what God has to say to you through his Word. Rather than skimming the Bible like you might skim the newspaper, approach it as you would a letter from someone you love deeply—and who deeply loves you.

Imagine yourself in the passage or in the setting of the story you are reading. Ask questions that help you reflect on the meaning of the passage for your own life:

- Where do I see myself in this passage?
- Which character do I relate to most?
- What thoughts or emotions surface as I envision myself there?
- Which aspect of what is being said here do I need or desire most?
- What is most challenging?

5. Be fully present

One of the most important things you can do to be fully present with God is to be yourself. The woman in the video had trouble with this. She seemed to feel that she had to censor her truest feelings about her life, her husband, and her friends. No wonder her times with God felt like an obligation rather than an opportunity.

Sometimes we fall into the trap of only praying about "spiritual-sounding" things, as if God didn't know all our thoughts anyway! This is deadly to prayer. C. S. Lewis wrote that we must speak to God "what is in us, not what ought to be in us."

Being fully present involves knowing what to do with distractions. The truth is that all of us struggle from S-A-D-D or "spiritual attention deficit disorder" from time to time. There are several things you can do to bring yourself back to your intent to be fully present with God. If your wandering thoughts really do seem like a distraction—like a to-do list—you can jot them down and then let them go, knowing that you can return to them at an appropriate time.

Some distractions, though, are not distractions at all; they could be promptings from the Holy Spirit. What we often think of as distractions might be thoughts and feelings we need to bring to God in prayer. Then we need to listen for what he has to say about them. The woman in the video could have done this with her feelings about her husband. Rather than dismissing her feelings of frustration about her husband and pretending that they were different than they were, she could have shared her feelings with God and asked him for truth and wisdom about what she should do with them.

If you give some thought to how you want to handle distractions before you begin your time in solitude, you can deal with them and still remain fully present with God.

6. Respond to what you hear God saying to you through Scripture or in prayer

Speak to God about what you are sensing, feeling, and hearing. Some people find it helpful to respond verbally in prayer while others write out their prayers in a journal. Experiment by addressing God as if you were writing a letter, or writing what you think God is saying to you.

If you choose to write your prayers, it is important to do so without censoring yourself. Sometimes people burn their journals when they are full to make sure they are free to be totally honest rather than afraid that someone else will read their words. However, if you keep your journals, over time they can become a rich history of your private times with God.

7. Express gratitude and commitment

Close your time in solitude by thanking God for his presence with you. Let him know you intend to respond faithfully to whatever you heard from him—and then do it.

Spiritual Pathway Assessment

1. Respond to each statement below according to the following scale:

   3 = Consistently/definitely true of me

   2 = Often/usually true of me

   1 = Once in a while/sometimes true of me

   0 = Not at all/never true of me

   Put the number in the blank before each statement.

2. Transfer the numbers you gave for each assessment statement to the grid on page 328.

3. Total each column. The highest number identifies your preferred spiritual pathway; the next highest number, your secondary pathway.

☐ 1. *When I have a problem, I'd rather pray with people than pray alone.*

☐ 2. *In a church service, I most look forward to the teaching.*

☐ 3. *People who know me would describe me as enthusiastic during worship times.*

☐ 4. *No matter how tired I get, I usually come alive when a challenge is placed before me.*

☐ 5. *Spiritual reality sometimes feels more real to me than the physical world.*

☐ 6. *I get distracted in meetings or services if I notice details in the surroundings that haven't been attended to.*

☐ 7. *A beautiful sunset can give me a spiritual high that temporarily blocks out everything bothering me.*

☐ 8. *It makes me feel better about myself to hang out with people I know and like.*

☐ 9. *I've never understood why people don't love to study the Bible in depth.*

10. *God touches me every time I gather with other believers for praise.*

11. *People around me know how passionate I feel about the causes I'm involved in.*

12. *I experience a deep inner joy when I am in a quiet place, free from distractions.*

13. *Helping others is easy for me, even when I have problems.*

14. *When faced with a difficult decision, I am drawn to walk in the woods, on the beach, or in some other outdoor setting.*

15. *When I am alone too much, I tend to lose energy or get a little depressed.*

16. *People seek me out when they need answers to biblical questions.*

17. *Even when I'm tired, I look forward to going to a church service.*

18. *I sense the presence of God most when I'm doing his work.*

19. *I don't understand how Christians can be so busy and still think they're hearing from God.*

20. *I love being able to serve behind the scenes, out of the spotlight.*

21. *I experience God in nature so powerfully I'm sometimes tempted not to bother with church.*

22. *I experience God most tangibly in fellowship with a few others.*

23. *When I need to be refreshed, a stimulating book is just the thing.*

24. *I am happiest when I praise God together with others.*

25. *"When the going gets tough, the tough get going"—that's true about me!*

26. *My family and friends sometimes tease me about being such a hermit.*

27. *People around me sometimes tell me they admire my compassion.*

28. *Things in nature often teach me valuable lessons about God.*

29. *I don't understand people who have a hard time revealing personal things about themselves.*

30. *Sometimes I spend too much time learning about an issue rather than dealing with it.*

31. *I don't think there's any good excuse for missing a worship time.*

32. *I get tremendous satisfaction from seeing people working together to achieve*

a goal.

33. *When I face a difficulty, being alone feels most helpful.*
34. *Even when I'm tired, I find I have the energy and desire to care for people's problems.*
35. *God is so real when I'm in a beautiful, natural setting.*
36. *When I'm tired, there's nothing better than going out with friends to refresh me.*
37. *I worship best in response to theological truth clearly explained.*
38. *I like how all the world's problems—including mine—seem unimportant when I'm praising God at church.*
39. *I get frustrated with people's apathy in the face of injustice.*
40. *If the truth were told, I sometimes feel guilty for enjoying silence and solitude so much.*
41. *I am happiest when I find someone who really needs help and I step in and offer it.*
42. *Others know that if I'm not around, I'm most likely outside in a beautiful place.*
43. *People around me describe me as a people person.*
44. *I often read lots of books or articles to help me work through a problem.*
45. *When I get overwhelmed, there's nothing like a good worship service to get me back on track.*
46. *I should probably take more time to slow down, but I really love what I do, especially ministry.*
47. *Sometimes I spend too much time mulling over negative things people say about me.*
48. *I experience God's presence as I counsel someone who is struggling or in trouble.*
49. *When I see natural beauty, something wonderful stirs in me that is difficult to describe.*

Spiritual Pathway Assessment Scoring

Transfer the numbers from the assessment to this grid, and total each column.

1.	2.	3.	4.	5.	6.	7.
8.	9.	10.	11.	12.	13.	14.
15.	16.	17.	18.	19.	20.	21.
22.	23.	24.	25.	26.	27.	28.
29.	30.	31.	32.	33.	34.	35.
36.	37.	38.	39.	40.	41.	42.
43.	44.	45.	46.	47.	48.	49.
Total	Total	Total	Total	Total	Total	Total
A Relational	B Intellectual	C Worship	D Activist	E Contemplative	F Serving	G Creation

☐	*Relational—I connect best to God when I am with others.*	*A*
☐	*Intellectual —I connect best to God when I learn.*	*B*
☐	*Worship—I connect best to God when I worship.*	*C*
☐	*Activist—I connect best to God when doing great things.*	*D*
☐	*Contemplative—I connect best to God in silence.*	*E*
☐	*Serving—I connect best to God while completing kingdom tasks.*	*F*
☐	*Creation—I connect best to God in nature.*	*G*

Additional Ideas for Simplifying Your Pace of Life

Slowing

Deliberately drive in the slow lane for a day.

Chew your food slowly, putting down the utensil after every bite.

Focus for a day on listening more than speaking.

Pause for several breaks during the day.

Leave your watch off for a day.

Saying No

Skip lunch one day—say no to a meal and devote that time to prayer or journaling about your pace of life.

Keep a log of how you spend your time during a typical week. Ask someone to review it with you, looking for activities to eliminate.

Look in the mirror in the morning and watch yourself say "no," politely but firmly ten times. Then say no to something that day.

What is an activity or involvement you might stop doing eventually? Could you stop doing it now?

Cancel a magazine subscription, knowing you can start it up again in a few months if you really miss it.

Keep the Sabbath

Pick one day and devote it to nonwork. Instead, spend it remembering and thanking God.

Engage in activities that are life-giving to you.

Do one thing that is quite out of the ordinary for you.

Don't do one thing that you would typically do. For example, don't read any advertisements, don't check your e-mail, don't go shopping, etc.

Create time for prayer and solitude within this day.

De-clutter

Have a throw–away day. Ask every member of your household to fill a large garbage bag with stuff to give or throw away.

Go through one drawer in your house and organize it. If you have time, do another.

Go through your freezer and eat everything that's in it before you buy any more frozen foods—this includes ice cream!

Any time you receive a telemarketing call, ask to be removed from their list.

Throw away junk mail without opening it.

Use Leisure Time in Life-Giving Ways

Limit how much TV you watch—budget a certain number of hours per family member per week.

Go for a weekend or a whole week without TV—try a "media fast."

Make a list of twenty-five things you like to do other than watch TV. Do all of those things at least once within six months.

Invite to dinner a few people you really enjoy. Ask each one to bring pictures of themselves as teenagers. Tell stories of what you were like back then.

What is something you liked to do when you were a child? (Examples: fly a kite, dress up dolls, play board games, make a model, paint with watercolors, make a fort with blankets.) Plan to do it this weekend.

Who is someone you would like to do an outrageously kind act for? Send that person a note, do some work at their house, watch their kids, give them some money for no reason, surprise them with a gift, or come up with your own way to use a little of your free time to serve them. Does this leave you replenished or exhausted?

Additional Resources

SESSION 1: LIVING IN JESUS' NAME

The Imitation of Christ, Thomas á Kempis (Ave Maria Press, 1989)
Life Together, Dietrich Bonhoeffer (HarperCollins, 1954, 1978)
Living in the Presence, Tilden Edwards (HarperCollins, 1987, 1995)
The Practice of the Presence of God, Brother Lawrence (Whitaker House, 1982)
The Sacrament of the Present Moment, Jean-Pierre De Caussade (HarperCollins, 1989)

SESSION 2: EVERYDAY RELATIONSHIPS

Connecting, Larry Crabb (Word Books, 1997)
Family the Forming Center, revised edition, Marjorie J. Thompson (Upper Room, 1997)
Friends and Strangers, Karen Burton Mains (Word Books, 1990)
Life Together, Dietrich Bonhoeffer (HarperCollins, 1954, 1978)
Listening for Heaven's Sake, Gary R. Sweeten (Equipping Ministries International, 1993)
The Mystery of Marriage, Mike Mason (Multnomah Publishers, 1985, 1996)
Practicing the Presence of People, Mike Mason (Waterbrook Press, 1999)
The Safest Place on Earth, Larry Crabb (Word Books, 1999)

SESSION 3: WORK

Honest to God? (chapter 11), Bill Hybels (Zondervan, 1990)
Let Your Life Speak, Parker J. Palmer (Jossey-Bass, 1999)
Why You Can't Be Anything You Want to Be, Arthur F. Miller (Zondervan, 1999)
Your Work Matters to God, Doug Sherman and William Hendricks (NavPress, 1987)

SESSION 4: LEADINGS

Hearing God (previously published as *In Search of Guidance*), Dallas Willard (InterVarsity Press, 1999)
A Testament of Devotion, Thomas R. Kelly (HarperCollins, 1941, 1996)

SESSION 5: SOLITUDE

Answering God, Eugene H. Peterson (HarperCollins, 1991)
The Genesee Diary, Henri J.M. Nouwen (1981)
The Life of the Beloved, Henri J.M. Nouwen (Crossroad, 1992)
Love Beyond Reason, John Ortberg (Zondervan, 2000)
Prayer, Richard J. Foster (HarperCollins, 1992)
A Spiritual Formation Journal, Jana Rea with Richard J. Foster (HarperCollins, 1996)
Too Busy Not to Pray, Bill Hybels (InterVarsity Press, 1998)
The Way of the Heart, Henri J.M. Nouwen (Ballantine Books, 1991)

SESSION 6: SPIRITUAL PATHWAYS

Invitation to a Journey, M. Robert Mulholland (InterVarsity Press, 1993)
Sacred Pathways, Gary Thomas (Zondervan, 2000)
Windows of the Soul, Ken Gire (Zondervan, 1996)

SESSION 7: PACE OF LIFE

Freedom of Simplicity, Richard J. Foster (HarperCollins, 1981, 1998)
Margin, Richard A. Swenson (NavPress, 1992, 1995)
Practicing Our Faith, Dorothy Bass, editor (Jossey-Bass, 1997)
Sabbath Time, Tilden Edwards (Upper Room, 1992)

SESSION 8: MAKING THE ORDINARY EXTRAORDINARY

The Divine Conspiracy, Dallas Willard (HarperCollins, 1998)
If You Want to Walk on Water, You've Got to Get Out of the Boat, John Ortberg (Zondervan, 2001)
The Life You've Always Wanted, John Ortberg (Zondervan, 1997)
Receiving the Day, Dorothy Bass (Jossey-Bass, 1999)
The Spirit of the Disciplines, Dallas Willard (HarperCollins, 1991)

Willow Creek Association

Vision, **Training,** **Resources**

for Prevailing Churches

This resource was created to serve you and to help you in building a local church that prevails!

Since 1992, the Willow Creek Association (WCA) has been linking like-minded, action-oriented churches with each other and with strategic vision, training, and resources. Now a worldwide network of over 6,400 churches from more than ninety denominations, the WCA works to equip Member Churches and others with the tools needed to build prevailing churches. Our desire is to inspire, equip, and encourage Christian leaders to build biblically functioning churches that reach increasing numbers of unchurched people, not just with innovations from Willow Creek Community Church in South Barrington, Illinois, but from any church in the world that has experienced God-given breakthroughs.

Willow Creek Conferences

Each year, thousands of local church leaders, staff and volunteers—from WCA Member Churches and others—attend one of our conferences or training events. Conferences offered on the Willow Creek campus in South Barrington, Illinois, include:

- Prevailing Church Conference—Foundational training for staff and volunteers working to build a prevailing local church.

- Prevailing Church Workshops—More than fifty strategic, day-long workshops covering seven topic areas that represent key characteristics of a prevailing church; offered twice each year.
- Promiseland Conference—Children's ministries; infant through fifth grade.
- Student Ministries Conference—Junior and senior high ministries.
- Willow Creek Arts Conference—Vision and training for Christian artists using their gifts in the ministries of local churches.
- Leadership Summit—Envisioning and equipping Christians with leadership gifts and responsibilities; broadcast live via satellite to eighteen cities across North America.
- Contagious Evangelism Conference—Encouragement and training for churches and church leaders who want to be strategic in reaching lost people for Christ.
- Small Groups Conference—Exploring how developing a church of small groups can play a vital role in developing authentic Christian community that leads to spiritual transformation.

To find out more about WCA conferences, visit our website at www.willowcreek.com.

Prevailing Church Regional Workshops

Each year the WCA team leads several, two-day training events in select cities across the United States. Some twenty day-long workshops are offered in topic areas including leadership, next-generation ministries, small groups, arts and worship, evangelism, spiritual gifts, financial stewardship, and spiritual formation. These events make quality training more accessible and affordable to larger groups of staff and volunteers.

To find out more about Prevailing Church Regional Workshops, visit our website at www.willowcreek.com.

Willow Creek Resources®

Churches can look to Willow Creek Resources® for a trusted channel of ministry tools in areas of leadership, evangelism, spiritual gifts, small groups, drama, contemporary music, financial stewardship, spiritual transformation, and more. For ordering information, call (800) 570-9812 or visit our website at www.willowcreek.com.

WCA Membership

Membership in the Willow Creek Association as well as attendance at WCA Conferences is for churches, ministries, and leaders who hold to an historic, orthodox understanding of biblical Christianity. The annual church membership fee of $249 provides substantial discounts for your entire team on all conferences and Willow Creek Resources, networking opportunities with other outreach-oriented churches, a bimonthly newsletter, a subscription to the Defining Moments monthly audio journal for leaders, and more.

To find out more about WCA membership, visit our website at www.willowcreek.com.

WillowNet www.willowcreek.com

This Internet resource service provides access to hundreds of Willow Creek messages, drama scripts, songs, videos, and multimedia ideas. The system allows you to sort through these elements and download them for a fee.

Our website also provides detailed information on the Willow Creek Association, Willow Creek Community Church, WCA membership, conferences, training events, resources, and more.

WillowCharts.com www.WillowCharts.com

Designed for local church worship leaders and musicians, WillowCharts.com provides online access to hundreds of music charts and chart components, including choir, orchestral, and horn sections, as well as rehearsal tracks and video streaming of Willow Creek Community Church performances.

The NET http://studentministry.willowcreek.com

The NET is an online training and resource center designed by and for student ministry leaders. It provides an inside look at the structure, vision, and mission of prevailing student ministries from around the world. The NET gives leaders access to complete programming elements, including message outlines, dramas, small group questions, and more. An indispensable resource and networking tool for prevailing student ministry leaders!

Contact the Willow Creek Association

If you have comments or questions, or would like to find out more about WCA events or resources, please contact us:

Willow Creek Association
P.O. Box 3188
Barrington, IL 60011-3188
Phone: (800) 570-9812 or (847) 765-0070
Fax (888) 922-0035 or (847) 765-5046
Web: www.willowcreek.com

Resources You've Been Waiting For . . .

To Build the Church You've Been Dreaming About

Willow Creek Resources

What do you dream about for your church?

At the Willow Creek Association we have a dream for the church . . . one that envisions the local church—your church—as the focal point for individual and community transformation.

We want to partner with you to make this happen. We believe when authentic, life-changing resources become an integral part of everyday life at your church—and when they become an extension of how your ministries function—transformation is inevitable.

It then becomes normal for people to:

- identify their personal style of evangelism and use it to bring their unchurched friends to Christ
- grow in their ability to experience God's presence with them in each moment of the day
- feel a deep sense of community with others
- discover their spiritual gifts and put them to use in ministry
- use their resources in ways that honor God and care for others

If this is the kind of church you're dreaming about, keep reading. The following pages highlight just a few of the many Willow Creek Resources available to help you. Together, we can build a local church that transforms lives and transfigures communities. We can build a church that *prevails.*

Experience the Reality of God's Presence Every Day

An Ordinary Day with Jesus

John Ortberg and Ruth Haley Barton

An Ordinary Day with Jesus uses aspects of an ordinary day and illustrates how we can connect with Jesus in those moments. Participants will learn how to:

- wake up and go to sleep in Jesus' name
- review their day with God
- silence competing voices in order to hear God's leadings
- experience time alone with God as an opportunity not an obligation
- use their own unique spiritual pathway to connect with God
- eliminate hurry and simplify their pace of life
- and much more!

Kit	0310245877
PowerPoint® CD-ROM	0310245885
Video	0310245575
Leader's Guide	0310245850
Participant's Guide	0310245869

Link People and Their Gifts with Ministries and Their Needs

Network

Bruce Bugbee, Don Cousins, Bill Hybels

This proven, easy-to-use curriculum helps participants to discover their unique spiritual gifts, areas of passion for service, and individual ministry style.

Network helps believers better understand who God made them to be, and mobilizes them into meaningful service in the local church.

Using *Network,* your whole church can share a vision for each member and understand the vital role each plays in building God's Kingdom.

Leader's Guide	0310412412
Participant's Guide	0310412315
Drama Vignettes Video	0310411890
Overhead Masters	0310485282
Consultant's Guide	0310412218
Vision/Consultant Training Video	0310244994
Implementation Guide	0310432618
Complete Kit	0310212790

Train Believers to Share Christ Naturally

Becoming a Contagious Christian

Mark Mittelberg, Lee Strobel, Bill Hybels

Over 500,000 believers have been trained to share their faith confidently and effectively with this proven curriculum. In eight, fifty-minute sessions, participants experience the joy of discovering their own unique evangelism style, learn how to transition conversations to spiritual topics, present gospel illustrations, and more.

Leader's Guide 0310500818
Participant's Guide 0310501016
Drama Vignettes Video 0310201691
Overhead Masters 0310500915
Complete Kit 0310501091

Also available—*Becoming a Contagious Christian* University Edition Video. Developed in partnership with InterVarsity Christian Fellowship, these drama vignettes feature college students building relationships with seekers. Designed to be used with the adult version of the curriculum.

Equip Students to Lead this Generation to Christ

Becoming a Contagious Christian Youth Edition

Mark Mittelberg, Lee Strobel, Bill Hybels

Revised and expanded for students by Bo Boshers

The award-winning *Becoming a Contagious Christian* curriculum has been revised and expanded to equip junior high and high school students to be contagious with their faith.

In eight, fifty-minute sessions, students learn how to:

- Develop relationships intentionally
- Transition an ordinary conversation to a spiritual conversation
- Tell their personal story of meeting Christ
- Share the gospel message using two different illustrations
- Answer ten common objections to Christianity
- Pray with a friend to receive Christ

Real stories of students who have led their friends to Christ make the material come alive as students see how God can work through them.

Leader's Guide	0310237718
Student's Guide	0310237734
Drama Vignettes Video	0310237742
Complete Kit	0310237696

Bestselling Books by John Ortberg

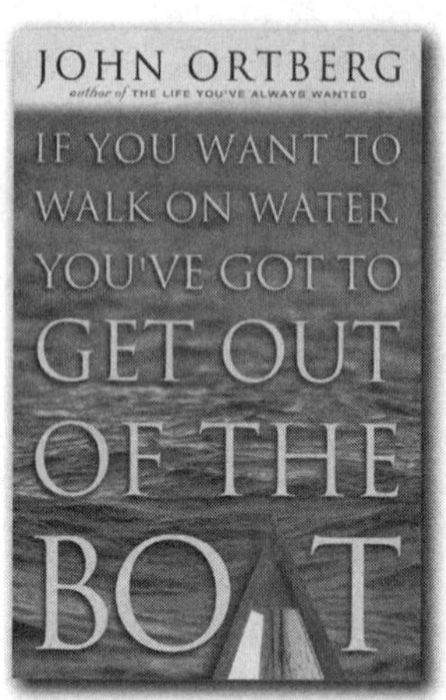

If You Want to Walk on Water, You've Got to Get Out of the Boat

With engaging illustrations, humor, and relevant applications, John Ortberg explains how discerning God's call, rising above fear, and taking next steps can strengthen your faith.

Hardcover 0310228638
Audio Pages®
Abridged Cassettes 0310234786

The Life You've Always Wanted

Gain a fresh perspective on the power of spiritual disciplines and how God can use them to deepen your relationship with him.

Hardcover 0310212146
Softcover 0310226996

Love Beyond Reason

Filled with poignant illustrations, real-life applications, and humor, *Love Beyond Reason* describes the numerous facets of God's reason-defying, passionate love.

Hardcover 0310212154
Softcover 0310234492

Experience Transformation in Community with Others

Pursuing Spiritual Transformation Series

John Ortberg, Laurie Pederson, Judson Poling

Explore fresh, biblically-based ways to think about and experience life with God through Willow Creek's Five Gs: Grace, Growth, Groups, Gifts, and Good Stewardship (Giving). Each study challenges the popular notion that merely "trying harder" will lead to Christlikeness. Instead, this series helps you identify the practices, experiences, and relationships God can use to help you become the person he longs for you to be.

Fully Devoted	0310220734
Grace	0310220742
Growth	0310220750
Groups	0310220769
Gifts	0310220777
Giving	0310220785

Life-changing Small Group Resources

InterActions Series

Bill Hybels

InterActions studies encourage participants to share interests, experiences, values, and lifestyles, and uses this common ground to foster honest communication, deeper relationships, and growing intimacy with God.

Authenticity	031020674X
Community	0310206774
Lessons in Love	0310206804
Marriage	0310206758
The Real You	0310206820
Commitment	0310206839
Essential Christianity	0310224438
Evangelism	0310206782
Freedom	0310217172
Getting a Grip	0310224446
Parenthood	0310206766
Serving Lessons	0310224462
Overcoming	0310224454
Character	0310217164
Fruits of the Spirit	0310213150
Jesus	0310213169
Prayer	0310217148
Psalms	0310213185
Transparency	0310217156
Transformation	0310213177

New Community Series

Bill Hybels, John Ortberg

New Community studies provide in-depth Bible study, thought-provoking questions, and community building exercises so groups can grow in faith together.

1 John: Love Each Other	0310227682
1 Peter: Stand Strong	0310227739
Acts: Build Community	0310227704
Colossians: Discover the New You	0310227690
Exodus: Journey Toward God	0310227712
James: Live Wisely	0310227674
Philippians: Run the Race	0310233143
Romans: Find Freedom	0310227658

Walking with God Series

Don Cousins, Judson Poling

Practical, interactive, and biblically based, this dynamic series follows a two-track approach. Series 1 plugs new believers into the transforming power of discipleship to Christ. Series 2 guides mature believers into a closer look at the church.

Series 1		Series 2	
"Follow Me"	0310591635	Building Your Church	031059183X
Friendship with God	0310591430	Discovering Your Church	0310591732
The Incomparable Jesus	0310591538	Impacting Your World	0310591937
Leader's Guide	0310592038	Leader's Guide	0310592135

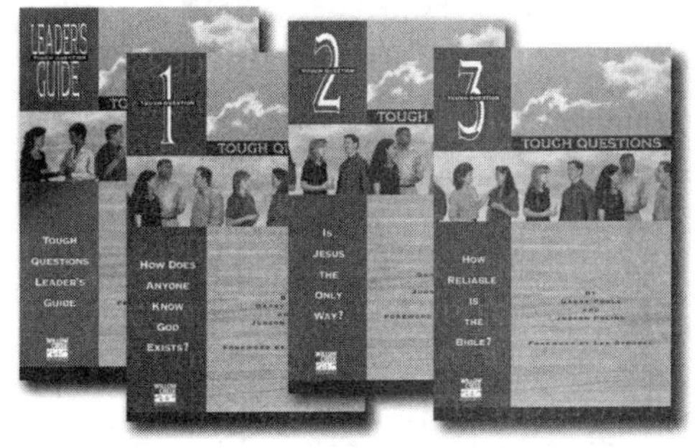

Tough Questions Series

Garry Poole, Judson Poling

Created for seeker small groups, this series guides participants through an exploration of key questions about and objections to Christianity.

How Does Anyone Know God Exists?	0310222257	Don't All Religions Lead to God?	031022229X
Is Jesus the Only Way?	0310222311	Do Science and the Bible Conflict?	031022232X
How Reliable Is the Bible?	0310222265	Why Become a Christian?	0310222281
How Could God Allow Suffering/Evil?	0310222273	Leader's Guide	0310222249

Build a Church Where Nobody Stands Alone

Building a Church of Small Groups

To provide the kind of authentic community people are hungry for, churches must be built on the foundation of little communities—small groups. Experience the vision, values, and necessary initial steps to begin transitioning your church from a church *with* small groups to a church *of* small groups in this groundbreaking book.

Hardcover 0310240352

The Connecting Church

Randy Frazee

Pastor Randy Frazee explores the three essential elements of connecting churches: Common Purpose, Common Place, and Common Possessions. An excellent resource to help leaders create the kind of church where every member feels a deep sense of connection.

Hardcover 0310233089

Leading Life-Changing Small Groups

Bill Donahue

Used by thousands of leaders at Willow Creek and around the world, *Leading Life-Changing Small Groups* covers everything from starting, structuring, leading, and directing an effective small group, to developing effective leaders.

Softcover 0310205956

Evangelistic Resources—for Believers and Seekers

Building a Contagious Church

Mark Mittelberg with contributions from Bill Hybels

Building a Contagious Church offers a proven, six-stage process to help your church become evangelistically contagious.

Hardcover 0310221498

Becoming a Contagious Christian

Bill Hybels and Mark Mittelberg

This groundbreaking book offers practical insights and real-life applications on how to reach friends and family for Christ.

Softcover 0310210089
Hardcover 0310485002

Inside the Mind of Unchurched Harry and Mary

Lee Strobel

Learn how to build relational bridges with friends and family who avoid God and the church.

Softcover 0310375614

The Case for Christ

Lee Strobel

Award-winning investigative reporter Lee Strobel puts the toughest questions about Christ to acclaimed psychology, law, medicine, and biblical studies experts.

Softcover 0310209307

The Case for Christ Student Edition

Lee Strobel with Jane Vogel

Based on the bestselling book for adults, the student edition is a fast, fun, informative tour through the evidence for Christ designed especially for students.

Softcover 0310234840

The Case for Faith

Lee Strobel

Tackles eight obstacles to faith, such as suffering, the doctrine of hell, evolution, and more.

Softcover 0310234697

The Journey

Uniquely designed to help spiritual seekers discover the relevance of Christianity.

Softcover 031092023X

Christianity 101

Gilbert Bilezikian

Explores eight core beliefs of the Christian faith. A great resource for both seekers and believers.

Softcover 0310577012

Proven Resources for Church Leaders

Rediscovering Church

Lynne and Bill Hybels

Rediscovering Church relates the beginnings of Willow Creek Community Church as well as its joys and struggles, and the philosophy and strategies behind its growth.

Softcover 0310219272

An Inside Look at the Willow Creek Worship Service

Featuring John Ortberg

Experience Willow Creek's weekly worship service, New Community. Featured is a look at Willow Creek's worship style with patterns and ideas that can be integrated into your church's unique worship style.

Video 0310223571

The Heart of the Artist

Rory Noland

Willow Creek's music director looks at the unique gifts and challenges artists bring to spiritual life.

Softcover 0310224713

Drama Ministry

Steve Pederson

A powerful and practical "how-to" book for drama directors from the director of Willow Creek's drama ministry.

Softcover 0310219450

The Source

Scott Dyer and Nancy Beach

Whatever the size of your church, this book will help you and your staff plan creative, impactful services.

Softcover 0310500214